35.16
9-21-88

D0903961

509132

Justifying Toleration

Justifying Toleration

Conceptual and Historical Perspectives

edited by
SUSAN MENDUS
University of York

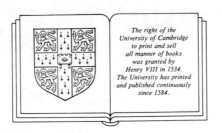

The right of the
University of Cambridge
to print and sell
all manner of books
was granted by
Henry VIII in 1534.
The University has printed
and published continuously
since 1584.

CAMBRIDGE UNIVERSITY PRESS

CAMBRIDGE

NEW YORK   NEW ROCHELLE   MELBOURNE   SYDNEY

CENTRAL MISSOURI
STATE UNIVERSITY
Warrensburg,
Missouri

Published by the Press Syndicate of the University of Cambridge
The Pitt Building, Trumpington Street, Cambridge CB2 1RP
32 East 57th Street, New York, NY 10022, USA
10 Stamford Road, Oakleigh, Melbourne 3166, Australia

© Cambridge University Press 1988

First published 1988

Printed in Great Britain at the University Press, Cambridge

British Library cataloguing in publication data

Justifying toleration: conceptual and
historical perspectives.
1. Toleration
I. Mendus, Susan
179'.9 BJ1431

Library of Congress cataloguing in publication data

Justifying toleration.
1. Liberty – History. 2. Civil rights – History.
3. Toleration – History. I. Mendus, Susan.
JC585.J87 1988 323.44 87–26815

ISBN 0 521 34302 X

BO

JC
585
J87
1988

Contents

509132

Preface

All but one of the chapters in this volume were first presented at the annual C. and J.B. Morrell Conferences on Toleration at the University of York. Since 1981 the Morrell Trust has sponsored a wide programme of research at the University of York into the philosophical and practical problems of toleration. This has included the funding of an annual Memorial Address and conference, five graduate studentships, a fellowship, and a programme of staff seminars. During the academic years 1985–7 I held the post of Morrell Fellow in Toleration at York, and I would like to take this opportunity to express my gratitude to the Trustees, both for their generosity and for their sustained interest.

The paper which was not delivered at one of the annual conferences is the one by David Edwards. His paper on Mill was presented to the York Political Theory Workshop and is included here because it seemed wholly appropriate that a volume on toleration should include at least one piece on John Stuart Mill.

In editing this volume, I have been greatly assisted both by the patience and understanding of the contributors, and by the encouragement of my colleagues at the University of York. In particular, my thanks go to John Horton for his characteristically generous assistance.

I am grateful to the Cambridge University Press reader for helpful and constructive comments on an earlier draft of the Introduction. Finally, I wish to acknowledge the efficient editorial work done by Pauline Marsh for Cambridge University Press.

Susan Mendus

Introduction

SUSAN MENDUS

This collection of papers traces the philosophical history of the concept of toleration, its justification, and its limits. The contributors discuss the theories advanced by philosophers from the seventeenth century to the present day, and it is remarkable, but perhaps not surprising, that in examining the concept of toleration, these philosophers were acutely aware of the particular practical form which problems of toleration took in their own societies. Thus, for example, John Locke placed emphasis on that religious intolerance which was so problematic in seventeenth-century Britain. Similarly, Hannah Arendt's writings on the topic were profoundly influenced by her own experience as a Jew forced to flee from her native Germany, and John Stuart Mill's views in his essay *On Liberty* are famously informed by his own concerns about the tyranny of public opinion which he felt to be prevalent in Victorian Britain. In these respects, the writings of the philosophers discussed here are historically specific. At the same time, however, they are of continuing and universal importance. This is not simply because these are great philosophers, whose views we should understand, but also because the general nature of the problem of toleration persists, even when its specific occasion has disappeared. Thus, those historically specific events which prompted Locke's *Letter concerning Toleration*, or Mill's *On Liberty*, are matters for history, but the general problems of what grounds and what sets limits to toleration are as pressing now as they ever were.

This last fact is emphasised by reflection on the extent of intolerance in the modern world: religious intolerance is still evident in Northern Ireland, in the Middle East, and in some Eastern bloc countries. To discover examples of racial intolerance we do not need to look further than Britain itself, and political oppression is common in many parts of the world. However, much as we may regret these instances of intolerance, we may still feel that toleration is not an unqualified good. For example, the toleration of expression of opinion has limits which are drawn by the laws of libel and of blasphemy. Similarly, laws governing the availability of pornography may be seen as necessary restraints within any society. And when we move from the realm of opinion to the realm of action, the limits of toleration become yet more apparent, for whilst we may, in the name of toleration, advocate free expression of opinion, we are markedly more reluctant to extend that toleration to actions performed on the basis of the opinions (indeed, it is notoriously difficult in many cases even to distinguish clearly between opinion and action). Nevertheless, if we believe toleration to be an important moral and political value, then we must say what its justification is, whilst at the same time distinguishing it from mere indifference, or unbridled licence. There are therefore two central questions which must be addressed. They are:

1. What are the grounds of toleration? and
2. What are the limits of toleration?

The first question prompts two distinct responses: firstly, that toleration is rooted in moral or religious scepticism, and secondly that toleration is rooted in respect for persons. In the papers gathered here a recurring theme is the traditional link between toleration and moral or religious scepticism. As Richard Tuck points out, it is often thought that there is at least an emotional kinship between toleration and scepticism, and belief in the connection between the two was powerful in the seventeenth century and persisted through the nineteenth century (in the writings of Mill), into the twentieth century (in the philosophy of Hannah Arendt). Scepticism is also a prominent feature of twentieth-century liberalism, which frequently bases its commitment to toleration on moral scepticism.

Nevertheless, the link between scepticism and toleration is not unproblematic: several of the chapters consider in detail the conceptual and historical connection between the two and suggest that there is in fact no straightforward move from moral or religious scepticism to toleration. Richard Tuck notes that seventeenth-century sceptics were just as likely to be intolerant as tolerant, and he suggests that this historical fact highlights a conceptual problem which persists for modern sceptics. In brief, the problem is that scepticism presents at best a pragmatic defence of toleration, not a principled one. Historical scepticism shows only why intolerance is

2

imprudent, not why it is morally wrong. Moreover, the focus of its attention tends to be the perpetrators of intolerance, not its victims. So what was originally required was an explanation of the wrong done to the victims of intolerance, whereas what is delivered is an explanation of the imprudence of the agents of intolerance.

These difficulties, prominent in seventeenth-century political thought, give rise to the second kind of justification of toleration, one meant to remedy the defects of the sceptical approach. Here the argument for toleration is founded on the principle of respect for persons. Where scepticism adduces pragmatic and prudential considerations, this argument adduces moral ones, and where scepticism characteristically construes toleration as, at best, an instrumental value, this argument insists that it be construed as a good in itself and independent of considerations of public order and peace in society.

The distinction between these two types of defence of toleration is obviously very crudely drawn here, and the aim of the chapters in this volume is to analyse them in greater detail and explain the ways in which they overlap and sometimes complement one another. Nevertheless, the distinction remains and may be seen not merely as a description of the history of political thought, but also as a response to a conceptual problem generated by the concept of toleration itself. As we have seen, seventeenth-century respect for scepticism gave rise to prudential justifications of toleration, and recognition of the problems inherent in this led to justifications in terms of respect for persons. Yet this historical movement was also a reflection of conceptual difficulties inherent in the notion of toleration. To understand this, we need to say something more about the concept of toleration itself.

WHAT IS TOLERATION?

Earlier in this Introduction, it was noted that toleration is distinct from unbridled licence. This is so both because toleration has its limits, and because toleration is conceptually linked to disapproval, or at least to dislike. We cannot, properly speaking, be said to tolerate things which we welcome, or endorse, or find attractive. Implicit in this conceptual claim is a statement of the problem which forced the historical movement mentioned above. If toleration implies moral disapproval, and disapproving of something involves thinking it to be wrong, then the question arises, why should I tolerate or permit that which I believe to be wrong, and how could it be right to do so? As D. D. Raphael puts it in Chapter 6, 'The intolerable',

> to disapprove of something is to judge it to be wrong. Such a judgement does not express a purely subjective preference. It claims universality; it claims to be the view of any rational agent. The content of the judgement, that something is wrong, implies that the something may properly be prevented. But if your disapproval is reasonably grounded, why should you go against it at all? Why should you tolerate?

On this account, toleration involves refraining from preventing that which may properly be prevented. This seems to amount to the claim that it may sometimes be proper not to prevent that which may properly be prevented, and herein lies the paradox. To draw its sting, we must either insist that moral disapproval does not imply the propriety of prevention; or that there is some other (external) justification of toleration, limiting its application; or that toleration is not a good after all. I shall consider these in turn. The first alternative (denying that moral disapproval implies the propriety of prevention) is commonly associated with scepticism. Here the thought is that moral disapproval does not spring from knowledge and that the suppression of hostile opinions is consequently unjustified. However, different writers approach this point in different ways and the claim is not invariably associated with moral scepticism. Scepticism is simply one way (amongst others) of denying the propriety of the move from moral disapproval to suppression or prevention of the act or opinion disapproved of. Other possibilities include, for example, the Lockian insistence that although there is moral and religious truth, such truth cannot be imposed forcibly and it is therefore not merely improper, but irrational to attempt, by intolerance, to impose the truth on others. In similar vein, John Stuart Mill often implies that there is such a thing as moral truth, but he insists that the road to truth is the road of toleration. These, then, are some of the ways in which philosophers have sought to deny the propriety of preventing that of which one morally disapproves. More will be said about each of these in a moment. For now it is enough simply to note that this is one way of attempting to solve the problem with which we began.

The second alternative (which seeks some further justification of toleration) is commonly associated with the doctrine of respect for persons. Here it is argued that the propriety of not preventing that which is disapproved of is explained by reference to what persons essentially are. Most commonly, toleration is of and by persons, and the tolerator's disapproval of the tolerated is compatible with his acting virtuously in tolerating precisely because such action alone can show due and proper respect for persons. A belief in persons as essentially autonomous (self-legislating) agents, entitled to direct the course of their own lives, generates an argument for toleration as distinct from indifference or licence, since what is required by such an ethic is precisely that I act morally well in allowing others to dictate their own actions, even though I morally disapprove of such actions. Indeed, arguments from autonomy tend to construe toleration as the right of the tolerated, not merely as a virtue in the tolerator: toleration is something which may be claimed as an entitlement, since it is this alone which displays due and proper respect for persons in all their diversity.

The fundamental requirement of respect for persons thus incorporates and explains the necessity of allowing actions of which we disapprove morally. Moreover, this justification offers an explanation of the limits of toleration: toleration is a good in so far as it is required by the principle of respect for persons. It is, however, also limited by that principle, and actions which fall within the ambit of the intolerable are all and only those which fail to show respect for persons. Thus, where the first kind of justification appeals, at least sometimes, to scepticism or moral relativism, the second kind of justification appeals to an over-arching moral principle, the principle of respect. Additionally, where the first justification concentrates on the status of the tolerator, and construes him as acting virtuously in refraining from preventing that of which he disapproves, the second justification concentrates on the status of the victim of intolerance, and emphasises the wrong which is done to him by intolerance. This second strand of thought is considered by several of the contributors: Nicholas Dent, D. D. Raphael, and Joseph Raz all discuss the nature and extent of the principle of respect for persons as a justification of toleration.

This brings us to the final route by which the problem of toleration may be solved: the denial that toleration is a good at all. Such a solution is characteristically associated with writers outside the liberal tradition, particularly marxist writers. Toleration is often presented as a quintessentially liberal value, and some liberal writers go so far as to suggest that liberalism has a virtual monopoly on toleration. The diverse, open, pluralist character of liberal societies is frequently contrasted with the unified, closed, monolithic character of socialist, particularly marxist, societies. Yet here two questions arise: are liberals as successful as they claim to be in providing a coherent justification of toleration, and is it impossible that marxist theories should also incorporate the value of toleration? The former question arises naturally from examination of the problems inherent in liberal accounts of toleration; the latter question involves examination of the basic tenets of socialism and marxism. The former question is raised and considered by Margaret Canovan in her paper on Hannah Arendt; the latter question is discussed in the papers by G. W. Smith, David Miller, and Graeme Duncan and John Street.

We began with the question 'what is toleration?' and it has been suggested that toleration consists in refraining from preventing that of which one morally disapproves. However, this suggestion raised a serious problem as to how it could be right to refrain from preventing that of which one morally disapproves. Three tentative ways of solving the problem were advanced:

1. to deny that thinking something morally wrong involves thinking it would be proper to prevent it;
2. to insist that the principle of toleration is justified and restricted by a wider principle, the principle of respect for persons;
3. to deny that toleration is an important value at all.

Characteristically, the first two suggestions are favoured by writers in the liberal tradition, whereas the third suggestion is associated with marxist thought. However, as the papers in this collection stress, the associations are rarely as clear as they first seem, nor are the liberal defences of toleration as successful as some liberal writers claim. We must therefore now look in more detail at the proposed justifications of toleration and assess their merits.

TOLERATION AND TRUTH

The first justification, and the first attempt to solve the problem of toleration, concentrated on the supposed move from thinking something morally wrong to believing it proper to prevent that thing. It has been proposed that one way of solving the problem involves denying the propriety of making that move, and several of the chapters presented here consider this approach. As was mentioned earlier, the approach is very often associated with a commitment to moral and religious scepticism. The thought here is that toleration is the child of doubt and that those who doubt whether we can know moral and religious truths will tend to favour a *laissez-faire* attitude towards diverse and disparate beliefs. In Chapter 1, 'Scepticism and toleration in the seventeenth century', Richard Tuck discusses this theme and points out that historically sceptics were just as frequently advocates of repression as of toleration. Seventeenth-century scepticism involved commitment to a life of *ataraxia* (imperturbability). Such a life involved the abandonment of strong beliefs of any sort, since the holding of strong beliefs was inimical to *ataraxia*. However, whilst sceptics themselves abandoned strong beliefs, their contemporaries did not, and this fact raised a serious problem: what should the sceptical response be to those who held strong beliefs? To suppress such beliefs would be to take them too seriously, yet to neglect to suppress them would be to risk just the sort of civil strife which would jeopardise the life of *ataraxia*. In pursuit of such a life, they insisted that moral beliefs must be subordinated to the political principles required to secure civil peace. It followed that seventeenth-century scepticism might just as easily dictate repression as toleration, for if civil order is what matters most, then different circumstances might require more or less tolerant attitudes, and Tuck argues that it was this same pragmatic consideration which produced both Lipsius' rejection of toleration and Locke's acceptance of it. The only thing that changed was the situation within society, which dictated that in Lipsius' day peace would best be fostered by intolerance, whereas in Locke's day it would best be fostered by tolerance.

Tuck's paper traces the historical progress of the link between toleration and scepticism and points out that the latter did not always generate arguments in support of the former. In addition, however, what is highlighted here is a quite general difficulty for any justification of toleration which rests on scepticism. Tuck questions whether toleration really is the child of doubt, but argues that even if it is the child of doubt, the kind of defence of toleration which scepticism can furnish will be limited and possibly unsatisfactory. Both conceptually and historically the defence of toleration offered by the sceptic will be a pragmatic, not a principled defence.

Alan Ryan takes up this same theme in Chapter 2, 'A more tolerant Hobbes?' He too points to the fact that the enforcement of orthodoxy in seventeenth-century England might be supported either by appeal to the truth of religion or by appeal to religious and moral scepticism, and where scepticism was adopted considerations of peace and good order might lead to oppression in just the same way as did considerations of religious truth. Ryan points out that Hobbes's central claim was that enforcement of orthodoxy must be limited by considerations of good order and thus, in the Hobbesian canon, toleration becomes a police matter. 'Uniformity in matters of worship is about manners in public rather than about anything deeper; just as obscenity is in itself no offence but only so when brought to notice, so is eccentricity of worship . . . public order trumps any notion of a right to free speech.'

These two chapters together indicate

1. that toleration is not necessarily the child of doubt and that, depending on social and political circumstances, scepticism may lead either to toleration or to the enforcement of orthodoxy;
2. that even where scepticism does favour toleration, that will be on pragmatic, not principled grounds. Considerations of peace and public order will dictate the need (or otherwise) for toleration.

This line of thought is further pursued by Jeremy Waldron in Chapter 3, 'Locke: toleration and the rationality of persecution'. Concentrating on the argument of the *Letter concerning Toleration* Waldron suggests that the central difficulty in Locke's account is that it shows at most that intolerance is irrational, not that it is morally wrong. Waldron raises two points which are particularly pertinent here: like Tuck and Ryan he questions the traditional claim that toleration is allied to scepticism and he goes on to suggest that a central defect in Locke's argument is that it fails adequately to explain the moral wrongness of intolerance. However, unlike his predecessors, Locke does not exhibit any commitment to pragmatism or prudence. He does not see toleration as a 'police matter'. Rather his argument rests on a belief in ethical rationalism. The basic form of Locke's argument is that coercion works on the will and belief is not subject to the will. Whatever we may think of the truth of this latter claim, it does, if true, entail the irrationality of attempting to coerce religious conformity. The consequences of this form of argument are, moreover, far-reaching. We have already seen that Locke's defence is not based on any commitment to scepticism and that, in common with other seventeenth-century writers, he does not present a principled justification of toleration as a virtue. However, where other seventeenth-century writers advocate toleration in the name of civil peace and good order, Locke advocates toleration in the name of rationality and, as Waldron points out, this separates him from the conventional 'saints of liberalism' in several important ways.

In the first place, Locke's defence is a defence not against coercion as such, but against certain *reasons* for coercion. Thus, as Waldron remarks, 'it is not a right to freedom of worship as such [which Locke defends], but rather, and at most, a right not to have one's worship interfered with for religious ends'. It follows from this that where reasons for coercion are not religious, but political or economic, Locke's defence gets no grip at all. Toleration is, for him, a rational requirement in respect of religious belief only.

The second crucial feature of Locke's account is that it has nothing to say about the intrinsic value of autonomy or individual self-development. The neutrality required by him is simply neutrality with regard to reasons and exhibits no commitment to the value of autonomy at all. It follows from this that Locke places no weight on the value of diversity as such.

These features of Locke's account exhibit a fundamental gap in his defence of toleration. For him, toleration is justified by appeal to appropriate or rational procedures which the perpetrators of intolerance might employ, given the truth of ethical rationalism and given that belief is not subject to the will. It says nothing about the wrong done to the victims of intolerance.

The chapters by Tuck, Ryan, and Waldron examine the shortcomings of two of the three ways of denying the move from thinking something wrong to thinking it may properly be prevented: Tuck and Ryan argue that where that move is based on moral or religious scepticism, it will provide at best a partial and pragmatic defence of toleration: at worst, it provides no defence of toleration at all. Waldron argues that where the denial of the move rests on rationalism (as it does for Locke), then again toleration cannot be advocated as a moral virtue, but only as a rational procedure in the case of religious belief.

What, then, of the third strategy for denying the implication? This is the strategy favoured by Mill in some sections of his essay *On Liberty*. Mill's claim is that we are not entitled to suppress an action or opinion simply because we believe it to be morally wrong, and that we are not entitled is a consequence of the fact that, whilst there is truth, the road to truth is the road of toleration.

In Chapter 4, 'Toleration and Mill's liberty of thought and discussion', David Edwards discusses Mill's defence of toleration and points to an apparent tension in his thinking – the tension between the belief that toleration is the royal road to truth and the belief that toleration is a good in itself because diversity is an intrinsic and irreducible value. Sometimes Mill resists the move from thinking something morally wrong to preventing it, on the grounds that we cannot be sure that what we think to be morally wrong actually is morally wrong. At other times, however, he resists the move on the grounds that diversity is itself an important and valuable feature of social life. In other words, sometimes Mill defends toleration as an instrumental value, while at other times he defends it as an intrinsic good. Concentrating on these two aspects of Mill's account, Edwards asks, 'Does Mill have two views of toleration, one of a provisional and instrumental character, the other involving a recognition of the intrinsic value of human diversity that will never lose its force?' If the former view is accepted then toleration will ultimately yield to truth and, presumably, to uniformity, but if the latter view is accepted, then we must face up to the difficulty of finding arguments for valuing sheer diversity for its own sake.

The starting-point of this discussion was the thought that we might solve the problem of toleration by insisting that someone might believe an action or opinion to be morally wrong, yet not believe that it follows from that that it would be proper to prevent or suppress it. Three main ways of resisting the implication were considered: denying that there is such a thing as moral truth; denying the rationality of attempting to compel others to the truth in religious or ethical matters; denying that truth is to be obtained other than by the practice of toleration. However, as we have seen, each strategy is problematic. Crucially, it has been argued that these strategies will not always generate a defence of toleration and that, even where they do generate a defence, it is the wrong kind of defence which is offered. We needed a non-instrumental account of the wrong done to others by treating them intolerantly. We received instead, and at best, an instrumental account of the imprudence (or even irrationality) of intolerance. The time has come, therefore, to turn to the second method of solving the problem of toleration: the claim that toleration is indeed an important value of a liberal society, but that it is grounded in and restricted by an over-arching requirement to show respect for persons.

TOLERATION AND RESPECT FOR PERSONS

The general form of the argument is as follows: intolerance is indeed morally wrong and not merely imprudent. Its moral wrong-

10

ness is a consequence of its failure to treat persons as autonomous, self-legislating beings who are worthy of respect. Three of the chapters in this book deal directly with this defence of toleration: Nicholas Dent's chapter considers the theme of respect for persons as it appears in the philosophy of Jean-Jacques Rousseau, whilst the chapters by D. D. Raphael and Joseph Raz deal with modern interpretations of the concept. One major advantage of a defence of this sort is that, if successful, it would overcome the defects of the earlier accounts. That is to say, it would show that toleration is a virtue, that it has intrinsic and not merely instrumental value, and that its pursuit is not only rational but morally right. Although the argument from respect for persons is most often associated with the philosophy of Immanuel Kant, Nicholas Dent points out that this strand is also present in the writings of Kant's predecessor, Rousseau. Two crucial points emerge in Dent's discussion of Rousseau and respect for persons: firstly, that Rousseau's concern in his political philosophy is not simply with good *order* in society, but with a good society. Immediately this marks a contrast with the seventeenth-century philosophers discussed earlier. For Rousseau, the wrongness of intolerance lies not solely or centrally in its tendency to promote social unrest and disorder, but in its manifestation of contempt for others within society. As Dent notes, the presence of tolerance is not, for Rousseau, simply the absence of intolerance. 'Rather, tolerance will be a matter of the positive welcoming and prizing of human individuality where that is expression of that integrity of mind and spirit of life which is facilitated by affording to everyone a fundamental confidence in their value and worth as persons with a life to make for themselves.' This marks the second important point in Rousseau's account, namely the value placed on individuality and on diversity. In showing respect for persons one is thereby showing respect for their individual differences – for their diversity. So where seventeenth-century writers see the worth of toleration as lying in its tendency to promote social order, Rousseau sees toleration as expressive of respect for others and their views even though those differ from one's own.

In this account, then, we find both an assertion of the intrinsic value of toleration and an explanation of the value of diversity. Diversity is to be valued not merely as an aesthetic preference but as an important concomitant of respect: to respect others is, ipso facto, to respect the ways in which they differ from one another and from oneself and the principle of respect thus involves valuing diversity, at least within certain limits. Additionally, the principle of respect suggests what the limits of toleration might be. If toleration is a good in so far as it exhibits respect for others, then the limits of toleration are also set by considerations of respect for others. Dent puts the matter this way:

one may say that one does not at all fail in showing the respect due to another if one violently intervenes to stop them acting like this (committing murder). It never was part of what respect for them implied that one should honour their murderous projects. Similarly, one may be faced with a signal instance or a general habit of intolerance and it is certainly not clear that one is obliged to show tolerance towards this, for example by way of non-interference with the expression of intolerant views or with the carrying out of actions consequent on that intolerance.

Thus the argument from respect for persons both grounds and sets limits to toleration. In addition, it explains why diversity should be valued as something more than a mere aesthetic preference. The limits of toleration and the connection between it and diversity are discussed by D. D. Raphael and Joseph Raz respectively.

Raphael concentrates on the interpretation to be given to the principle of respect for persons. The suggestion is that the goodness of toleration is to be explained by the fact that it shows such respect. However, it is this explanation which generates the problem of toleration mentioned at the outset. As Raphael says:

If toleration implies moral disapproval of what you tolerate, and if the criterion of moral disapproval is conformity to the principle of respect for persons, then toleration presupposes that what you tolerate does not conform to the principle of respect for persons. But on the other hand, so it is suggested, we ought not to tolerate whatever contravenes the principle of respect for persons. Then how can there be toleration at all? We cannot, as a matter of logic, tolerate anything unless it goes against respect for persons, and yet we ought not to tolerate anything that does that.

Raphael proposes that the apparent self-contradiction be removed by distinguishing between more and less stringent categories of moral obligation: failures in the more stringent being both wrong and intolerable, failures in the less stringent being wrong but tolerable. In particular, he suggests a distinction between duties of perfect and imperfect obligation, understood as a distinction between duties that are non-discretionary and imply corresponding rights, and duties that are discretionary and do not imply corresponding rights. Toleration is appropriate in all and only those cases where the actions of others, although morally wrong, do not infringe rights:

Acts of which we disapprove but which do not infringe rights may be tolerated despite our belief that they are wrong, and should be tolerated if those who do the acts have deliberately chosen to do them. In the latter event toleration is called for because it shows respect for the ends (the choices) of those who do the acts.

The move from thinking something morally wrong to preventing it is thus circumscribed by the principle of respect. I may properly prevent that of which I disapprove only when the act involves failure to show respect for persons and it fails in that way only when it constitutes an infringement of rights. This account marks a clear distinction between the morally wrong but tolerable, and the morally wrong and intolerable. Nevertheless, it is not unproblematic, as Raphael makes clear. One central difficulty here is that of deciding on the application of the distinction between duties of perfect and imperfect obligation. In this area we seem to be thrown back on intuition, and notoriously intuitions differ from person to person and from society to society. So the principle of respect, while offering a defence of toleration as a moral virtue, is dogged by difficulties of application.

The connection between toleration and the value of respect for persons is further explored by Joseph Raz in Chapter 7, 'Autonomy, toleration, and the harm principle'. He argues that the principle of respect for persons as autonomous moral agents (which he calls 'the autonomy principle') generates a characteristically liberal justification of toleration, one not readily available to non-liberal writers. Like Raphael and Dent he construes toleration as an aspect of respect for others and argues that this has two implications: firstly, it implies moral pluralism, and secondly it yields a set of duties more wide-ranging than the duty of non-interference. Pluralism is implied simply because the requirement to respect others as autonomous agents carries with it the recognition that they may have ideals different from and in conflict with one's own, but that those ideals are, nevertheless, moral virtues. In other words, pluralism requires not simply the existence of incompatible forms of life, but the existence of incompatible forms of life each of which is capable of being pursued for its own sake.

This commitment to pluralism is implied by considerations of autonomy, since the development of autonomy requires that the agent have a choice between goods. One cannot be autonomous if presented only with choices between good and evil. 'A choice between good and evil is not enough.' It requires a plurality of incompatible and yet morally acceptable forms and styles of life. So

13

509132

respect for autonomy implies moral pluralism and, Raz notes, it is often suggested that moral pluralism alone establishes the value of toleration. If autonomy requires moral pluralism and moral pluralism establishes toleration, then the argument from autonomy is complete. However, Raz urges that what is in fact required for the value of toleration is *competitive* moral pluralism and it is in the nature of competitive moral pluralism that it not only encourages distinct and incompatible moral virtues, but also virtues which tend, given human nature, to encourage intolerance of other virtues. If this is correct, then the problem of toleration arises yet again, for we need to know when it is appropriate to tolerate ideals which conflict with one's own and when it is not. Raz suggests that the limits of toleration are themselves provided by appeal to the principle of autonomy. Since an autonomous life is valuable, governments have duties to promote and foster conditions in which agents may develop their autonomy. However, the autonomy principle is, says Raz, a perfectionist principle. Autonomous life is valuable only if it is spent in the pursuit of acceptable and valuable projects. Thus the principle requires not only the promotion of valuable projects, but the elimination of repugnant ones. As well as justifying toleration, it also circumscribes it.

The arguments presented in these three chapters – by Dent, Raphael, and Raz – all suggest that the proper defence of toleration is to be given by reference to a principle of respect for persons as autonomous agents. Such a defence purports to explain why toleration is a central value of a liberal society and also to explain when and why it is to be limited. We have seen, however, that there are difficulties inherent in such an account. Despite its attempt to present toleration as good in itself and not merely a prudential policy, the argument from respect must, ultimately, depend upon an analysis of rights and duties and we have seen that such analysis may often simply take the form of appeal to intuition, where intuitions differ from one person to another and from one society to another. Similarly, the claim that toleration is an aspect of the principle of autonomy and that societies have autonomy-based duties needs elaboration and explanation: what constitutes failure of duty and why? The argument from respect, in attempting to justify toleration by reference to a wider principle, inevitably generates the question, 'what grounds that wider principle?' Nevertheless, this is a more satisfactory form of defence than the earlier argument. We do here have an account which attempts to explain why toleration is something more than a merely prudential policy. Moreover, as Raz

14

remarks, this justification often seems to be the paradigmatic liberal account of toleration, emphasising as it does plurality, autonomy, and individual rights. We must now ask whether it really is what it appears. We must return to the two questions mentioned earlier: how successful is liberalism in justifying toleration, and is the justification of toleration the exclusive preserve of liberals?

THE DENIAL OF TOLERATION

In the second section of this Introduction it was suggested that there are, broadly speaking, three ways of solving the problem of toleration. Two of these have already been covered. The denial of the move from thinking something morally wrong to thinking it proper to prevent it was discussed in the section 'Toleration and truth'. The claim that toleration is circumscribed by a wider principle, the principle of respect for persons as autonomous agents, was considered in the last section. What of the third strategy, the denial that toleration is an important value at all? This claim is most often associated with non-liberal, particularly marxist writers, and the suggestion is that where liberals value plurality and hence value toleration, marxists do not value plurality and hence cannot construe toleration as either a right or a virtue. Furthermore, it has been said that the value of autonomy is a peculiarly liberal value and that, in so far as marxism does not value autonomy, it cannot value toleration. These claims are taken up in three of the chapters: Graeme Duncan and John Street ask whether there is any place for liberal tolerance within marxist theory; G. W. Smith discusses the relationship between marxism and autonomy; and David Miller considers the connection between socialist toleration and pluralism.

Before looking in detail at these three chapters, however, we should first ask how successful liberalism is in defending and explaining the value of toleration. In particular, we should ask what warrant there is for the liberal claim to justify a diverse, open, tolerant society – for liberal criticisms of marxism can be fully sustained only if liberalism itself can provide a coherent justification of toleration.

In Chapter 8, 'Friendship, truth and politics: Hannah Arendt and toleration', Margaret Canovan questions whether liberals really are as tolerant as they claim to be. She finds within liberal writings 'an unconscious commitment to uniformity which is similar to the outlook of the orthodox save for the important qualification that this uniformity is thought of as something to be achieved gradually and by peaceful means'. Even John Stuart Mill's praise of individuality and eccentricity is underpinned by his belief that opinion will gradually 'yield to fact and argument', and in this respect, Canovan suggests, 'the literature gives one the impression that the tolerant and the intolerant disagree about means rather than ends, since the ideal for both is a united mankind, living in harmonious brotherhood in accordance with agreed principles'. Of course it is true, and she says so, that some liberal writers have favoured diversity not as a means to the attainment of truth, but as an end in itself. We have already noted that Mill sometimes appears sympathetic to this approach, but, as Mill discovered, it is hard to justify such a view, and the history of liberalism suggests that writers who claim to value diversity for its own sake are (with the notable exception of the Romantics) often being somewhat disingenuous. On inspection, what they tend to value is truth – the diversity which culminates in uniformity – or, at best, diversity of *goods*, where what counts as a good is limited and defined by the premises of liberalism itself.

Canovan argues that one of Hannah Arendt's major contributions to this discussion lies in her denial that controversy is valuable only when it leads to truth, and her insistence that plurality and freedom, not unanimity and constraint, are the basis of the political condition. For Arendt, truth is certainly valuable, yet its value is subservient to the value of 'unending discourse among men'. Consequently, toleration is not to be defended because it is the royal road to truth, nor must failure to arrive at truth generate despair. Value lies in the very activity of discussion and debate, and this value is superior to truth. This insistence on the intrinsic value of toleration points up a difficulty inherent in monist liberalism which casts doubt upon liberalism's claim to superiority over marxism. Reporting the standard view about the differences between marxism and liberalism, Duncan and Street say, 'where liberalism emphasises intellectual and moral agnosticism and political pragmatism, marxism stresses intellectual certainty and politically centralised control in pursuit of the truth'. Yet Canovan's chapter suggests that intellectual and moral agnosticism is only the superficial character of liberalism and that toleration is consequently a temporary expedient against the day (however distant) when moral certainty is attained.

Where Canovan questions the ability of liberalism genuinely to justify toleration as a virtue, Duncan and Street question the inability of marxism to accommodate it. They consider three contexts in which marxist toleration might be expected – in capitalism, in revolution, and in communism, and they note that in capitalism toleration is construed as thinly disguised oppression; in revolution it is considered inefficacious; and in communism, unnecessary. It seems, then, that marxism really does outlaw toleration, and yet the manner in which it does so is interestingly paralleled by liberal theories of toleration. In monist liberalism, where toleration is justified instrumentally, it will be a matter of political judgement whether to be tolerant or not. In this respect, marxism is no worse off than liberalism and the marxist judgement that toleration in revolution is inefficacious exactly parallels the seventeenth-century liberal judgement that toleration is a police matter. So the instrumental character of monist liberalism precludes its claiming any superiority over marxism with respect to toleration. What of pluralist liberalism? Here the problem is that of showing why diversity might be valued for its own sake, and the chapters discussed in the preceeding section, 'Toleration and respect for persons', presented some arguments for so valuing diversity. Chief amongst these was respect for persons as autonomous, self-legislating beings. Discussing this justification, Joseph Raz remarked that the autonomy principle appears to be the quintessentially liberal defence of toleration – a defence not available to writers outside it.

G. W. Smith enquires into the exclusively liberal character of the autonomy principle and asks whether there is room for it within marxism. He argues that Marx's philosophy is essentially an intolerant one in which heterodoxy on matters of communist value must be treated as a symptom displayed by a subject who, by his dissent, has placed himself outside the community and outside reason. It follows from this that the adoption of a 'psychiatric attitude' to dissentients in communist countries is not an aberration, but an implication of Marx's principles. This implication follows directly from Marx's insistence on uniform moral consensus and his restrictive conception of what can count as the rational ends of human beings. When put together these imply that the prospect for individual rights (the rights of autonomous human beings) will be bleak indeed. The papers by Duncan and Street, and Miller, suggest that where toleration is defended as the royal road to truth, marxism is not irredeemably worse off than liberalism. However, where toleration is defended on grounds of individual autonomy, marxism does emerge as an essentially intolerant ideology, but it is important to note that the intolerance is generated, as Smith points out, by the combination of insistence on moral consensus and a very restricted view of what can count as the rational ends of human beings. The latter, as we shall see, is not a necessary concomitant of all socialist theories.

The final paper in this collection is David Miller's 'Socialism and toleration'. Unlike Duncan and Street, and Smith, Miller does not consider the relationship between marxist writings and toleration. Rather, his emphasis is on the ways in which contemporary socialism may deal with practical political problems of toleration. He urges that there is no need for contemporary socialism to follow the 'Eastern road' of cultural and religious oppression. Such oppression is required only by a full-blown conception of the good life, which socialists need not adopt. Thus Miller concurs with Smith in thinking that intolerance and oppression are a consequence of holding a restricted view of what can constitute the good life. Nevertheless, a troublesome feature of marxism, picked out by Smith, does carry over to socialism generally. Smith notes that the coherence of socialist societies must rest largely on the existence of a uniform moral consensus as to its basic values. In similar vein, Miller remarks upon the need for all socialist societies to foster, as a basic value, a sense of common citizenship. At root, socialism is communitarian, and in this lies the problem for a genuinely socialist account of toleration: for the kind of common identity which socialism requires may simply rule out the possibility of genuinely fostering diverse cultural identities. This will be the case when, for example, elements within a particular culture are at odds with the requirements of loyalty to and identity with the larger community. As Miller says, political education

must try to present an interpretation of, let us say, Indian culture in Britain that makes it possible for members of the Indian community to feel at home in, and loyal to, the British state. In so far as there are elements in Indian culture that are at odds with such a reconciliation, the interpretation must be selective or, if you like, biased.

On this account, socialism will limit the scope of toleration, but this is equally true of liberalism. Neither can claim to have the monopoly on the virtue of toleration, yet neither is committed, necessarily, to denying the value of toleration. Of course, the reasons which socialism has for restricting the scope of toleration will differ from the 'quintessentially liberal' reasons. However, as Miller points out, the features of community and civic participation which are now so strongly associated with socialism were in fact taken over by socialists from the civic humanist strand of liberalism. Thus, the socialist will restrict toleration for reasons different from those adduced by the republican liberal, but for reasons similar to those adduced by the liberal operating in the civic humanist tradition.

CONCLUSION

The discussion here, and in the papers gathered in this volume, has centred around two questions:

1. What are the grounds of toleration?
2. What are the limits of toleration?

In the liberal tradition toleration is sometimes associated with scepticism, yet we have seen that a sceptical defence justifies toleration only as an instrumental, not as an intrinsic value. Similarly, the claim that toleration is the royal road to truth will deliver at best a justification which fails to distinguish, in terms of ends, between the tolerant and the intolerant. If we wish to count toleration as a genuine virtue, then its justification must make reference to the value of persons as essentially autonomous, self-legislating beings who are worthy of respect. This justification is standardly thought to be *the* liberal justification of toleration, the one justification not available to writers outside the liberal tradition. However, some of the chapters presented here question this and suggest that liberals are not as well equipped as they imagine to defend toleration, nor are socialists as ill equipped. Both socialism and liberalism carry with them moral commitments which limit the scope of toleration and neither can promise universal tolerance. Perhaps this conclusion is not wholly surprising. Neither should it be depressing. After all, toleration is distinct from indifference: it implies moral commitments and judgements which will serve both to explain the nature of toleration as a good, and to set limits to its proper employment. Where the basic values differ, as they do between socialism and liberalism, the nature and extent of what is tolerated will also differ, and this shows us that disputes about toleration are disputes about ends and not merely about means.

1

Scepticism and toleration in the seventeenth century

RICHARD TUCK

It is natural to suppose that there is – at the very least – a certain emotional kinship between a belief in the desirability of toleration and a sceptical attitude towards religious or ethical beliefs. At the back of many people's minds is a rough history of the modern world in which the dissolution of strongly held beliefs (typically, the relatively unified Christianity of the Middle Ages) was a precondition for extending toleration to men who would once have been attacked as heretics. This view has been given a more precise expression by a number of writers, particularly on the sixteenth century, who have pointed to the religious scepticism of figures such as Bodin or Castellio as an explanation of their advocacy of toleration as a solution to the religious wars of their time.[1] I do not want in this paper to question the naturalness of this linkage, seen from some very long perspective; but I do want to remind us that the path to toleration through the meadows of late sixteenth- and early seventeenth-century scepticism was a surprisingly treacherous one, and that moral and religious scepticism may often be linked with a programme of what we would take to be excessive ideological repression. This in turn raises (I shall suggest) some problems for twentieth-century sceptics like (I imagine) most of us.

I want to begin with one of the first and most influential debates about toleration in post-Reformation Europe, which in many ways set the scene for writers during the next hundred or even two hundred years. In 1589 Justus Lipsius, professor at Leiden University, published a volume of political observations, *Politicorum libri sex*. This contained an eloquent defence of the need to repress heretical opinions: 'here is no place for clemencie, burne, sawe asunder, for

---

[1] This has, for example, been argued by Quentin Skinner in his *The Foundations of Modern Political Thought* (Cambridge, 1978), II, 247–9.

21

it is better that one member be cast away, than that the whole body runne to ruyne'.[2] This passage was picked on by another Netherlander, Dirck Coornhert, the secretary to the States of the province of Holland, who published an equally eloquent defence of the principle of religious toleration. Lipsius answered him in a later work, and the controversy continued for a couple of years.[3]

This argument has sometimes been presented as a clash between a liberal and even rather sceptical humanist, in the person of Coornhert, and a rigid neo-Stoicism in the person of Lipsius; but the truth is far more complex and even in a way the opposite. To understand it, we need first to consider more fully the philosophical attitudes of Lipsius.[4] He was born near Brussels while Charles V still ruled a united Netherlands, and was educated at Louvain; throughout his life he saw himself as a citizen of the Netherlands, and regarded what we call 'the Dutch Revolt' as a civil war within the Netherlands (which indeed it was). During this civil war, which lasted for the last three decades of the century, he moved between the Dutch and the Spanish sides, and between Protestantism and Catholicism, in an apparently bewildering way – but in fact he sought always to lend his support to the side which at any time looked more likely to secure a negotiated and non-military solution to the war. He thought and wrote constantly on the political problems thrown up by the Netherlands civil war, and he had a very clear picture of where he was himself to be located in the intellectual history of Europe. He is most famous for two features of his writings: one is his reconstruction of ancient Stoicism and its application to the modern world, and the other is his study and use of Tacitus as the central political text from antiquity (the *Politicorum libri sex* consist largely of a complicated network of quotations from Tacitus marshalled into a coherent text).

The character of Lipsius' neo-Stoicism is often misunderstood, and confused with the kind of Stoic ideas which we can find either in the Ciceronian humanists of the early Renaissance or in the post-

[2] Justus Lipsius, *Sixe bookes of politickes or civil doctrine . . . done into English by William Iones* (London, 1594), 64 (Book IV, 3).
[3] Coornhert's responses to Lipsius were the *Defensio processus de non occidendis haereticis* (Gouda, 1591), and the *Epitome processus de occidendis haereticis, at vi conscientiis inferenda* (Gouda, 1592). An earlier work of his in a modern edition is *A L'aurore des libertes modernes: synode sur la liberté des consciences*, 1582, ed. Joseph Leclerc and Marius-François Valkhoff (Paris, 1979). The debate with Lipsius is surveyed in G. Guldner, *Das Toleranz-problem in den Niederlanden im Ausgang des 16 Jahrhunderts* (Lubeck, 1968).
[4] The most important study of Lipsius is Gerhard Oestreich, *Neostoicism and the Early Modern State* (Cambridge, 1982).

Grotian modern natural law writers of the seventeenth century. But Lipsius' version of Stoicism was very close to that of his great contemporary Montaigne, and shared with Montaigne's an intimate relationship with a kind of scepticism. When Lipsius read Montaigne's *Essayes*, he wrote to their author that he was the one man in Europe who shared his own ideas, while he described him elsewhere as 'the French Thales' – implying that Montaigne was the first of a new kind of thinker. He also tried to get Montaigne into the group of scholars and philosophers published by his printer, Christopher Plantin.[5] Montaigne and Lipsius remained intellectually very close until Montaigne's death. Although Lipsius never wrote anything as full on ancient scepticism as Montaigne's *Apologie pour Raimond Sebond*, he often revealed his sympathy for it, remarking for example in one of his works on ancient philosophy (the *Manductio ad Stoicam Philosophiam* of 1604) that the sceptics'

aim is a high and laudable one; which is *ataraxia* or *Imperturbability*, with nothing that we experience through our senses affecting us. I will bravely declare that the sceptics are not to be rejected for this: it is merely that they should have ensured that they were not carried away by their zeal for debating things. Even Seneca seems to have regretted the disappearance of the sceptics, and to have mourned their passing.[6]

This passage goes to the heart of the matter: for what both Montaigne and Lipsius indeed advocated was the life of *ataraxia*, of detachment from the passions which brought pain and destruction to their possessors. But detachment from passion was for both of them detachment also from *belief*, and that was the emotional point of their scepticism. Like the sceptics of antiquity, the sceptics of the late sixteenth century were struck most forcibly by the absence of any secure criterion for discriminating between rival theories about the physical and moral worlds. The brute fact of radical moral disagreement, both between societies and, now, within their own society, was the starting-point for their moral relativism; their scepticism was thus not of the modern, post-Humean kind, in which even if there were universally agreed practices or beliefs, this would

---

[5] (My translation) 'In Europa non inveni, qui in his talibus sensu mecum magis consentiret.' Lipsius, *Epistolarum Selectarum III Centuriae* (Antwerp, 1601), 234 (Cent. II. 55). His remark about the French Thales and his suggestion about Plantin is in his *Epistolae*, I, ed. A. Gerlo et al. (Brussels, 1978), 433 and n. 12.

[6] (My translation) 'Neque non finis etiam eorum altus & laudabilis, qui est ataraxia sive *Imperturbatio*, & ut ne nulla re sensibus obiecta moveantur. Ego vera audacter eloquar, non sic abiiciendos esse: modum tantum tenuissent, nec disputandi studio ablati extra fines fuissent. Quin & Seneca requirere eos videtur, & dolere quod periisent.' Lipsius, *Manductionis ad Stoicam philosophiam libri tres* (Antwerp, 1610), 73.

not be sufficient to establish the existence of any absolute *moral* truths. But although the post-Humean position is far more subtle, the emotional force of moral relativism even today for many people is still what it was for Montaigne – 'what truth is that, which these Mountaines bound, and is a lie in the World beyond them?'[7] Despair at the variety and irreconcilable character of moral beliefs was, however, only the starting-point of the sixteenth-century sceptics' argument: a consciousness of the local character of one's beliefs could be a kind of therapy, in which one was liberated from the fears and anxieties which unreflective possessors of those beliefs felt. Montaigne's *Essayes* are full of statements of this kind, but an equally good example can come from Lipsius' first major work, his *De constantia in publicis malis* of 1584. In this he (among other things) attacked the idea of *patriotism*, and the belief that one's own country should in some way be an object of regard. Instead, he insisted that *self*-interest was crucial – one should only be concerned about civil war when one's *own* preservation was threatened, and anything beyond that was an unnecessary hostage to fortune in the form of ties of affection which would lead to suffering.

What both Montaigne and Lipsius had noticed, and what the latter documented with massive scholarship, was that classical Stoicism had two sides to it. Reading Seneca and the account of Stoicism in Diogenes Laertius, they saw that the central theme of Stoicism was *self-preservation*, the preservation of the self not merely from external attack but also from the passions which might leave it open to attack in some way. Many Stoic writers (though Seneca was not prominent among them) tried to combine this with an account of men as naturally desirous of the preservation of their fellow-creatures, particularly those close to them by blood or residence. But this was always seen as a problematical extension of the basic theory, even in antiquity. The head of the sceptical Academy, Carneades, pointed out the problem in a speech in 155 B.C. which became crucial to early modern moral scepticism (though it was recorded only at third hand, in Lactantius' quotations from Cicero's account of the speech). Carneades remarked that if one accepted the Stoic view – as, in this speech, he professed himself willing to do – then obvious dilemmas arose such as the case of two men after a shipwreck:

What will the just man do, if he shall happen to have suffered shipwreck, and some one weaker than himself shall have seized a plank? Will he not

---

[7] Michel de Montaigne, *Essayes*, trans. John Florio (London, n.d.), 524 (Book II.12).

thrust him from the plank, that he himself may get upon it, and supported by it may escape, especially since there is no witness in the middle of the sea? If he is wise, he must do so; for he must perish himself unless he shall thus act. But if he choose rather to die than inflict violence upon another, in this case he is just, but foolish, in not sparing his own life while he spares the life of another.[8]

The primacy of self-preservation was thus compatible with a strong degree of scepticism about universal and objective ethical principles, and it was in effect Carneades' blend of Stoicism and scepticism which was canonical for the neo-Stoics of the late sixteenth century, rather than (say) Cicero's much less morally relativist approach.

Given that the truth of religious or moral beliefs is a matter of indifference to the sceptic, but given also that this detachment is a very unusual mental attitude, what is the sceptic to do about the beliefs strongly held in his society? Montaigne and Lipsius continually emphasised (as Descartes in his sceptical mode was to do later) that the wise sceptic must abide by the public requirements of his society, both in morality and religion. To oppose himself to them would both be to take their truth value *seriously*, and also to run a direct physical risk to his own serene existence. But each of them went further, in a way that had immense implications for European political thought. If there is a set of political techniques available which can be used to secure civil peace, such that the private individual is no longer threatened with attack, then those techniques must be used by the state or the prince, and no general moral or legal principles have any standing against them. To be a constitutionalist was once again to take unfounded principles seriously, and by doing so to run the risk of disorder or death (as the constitutional resistance of the French Huguenots had done). This is the source of Lipsius' well-known 'Machiavellianism'; he certainly praised Machiavelli, describing him as 'the Tuscan master' and 'the Italian *faulte-writer*, (who poore soule is layde at of all hands)', though his reading of Tacitus was more important to him than his reading of Machiavelli in helping to form this attitude.[9] Once again, Descartes was to share this approach. Machiavelli being almost the only political theorist in whom he took any interest.

It was the application of this political principle to religion which

---

[8] Lactantius, *Works*, I, trans. William Fletcher, Anti-Nicene Christian Library, xxi (Edinburgh, 1871) 329 (*The Divine Institutes*, Book V.17).
[9] 'Etruscus magister', Lipsius, *Epistolae*, I, 412. 'Faultewriter', Lipsius, *Sixe bookes*, 62–3.

led Lipsius into his confrontation with Coornhert. What he argued was that in practice religious multiplicity led to civil strife, for religious beliefs were upheld by fanatics who cared about their public expression and about the immorality of other people's religious observances. 'One religion is the author of unitie; and from a confused religion there alwayes groweth dissention.' Religious fanaticism had done untold damage: 'Good Lord, what firebrands of sedition hath religion kindled in this fayrest part of the world? The chiefe heads of our christian common wealths are at strife amongst themselves, and many millions of men have bin brought to ruine and do dayly perish, under a pretext piety.' And to support his insistence on savage repression if necessary, he quoted Aristotle: 'to swarve from, or violate the custome receaved in a Country, is amongst all Nations accoumpted a capitall crime'.[10] This made exactly the point that submission to a single religion was a special case of the general principle that one should abide by the laws and customs of one's country.

But the primacy of self-preservation cut two ways, and Lipsius also gave offence to radical supporters of the Counter-Reformation when he continued,

This course thou oughtest to take, so long as the disturbers may be quieted without any further trouble. But thou wilt say, what if it fall out otherwise? and what if the times be so disposed, *that a suddaine constraint will bring more domage than profit to the commonwealth?* Wherefore herein I do with reason doubt, whether it be not fit that the Prince do somewhat consider the times *(which all Politicians are of opinion he ought to yield unto) or that it be better to differ* [defer] *the suppressing of overgrowne vices, then to make it openly knowne, that our force is too weake to checke and controll them*. . . Others cry out, *weapons and warre*: But do we not see again, *that weapons and warre have bred resistance by force of armes?*[11]

If repression was politically impossible, toleration was justifiable: this message had a particular political point in 1589, for at just that moment the Spanish Governor of the Netherlands, Parma, was trying to persuade King Philip that a policy of partial recognition of Calvinism should be followed to end the war. Lipsius moved back to the Spanish side when this policy seemed to be on the point of success, and he continued to urge it until his death despite Madrid's unwillingness to listen to the advice coming from Brussels.

Like Lipsius, Montaigne saw the ambiguous character of toleration. In his essay *Of the Liberty of Conscience*, he praised Julian the

---

[10] Lipsius, *Sixe bookes*, 62–3.   [11] *Ibid.*, 64.

Apostate's high-principled and philosophical conduct, but continued,

this is worthy consideration, that the Emperor *Julian*, useth the same receipt of libertie of conscience, to enkindle the trouble of civill dissention, which our Kings employ to extinguish. It may be said on one side, that, *To give faction the bridle to entertaine their opinion, is to scatter contention and sow division,* and as it were to lend it a hand to augment and increase the same: There beeing no Barre or Obstacle of Lawes to bridle or hinder his course. But on the other side, it might also be urged, that to give factions the bridle to uphold their opinion, is by that facilitie and ease, the readie way to mollifie and release them; and to blunt the edge, which is sharpened by rarenesse, noveltie, and difficultie.[12]

Either way, as in Lipsius, the question of toleration is a *pragmatic* one, to be resolved in accordance with the particular social circumstances and the general principle of the priority of civil peace.

Both aspects of Lipsius' views on toleration came under attack from contemporary writers. A number of Jesuits wrote against the irreligious implications of his Tacitism, while Coornhert wrote against his remark on the need to extirpate heresy. But his opponents shared a common sense that what was offensive about Lipsius was his open subordination of the requirements of religion to the needs of policy, and that they themselves possessed a genuine and well-founded knowledge of religious truths. This may seem fairly obvious in the case of the Jesuits, but it is more surprising in the case of Coornhert. And yet Coornhert published alongside his attack on Lipsius a work explicitly defending the possibility of human knowledge of ethical truths, through the pellucid medium of Scripture.[13] He was in fact a straightforward heir of the Evangelical humanists of the early sixteenth century, who believed that uninterrupted access to Scripture permitted men to determine moral truths of an uncontroversial kind: controversy arose only because access was persistently interrupted either by the withholding of the text from its readers (as in the Catholic Church) or by a culture which encouraged self-evidently absurd ways of reading it.

His defence of toleration in the controversy with Lipsius was thus two-fold. One plank of it was his conviction that toleration would not engender discord precisely because the essence of toleration

---

[12] Montaigne, *Essayes,* 607 (Book II. 20).
[13] Coornhert, *Breve documentum de cogitationum observatione* (Gouda, 159[ ]).

was free access to the Scriptures, and what men would find there could not sow discord among them. The other was a conviction that one of the messages which Scripture carried was itself a call for toleration – as he pointed out to Lipsius, rather acutely, it was Lipsius' principles which were faithfully applied by Christ's executioners.[14] But each of these planks rested on a confidence that moral and religious truths could be known – the opposite of the sceptical approach of Montaigne and Lipsius.

The attitudes expressed by Lipsius were of fundamental importance during the following century. The vast literature of works on *ragion di stato* which flooded Europe (principally from Italy) from the 1590s onwards owed a great deal to Lipsius' perception that a powerful state was necessary to protect its citizens irrespective of their or its religious beliefs, and he himself contributed to the burgeoning literature analysing the powers and capabilities of such a state in two works, one an account of the Roman army's organisation, discipline and morale, and the other an explanation of the *magnitudo* of the Roman Empire (i.e. its *grandezza* – a theme which preoccupied the Italian writers from his contemporary Botero onwards and which again picked up some Machiavellian motifs).[15] Lipsius saw that the empire's *grandezza* rested on the size of its population, their economic activity and the taxation system which provided funds for the state, and he also saw that modern empires (particularly Spain) had to be much more careful about their economic and financial base than had hitherto been the case. Like Botero's better-known remarks on the same subject in his *Ragion di Stato* of 1589, this was an intimation of what was quickly to become the fully fledged ideology of what we can, I think, still fairly call mercantilism – of industry and commerce put to the service of military-minded and imperialist states in a battle which was eventually won conclusively not by Spain but by England.

The main target of Lipsius' and Montaigne's scepticism had been the great constitutional and ethical systems of the previous generation – notably the Aristotelian natural law theory of the neo-Thomists, which attempted to integrate both juridical and ethical principles into a single structure, and the more idiosyncratic but equally systematic syntheses of Bodin and his followers. It was going to be difficult for any writer on ethics or politics to take either of these systems seriously again, for the case of the moral relativist

---

[14] Coornhert, *Defensio processus*, 71.
[15] Lipsius, *De militia Romana libri quinque* (Antwerp, 1595); *Admiranda, sive, De magnitudine Romana libri quattuor* (Antwerp, 1598).

against (for example) the Aristotelian list of virtues seemed extremely strong: many societies had exhibited neither temperance, fortitude nor prudence, and some had survived without certain kinds of justice. Moreover, the relevance to contemporary conditions of the late sixteenth-century sceptics, and the emotional force of their case, was extremely compelling. But equally compelling was the fact that ethical discourse *at all* was endangered by the sceptical position, let alone the fact that it denied the possibility of any human science to set beside the mathematical and natural sciences which were beginning to deliver their extraordinary modern bounty. The great achievement of political philosophy in the first half of the seventeenth century was thus the construction of a new theory of natural law which was avowedly anti-Aristotelian and capable of absorbing within itself the principal insights of the sceptical state-builders.

When at the end of the century the history of this new 'science of morality' came to be written, there was no doubt in the minds of its historians that Hugo Grotius had been its inventor, and indeed Grotius signalled his intentions clearly enough in the Prolegomena to *De Iure Belli ac Pacis* when he selected Carneades as the man whose arguments had to be countered if an adequate theory of universal justice was to be advanced. Essentially, what Grotius did (though the process is rather clearer in his early *De Iure Praedae* than in his complex and allusive later work) was to argue that there are two moral universals upon which an adequate ethical structure can be raised: one is the universal right of self-defence, and the other is the universal condemnation of violence against other human beings *except* in self-defence. These were Grotius' minimal principles of 'sociability', very far removed from the much richer Aristotelian account of a sociable animal. But they were also intended to be principles which even sceptics could accept, for they corresponded precisely to the needs upon which Lipsius and the rest had constructed their account of the life of wisdom and political action – the need to protect oneself and to eschew any *other* moral grounds for violence, such as religious imperatives. 'Necessities' in Lipsius or the *ragion di stato* writers became 'rights' in Grotius and his successors.[16]

One object of this transformation was, as I have said, to permit the free passage into a moral science of the particular ideas on

[16] I have discussed this shift in 'Grotius, Carneades and Hobbes', *Grotiana*, New Series, 4 (1983), 43–62, and in 'The Modern Theory of Natural Law', in *The Languages of Political Theory in Early-Modern Europe*, ed. Anthony Pagden (Cambridge, 1987).

economics and statecraft found in the earlier writers. For our purposes, the important particular idea was of course the attitude towards religious toleration; and in Grotius we indeed find exactly the same ambivalence about the subject as in Lipsius. Like Lipsius, Grotius had himself lived through events which demonstrated vividly the complexity of the issue.[17] He had been a political aide to the Dutch statesman Jan van Oldenbarnevelt during the period when the Arminians in the United Provinces turned to the state for protection against the attacks of orthodox Calvinists, and he had toured the country making speeches in town assemblies and writing pamphlets urging the need for state control of the church. He narrowly escaped with his life when the orthodox turned against Oldenbarnevelt in 1619 and had him executed, and he spent the rest of his life an embittered exile.

He had thus been presented in the starkest possible way with the central dilemma of the age: if religious strife and persecution were to be avoided, the power of the state in religious matters had to be upheld. In *De Iure Belli ac Pacis* he argued the case out. In general in that work he accepted the legitimacy of war for self-defence, or for reasons which could be unpacked ultimately as those of self-defence, such as (he believed) punishment. Consequently, and very unusually for his time, he accepted the legitimacy of private war, without any state authority (a useful position to take up at a time of imperial activity by a company, the Dutch East India Company, rather than a state). But he was clear that there could be no *religious* grounds for warfare, other than against militant atheists. The only propositions about God to which all men would assent, and whose denial constituted a threat to social existence, were 'that there is a deity, (one or more I shall not now consider), and that this deity has the care of human affairs'. 'Those who first attempt to destroy these Notions ought, on the Account of human Society in general, which they thus, without any just Grounds, injure, to be restrained.' Beyond that there was no justification for the persecution of any religious beliefs.[18]

But this once again pointed in two directions. No individual (or state) was entitled to enforce more extensively specified religious opinions upon another merely because of their conviction that those opinions were *correct*; but neither were they entitled to resist the imposition of religious ceremonies and dogmas by the state if it

---

[17] For Grotius' involvement in Dutch politics, see Jan den Tex, *Oldenbarnevelt* (Cambridge, 1973).

[18] Grotius, *The Rights of War and Peace* (London, 1738), 444–5 (Book II.20.46).

believed that it was necessary to do so for *political* reasons, i.e. reasons of communal peace. In a work written in 1617 but published posthumously thirty years later, the *De Imperio Summarum Potestatum circa Sacra*, he had elaborated this second point. The rulers of a state had the power to establish its religion; they could take advice from theologians just as they might from engineers or doctors, but those theologians could have no independent authority. Grotius claimed that in modern European societies citizens need not worry too much about the exercise of these powers by their rulers, as they would have no desire to subvert the fundamental principles of Christianity, and equally no desire for political reasons to risk giving offence to the mass of their subjects. But the Calvinist readers of Grotius' works certainly worried very greatly about their implications; he was assailed as an 'atheist' – 'ill principled men such as Selden, Grotius and Hobbes, . . . as bad as can be' said one of them. [19] Laudian Anglicans and Catholics had a similar response; anyone who wished for their church to have some independence from the state would react against Grotius' arguments.

As in many other respects, the person who followed out Grotius' ideas in this area to their logical conclusion and thereby illustrated their radically disconcerting character was Thomas Hobbes. His political theory, as is well known, rests on the two fundamental principles which Grotius had singled out: for Hobbes too allows a universal right of self-defence, and he also *limits* it to self-defence (as a number of passages in his works illustrate). The difference between them in this area is simply that Hobbes saw more clearly than Grotius the (so to speak) *epistemic* uncertainty of this situation: all men might agree that they were each entitled to defend themselves, but they might still *disagree* about what constituted a threat to any particular person. Each man would be the judge of his own circumstances, and would err on the side of caution; pre-emptive strikes and the *bellum omnium contra omnes* would result. A universal right was no use without an equally universal consensus about the conditions for the exercise of the right, and because of the inherent uncertainty of our knowledge of the world, no such consensus was naturally possible. It was possible *artificially*, however, if all men agreed to give up their power of judgement in cases of some doubt to a common judge – the Leviathan. (In cases of absolute certainty, such as where an armed man was directly attacking them, they

[19] William M. Lamont, *Godly Rule* (London, 1969), 116.

31

could of course not be expected to withhold their own judgement about the danger involved.)

Hobbes thus argued that a universal moral science of the Grotian kind entailed a powerful state – a conclusion towards which Grotius himself had drifted. The morally unconstrained state of the *ragion di stato* writers whom Hobbes had studied in his youth then turned into the equally unconstrained sovereign of *Leviathan*; and like their state, Hobbes's was posited against a background of scepticism and uncertainty about traditional moral absolutes. But *Leviathan* was above all a treatise on church government (it is no accident that the longest chapter in the work is on 'Power Ecclesiastical'), and Hobbes produced in it the same kind of ambiguous account of toleration that we have already found in Lipsius and Grotius. The sovereign in Hobbes has of course complete power to determine not only religious observance but even the content of Christian dogma; but he has this power in order to protect his subjects from the claims to a similar power by bodies other than the state. *Leviathan* in fact contains an eloquent plea for freedom of philosophical enquiry, in which the attitudes which I have been surveying receive a compact expression.

Our own Navigations make manifest, and all men learned in humane Sciences, now acknowledge there are Antipodes: And every day it appeareth more and more, that Years, and Dayes are determined by Motions of the Earth. Neverthelesse, men that have in their Writings but supposed such Doctrine, as an occasion to lay open the reasons for, and against it, have been punished for it by Authority Ecclesiasticall. But what reason is there for it? Is it because such opinions are contrary to true Religion? that cannot be, if they be true. Let therefore the truth be first examined by competent Judges, or confuted by them that pretend to know the contrary. Is it because they be contrary to the Religion established? Let them be silenced by the Laws of those, to whom the Teachers of them are subject; that is, by the Laws Civill: For disobedience may lawfully be punished in them, that against the Laws teach even true Philosophy. Is it because they tend to disorder in Government, as countenancing Rebellion, or Sedition? then let them be silenced, and the Teachers punished by vertue of his power to whom the care of the Publique quiet is committed; which is the Authority Civill.[20]

Like Grotius, Hobbes handed over immense power to the state in religious or intellectual matters, in order that the power of fanatics arrayed in churches could be smashed by politicians who would

---

[20] Hobbes, *Leviathan*, ed. C. B. Macpherson (Harmondsworth, 1968), 703 (ch. 46).

(Hobbes thought) have no particular ideological axe to grind, for their objective was simply to secure the public peace.

So standard is this combination of respect for the arguments of the sceptic, acceptance of a minimalist morality, and support for a potentially intolerant state, that it comes as no surprise to find the young Locke expressing an identical set of attitudes. What is extraordinary about Locke, however, and fully justifies his key position in the history of ideas about toleration, is that he (and virtually he alone) came to cut the link between the first two elements in the set and the third. But in doing so he illustrated the uncertain foundations upon which the principle of toleration must rest in a society where scepticism is possible.

Locke's respect for scepticism is well illustrated by a famous letter which he wrote to a friend in October 1659.

When did ever any truth settle it self in any ones minde by the strength and authority of its owne evidence? Truths gaine admittance to our thoughts as the philosopher did to the Tyrant by their handsome dresse and pleaseing aspect, they enter us by composition, and are entertaind as they suite with our affections, and as they demeane themselves towards our imperious passions, when an opinion hath wrought its self into our approbation and is gott under the protection of our likeing tis not all the assaults of argument, and the battery of dispute shall dislodge it. Men live upon trust and their knowledg is noething but opinion moulded up betweene custome and Interest, the two great Luminarys of the world, the only lights they walke by.[21]

At the same time he could write to another friend, Henry Stubbe, criticising his programme of toleration for all religious groups including Catholics, precisely because he was unpersuaded that the interests of the various religious groups were such that they would 'quietly unite . . . under the same government and unanimously cary the same civill interest and hand in hand march to the same end of peace and mutuall society though they take different ways towards heaven'.[22] It is clear that in 1659 Locke wished that this could be so, but it is also clear that he thought it unlikely, and that a policy of toleration would encourage the development of competing religious groups.

This argument was spelt out in more detail in the so-called *Two Tracts* written during the following two years against another advocate of (a degree of) toleration, Edward Bagshawe. Locke pointed out that Christianity had become in the modern world 'a perpetual

[21] Locke, *Correspondence*, ed. E. S. De Beer (Oxford, 1976), I.   [22] *Ibid.*

foundation of war and contention' because of Christians' deeply
entrenched but false beliefs about the necessity of correcting heresy
by force of arms if necessary.[23] These beliefs could not be expunged
simply by an appeal to reason, for beliefs so closely aligned (now) to
interests of various kinds could not be changed by rational argument; the prudent course was therefore for the magistrate to prevent this destructive competition by imposing uniformity. So far,
Locke was entirely within the intellectual tradition of Lipsius or
Grotius, a fact emphasised by his endorsement of a strong
sovereign.

But in 1667 Locke wrote a draft *Essay concerning Toleration* in which
he completely changed his ideas.[24] The change is particularly striking given that he had not changed his general ideas about ethics or
politics during the previous five years: his new ideas on toleration
arose out of the same intellectual presuppositions as his old ones,
including an acceptance of a powerful sovereign – toleration was to
be introduced by royal prerogative. The central argument of the
Essay, moreover, rests in a way on the same foundations as the argument of the *Two Tracts*, for it too depends on the force of a simple
observation about how people behave in the modern world. In the
Tracts, Locke had been most struck by the competitive fury of modern churches; but in the *Essay* he was most struck by the
impossibility of forcing sincere believers to abandon what they took
– rightly or wrongly – to be necessary to their salvation. It is hard not
to accept that he had been influenced by the behaviour of Dissenters confronted with the Clarendon Code in England, as well as
by the successful practice of toleration which he had witnessed in
the Duchy of Cleves and about which he wrote admiringly to
Robert Boyle. But if sincere believers cannot be forced into uniformity, then an attempt to do so may produce more civil strife than
simply leaving them alone (and Locke began to suspect that
religious uniformity had often been used as a cloak for the
dominance of one interest group in the population over the others).
This is the argument which is richly and eloquently documented in
the *Letter on Toleration*, and which represents the most persuasive
defence of toleration to come out of the seventeenth century; in its
origins it clearly antedates Locke's liberal political theory of the *Two
Treatises*.

[23] Locke, *Two Tracts on Government* ed. Philip Abrams (Cambridge, 1967), 160.
[24] For a discussion of this and Locke's other writings on toleration (a discussion to which I
am greatly indebted) see Locke, *A Letter concerning Toleration*, ed. James H. Tully
(Indianapolis, 1983), 1–16.

We can now, I think, see more clearly the limited character of this argument. None of the ideas about toleration or uniformity we have been considering, all of which grew out of a more or less sceptical attitude towards traditional dogmas, present the issue as one of *high principle*. All the writers I have discussed would have agreed that there are not, and could not be, grounds for enforcing one's own beliefs upon another *simply because of the nature of those beliefs*; but beliefs *could* be enforced upon unwilling subjects for pragmatic or political reasons. Equally, they could be left alone to practise their own religion for the same reasons. The ambiguous character of Lipsius' remarks about toleration set the tone for all subsequent discussions of the issue in the seventeenth century, and even Locke can be read as simply moving from Lipsius' defence of repression to his defence of toleration as the circumstances in England changed.

Could we have expected more? In a way, the modern problem of toleration is an example of the general problem for the sceptic, originally put to him in antiquity, namely how can one *live* one's scepticism? If the sceptic is to live the life of *ataraxia*, then it is hard to see how he can emotionally respond to the sight of other people clinging passionately to their beliefs in the ideological storm, or feel that they should be protected from pain by having their *beliefs* protected. After all, the central assumption of the sceptic is that the only route to protection from pain is the *abandonment* of belief. It is untrue that a relativistic attitude to morality or politics necessarily and in itself implies a commitment to pluralism as a value: the history I have sketched illustrates how one powerful kind of relativism led to precisely the opposite commitment. Even the emergence of a new kind of scepticism with Hume does not obviously change this state of affairs: it remains true that strong beliefs are potentially dangerous things, and that the wise relativist may find himself defending intellectual repression on pragmatic grounds.

2

A more tolerant Hobbes?

ALAN RYAN

Hobbes's *Leviathan* is a book which catches the imagination for many reasons – the vigour of the prose, the confidence of the author, and, above all the scope of the argument. Hobbes begins with the first principles of meaning and knowledge, continues through an account of human nature, and after justifying absolute governments concludes triumphantly with an analysis of the nature of religion, the proper powers of the churches, and the sources of the improper powers of false prophets. One aspect of Hobbes's case which particularly catches the eye of the philosopher is his apparent espousal of a conventionalist theory of truth; he seems to believe that we *make* propositions true by deciding on definitions of terms, and that one task of the sovereign is to create moral truths by imposing rules for calling acts or states of affairs 'good' and 'bad'. It is an astonishingly bold, and implausible, view.[1]

Leviathan also sets great store by education – in a wide sense of that term. We are born unapt for society and are trained into sociability. Put Hobbes's conventionalism together with Hobbes's obsession with social training, and we see a philosophical totalitarian trying to ensure that the very language we use, and the propositions we take for true, make the project of rebellion against our rulers incoherent. Why else should he insist that the sovereign cannot act 'unjustly' or 'injure' his subjects? Is he not, like Rousseau after him, demanding that the sovereign should know how to remake human nature, and in the process make us unable to think rebellious thoughts?[2]

If there is that temptation in the text of *Leviathan*, much else sug-

---

[1] J. W. N. Watkins, *Hobbes's System of Ideas* (London, 1968), 99–118.
[2] Alan Ryan, 'The Nature of Human Nature in Hobbes and Rousseau', in Jonathan Benthall (ed.), *Nature and Human Nature* (London, 1974), 3–19; cf Marshall Berman, *The Politics of Authenticity* (New York, 1972).

gests that Hobbes's ambitions are less far-reaching. In a memorial volume to John Plamenatz I argued that Hobbes's philosophical account of the nature of science, morality, and religion left room for a large measure of toleration. The conventionalist theory of truth did not on closer inspection go deep – Hobbes's insistence that definitions had to be well chosen implied that where truth was in question at all it was not established by definitional fiat; his account of the way the sovereign lays down moral truths was not an attempt to turn moral judgements into necessary truths, and these into truths which were made true by convention or imposition; where Hobbes allowed for the 'imposition' of doctrine, this appeared to be because there was no question of truth at stake.[3]

The thought that there is room in Hobbes for a large measure of toleration will not surprise historians. The historians' Hobbes is a figure who wants peace for ordinary subjects and in addition wants intellectual freedom for scientists and philosophers. For all that, there remains a gap which even the historians have not done much to fill – for quite good reasons. We lack an answer to the question of what Hobbes's contemporaries thought he was saying – whether any of them thought he was defending an unusual degree of intellectual or moral or religious *laissez-faire*. My case was *a priori*; I tried to show that Hobbes's philosophical position left room for a greater degree of intellectual and religious *laissez-faire* than many commentators had suggested. It is not clear how consistent Hobbes's underlying philosophical position is or, therefore, just how naturally it lends itself to a positive defence of toleration, and this clouds the issue when one is assessing what Hobbes's contemporaries made of him. Nonetheless, one can make a start by seeing what they particularly disliked about his doctrines, and how that bears on plausible interpretations of his basic position.

Essentially, this chapter is such a start. It is no more than a start. It poses a question about Hobbes and his contemporaries which they never couched in the way I couch it, and their arguments do not yield a simple answer. What emerges clearly is that in an age when almost nobody asserted a natural right to free speech in general, Hobbes was denounced, not for asserting any such right but because his own pride on the one hand and his secularism on the other subverted *all* intellectual authority and religious authority along with it; much of the indignation lavished on *Leviathan* was directly self-interested, of course, because his defence of political

---

[3] 'Hobbes, Toleration and the Inner Life', in David Miller and Larry Siedentop (eds.), *The Nature of Political Theory* (Oxford, 1982), 197–218; for a very different view, see W. K. Jordan, *The Development of Religious Toleration in England* (Cambridge, Mass., 1938), IV, 299–320.

absolutism was conjoined with a fierce hostility to the power of the Anglican Church. Yet defenders of the Church of England monopoly could not help but adduce some general defence of ecclesiastical authority; Hobbes's truculent individualism, and his contempt for the authority of tradition made him an enemy to any principled – as opposed to pragmatically justified – case for requiring uniformity in thought.

Defenders of toleration – usually expressed as 'liberty of conscience' – were friends of religion. Hobbes had no time for liberty of conscience, and was, if anything, hostile to what his contemporaries (though not the ancient Romans) took to be religion. However, it did entail a large measure of intellectual *laissez-faire* for reasonable men. The enemies of this form of toleration in Restoration England were the defenders of the religious monopoly and the political power of the Church of England; an enemy of the Church of England such as Hobbes had more than adequate reason to argue in favour of toleration. It is apparent at first glance that Hobbes did not have an explicit doctrine of toleration, in the sense of 'liberty of conscience'; Hobbes does not devote his efforts to a defence of toleration in the way that Locke does. This then prompts the question what is a defence of toleration? What unprincipled defence might Hobbes have made? Until we have some view of the answer to these questions, we cannot get far in extending the *a priori* case that there was *room* for toleration in Hobbes's account by appealing to historical evidence to show that he used the room so created.

I adopt the following tactics. I begin with some dogmatic remarks about possible accounts of toleration and its grounds. These add nothing to the extensive literature on these matters, but draw a few distinctions to separate out Hobbesian 'laissez-penser' from Lockian and Millian ideal-based defences of freedom of thought, and separate out Hobbesian arguments for orthodoxy from the arguments of his contemporaries. This does not settle the old and absorbing question of Hobbes's atheism, though I should like to do so, if only because the most frequent charge levelled against Hobbes was precisely that he was an atheist. I end by stressing that Hobbes's account of the limits of toleration is political, instrumental and utilitarian. All the same, Hobbes's instrumental and utilitarian arguments for toleration are less ignominious than we tend to think, and are quite compelling in their own right.[4]

---

[4] But cf 'Hobbes and the Inner Life', 218.

I

Toleration is a topic with indefinite boundaries. Here it can be framed as a question of the following kind: 'how far ought the secular authorities to go in securing adherence to a particular religious creed?' Ought they to permit dissenters to publish their dissenting beliefs; ought they to permit dissenters to practise their non-conforming forms of worship, either publicly or in private? Whose view of what is essential to orthodoxy ought to be taken, and what qualifications do they need for dictating an orthodoxy? How extensive a range of doctrines falls within the scope of orthodoxy? What are the grounds for securing uniformity of belief, and are they the same as the grounds for seeking uniformity of practice? What benefits do individuals get from the enforcement of uniformity, and what price do they pay for it, if any?

There is a crucial feature of the case made by the saints of liberalism which is not often enough stressed; this is that their defence of toleration in all areas of life relies on considerations which are most at home in a religious context. This is obvious in the case of Locke, who defends toleration on the ground that God requires a willing belief and submission from his servants, not a forced and external obedience.[5] It is, however, equally true of Mill, whose defence of liberty of thought does not rest on the claim that by my mere thoughts I cannot damage anyone else's interests, but on the bolder and more interesting claim that unless I am exposed to challenge and counter-evidence, my beliefs are not really *my* beliefs at all, and cannot be held with the liveliness which alone makes them worth holding in the first place.[6]

There are many pragmatic reasons why governments might be ill advised to impose any great degree of religious orthodoxy – the most obvious is that the attempt secures no genuine uniformity of conviction but creates endless irritation and resentment. This is Hobbes's contention in *Behemoth* and in his essay on heresy.[7] The argument which takes hold in the liberal tradition, however, has stressed the peculiar damage which it does to someone to violate his or her intellectual integrity. In Locke's universe, this violation is

---

[5] John Locke, *The Second Treatise on Government and a Letter concerning Toleration*, ed. J. W. Gough (Oxford, 1956), 157–8.

[6] J. S. Mill, *Utilitarianism, Liberty and Representative Government* (London, 1910), e.g. 97, 105, 112.

[7] Thomas Hobbes, *Behemoth*, The English Works of Thomas Hobbes (London, 1840), VI, 174ff; 'An Historical Narration Concerning Heresy', E.W., IV, 385–408.

condemned twice over – God will not accept an unwilling or insincere submission; and the individual, whose primary duty is to employ his or her intellect, 'the candle of the Lord', in seeking out the path of duty and the road to salvation, is frustrated in the performance of this most important of all tasks.

This picture of the individual's fundamental duty is relied on by all subsequent liberals, even when they turn their backs on the Christian framework which sustains Locke's account of it. Kant's account of our duty to perfect ourselves and Mill's picture of man 'as a progressive being' are secularised versions of what earlier appeared in Locke's *Letters*. Hobbes's limited defence of toleration does not rest on anything of the sort. An account of the individual's duty of self-perfection answers the question I posed above about the damage which submission to intolerance does to the individual, but it does not answer it in a Hobbesian way.[8] Hobbes's answer is not based on the individual's duty of self-perfection but upon the foolishness of causing needless anxiety and resentment.

An aspect of the liberal position at which we must look more closely in due course is that for Locke, though not his successors, one danger to be set against any sort of conformity is the threat which subscribing to a false doctrine may pose to our immortal salvation. Since his or her final salvation is at stake, no individual can rationally hand over the care of his or her soul to anyone else. God has set us on the earth to go about His business, and He will enquire in due course into our stewardship of the life He gave us. No thinking person could rest easy with the fear that what the state commands us to do might be so displeasing in the eyes of God that our salvation was imperilled.

This argument is one that Hobbes considers, though as one might say, somewhat at arm's length; he is best known – and in general, rightly – for arguing that the state cannot command anything which genuinely threatens our salvation. This is only true in general terms; Hobbes objects to governments over-extending their search for doctrinal uniformity on the grounds that this sets a man to 'play for his salvation at pile and cross', and he admits at any rate one case – happily for him, a case of no continuing relevance – where the subject may challenge his ruler's account of what rule of public worship to follow.[9]

Academics writing in the safety of 1980s universities in America and Western Europe are ill placed to take Hobbes wholly seriously.

---

[8] *Utilitarianism*, 97.   [9] *De Cive* (Oxford, 1985), 203.

Utilitarian arguments for doctrinal uniformity and a uniform public worship imposed by a not too intrusive authority do not impress them, and they are almost invariably more impressed by appeals to human rights including therein the right to free speech and freedom of conscience. Were we to look further outwards and consider the doctrines of *Leviathan* in the context of Iran, say, we would be more impressed with the argument that the sovereign has the right and the duty to impose one system of public worship and one interpretation of Holy Writ, not for the sake of salvation or truth, but only in order that peace and prosperity should be preserved. Thomas Tenison complained of Hobbes that 'He hath subjected the Canon of Scripture to the Civil Powers and taught them the way of turning the Alcoran into Gospel'; we might, looking at the horrors of sectarian strife on our own doorstep in Ulster, in the streets of Beirut, and in much else of the world, think that turning the Alcoran into Gospel on the terms Hobbes had in mind would be no bad thing. For Hobbes tried to show how it could be turned into Gospel without limiting freedom of thought.

However, since liberal Britain has long taken religious toleration for granted, it is perhaps more interesting in the first place to turn to the case for the enforcement of orthodoxy. It comes in two versions. The first is the true believer's argument. Since the conditions of salvation are known, and the thing that matters most to anyone is whether or not he or she will be saved, it is evidently right and proper to bring sinners to salvation by any means possible. Did not Christ say 'compel them to come in'? 'To deny all coercive power' to the church 'is to deny the commission which the Great King, *Luke*, 14 gave to his servants, that they should compel those in the highwaies to come to his supper' said Alexander Ross in *Leviathan Drawn Out with a Hook*. It is not persecution but charity to prevent people imperilling their immortal souls; defending the duty of the sovereign to do just that John Shafto wrote.

he is not only by his private Conscience, but publick Ingagement obliged: For he who sees another man in his Opinion blind, and going directly upon a Pit, or Precipice, where he shall be sure to pitch upon his own death, is very much to blame if he do not hinder him from running thus foolishly to his destruction. . .

Since they are sinning either out of ignorance or bravado, they lose nothing by being made to conform to the true faith. *Compelle intrare* had long been the basis of Catholic thinking on the absurdity of tolerating heretics; neither the Puritan contemporaries of Hobbes, nor his Anglican assailants, were going to appeal to a Papal Bull for authority, but they were content with the same logic.

The second is the politician's argument. This admits from the outset that whether a given doctrine will lead to salvation is unknowable or at any rate debatable. What is knowable is that agreement in matters of religion leads to peace and good order, economic prosperity, military efficiency, and good private morals, while dissension leads to anarchy, civil war, libertinism, poverty, and a host of evils. It is therefore the duty of the state to impose one faith on the whole population in order that peace and plenty may be secured. This political argument occurs in writers like Machiavelli as often as in the devout; in these 'political' writers, it is religion as outward performance and the public avowal of respect for the Gods which is aimed at, and the degree of 'faith' instilled is a secondary matter entirely.

The obvious interpretation of Hobbes as a simple enemy to toleration rests on the fact that he produces just such a political case for the imposition of one doctrine by the sovereign.[10] Yet, seeing how hostile he was to classical political theorising, we cannot assume that he will adopt the classical concern for public profession and its unconcern with inward faith. The question the political defence of uniformity meets is, naturally, one about its scope – how *much* in the way of doctrine ought to be imposed? Those who fear that men will run amok if not tightly controlled in everything they think and do will no doubt be susceptible to arguments for expanding the range of imposition – de Maistre, many years later, is an instance, and so, perhaps, is Dr Johnson, though his enthusiasm for wholesale conformity perhaps owed as much to a feeling for the intellectual and emotional insecurities of individuals left to work out their own salvation as to any fear of social and political upheaval. Against this is the Machiavellian or classical republican view that so long as God and the commonwealth enjoin much the same things, a nice enquiry into doctrinal detail is a distracting waste of time. What emerges is that although Hobbes generally has no time for the ancients, this is one area in which he sides unequivocally with Machiavellian precepts.

We must tackle one further question before embarking on our main topic. This is the question of who is to decide what doctrines are to be enforced. There are two candidates and two only – in the modern world, that is, where direct instruction from God is no lon-

---

[10] *Leviathan* (London, 1914), 196.

ger to be looked for as it was under Abraham and his heirs. Either the state ought to decide or the church ought to be granted powers of its own to enforce orthodoxy. The two alternatives can, of course, be institutionalised in ways which make the alternatives less stark – there might be church courts such as the Inquisition which had the power to find people guilty of heresy and turn them over to the state for punishment, or there might be civil courts which could treat heresy as a civil offence using assessors and prosecutors provided by the church. Hobbes's position is, as is well known, that the power must remain firmly in the hands of the state; to separate the power to determine doctrine from other aspects of sovereignty would be as fatal as to separate any other powers.[11] What makes Hobbes distinctive and so offensive to his opponents is precisely the extent to which he insists on subordinating the church's authority to the state's.

Given this brief discussion, we need to ask Hobbes the following questions: ought the state to secure uniformity in matters of religion? Is this uniformity to be understood primarily in terms of practice or in terms of belief? Is there any way of telling what doctrines men must believe to secure their eternal salvation, and whether there are things they must not do or say or think if they are not to imperil that salvation? Is there anything to be said against the establishment of religious orthodoxy, either on religious or other grounds? Ought the state to listen to the church in deciding what the limits of religious toleration are to be?

The point of asking the questions in this form is to line up Hobbes and his opponents in face of the same questions. To put the matter peremptorily, Hobbes's opponents generally held some or all of the following things: that between the Bible, the tradition of the Christian churches, inspired thinking by individuals, and the enquiries of the philosophers, it was known what God required of us both for our earthly peace and our heavenly salvation, and it was therefore the business of the state to see that true doctrine on these points was taught and anything hostile was suppressed; that the best informed people on these matters were priests, or theologians, or a council of the church, and that the state therefore ought to take its cue from their deliberations and decisions; that individuals ought to be duly grateful to have their doubts and anxieties taken care of; and that the lower orders in particular ought to be given no opportunity to think for themselves on these issues: 'why should

[11] *Ibid.*, 178ff.

not therefore every Mechanick, with the same humility, submit to the Opinion of the Learned in points of Learning; and to the Exposition of the Scripture, in Scripture-Interpretation?' asked Shafto.[12]

There were inumerable preachers and writers who thought that they and others like them were the recipients of direct inspiration from God; this, though, did not lead to a demand for toleration, only to a demand that they should be listened to and nobody else. They particularly enraged Hobbes, and it was against them that many of his arguments about the nature of prophecy and about the knowability of God's commandments were directed. The immediate point is that they were not defenders of toleration, even if they were inadvertent defenders of a free for all. If we add to the basic enthusiasm of Hobbes's opponents for enforcing true religion the belief that true doctrine covers most aspects of life, we have a thoroughgoing theory of non-toleration which supports a large and active political role for the churches.[13]

What I hope to show is that whether Hobbes was or was not an atheist – the most common charge against him – he was by the standards of his age, and was seen to be, a defender of toleration. The clever and original part of his case was the way he combined a defence of scientific openness with an insistence on the state's duty to secure religious uniformity. The extent to which governments ought to interfere with the intellectual activities of their subjects was limited by prudential considerations, reinforced by scepticism about the extent to which theological issues were the subject of rational enquiry; conflict between the state's demands for uniformity and individual desire for liberty ought to be minimal. Nothing fit for the state to decide by decree impinges on genuine intellectual issues.

This eliminated any conflict between the search for salvation and our duty to obey the state in all things. Although it would be unreasonable for a man to obey the state at the cost of eternal damnation, there is no risk of that cost being incurred. (This claim has to be qualified a little, as suggested above, and explained below.) The state can demand obedience in matters of religion, because it can limit the impact of that demand. It ought to limit its demands for professions of belief since the way to advance science and thus in the end the well-being of mankind must be to allow scientists to

---

[12] John Shafto, *The Great Law of Nature* (London, 1673), 76.
[13] Thomas Tenison, *The Creed of Mr Hobbes Examined* (London, 1670) and John Dowel, *Leviathan Heretical* (London, 1683) make such a case.

investigate everything that it makes any sense to investigate. Moreover, it must be the state, not the church, which lays down the few fundamentals to which everyone must subscribe; to hand over the decision to the squabbling sectaries would be mad. Hobbes offended his contemporaries by his scepticism, his anti-clericalism, and his Erastianism; they could not help seeing that at the end of the Hobbesian road lay a wholly secular society, where religious belief is a matter of private inclination. This is not to say that Hobbes was identified as a 'liberal' by his contemporaries; given the absence of the term from the seventeenth-century vocabulary, it is hard to guess what they would have thought of our classificatory difficulties with him. He was rightly identified as a secular utilitarian, who would *generally* but not as a matter of principle side with intellectual *laissez-faire*.[14]

II

The peculiarities of Hobbes's views on the nature of God are well known. All we can know positively of God is that He exists.[15] What He is is unknowable, and speculation is even faintly impious, since all attribution is privative, and it insults God to suggest any deficiency in Him. The natural springs of religion are curiosity and fear. These combined with ignorance of secondary causes and the uncontrolled imagination of most men generate all sorts of superstitions. The existence of one God (as opposed to a riot of minor deities) is vouched for by reason rather than by fear, even though the role of fear in leading us to a belief in and submission to the deity is not to be under-estimated. Fear begets curiosity, reason begets an understanding of causes, and leads us back from effects to causes; eventually we come to the First Cause, which we denominate God.[16]

Hobbes insists – perhaps against Spinoza – that it is atheism to say that the world itself is God. (The charge was levelled against Hobbes himself that his materialism amounted to atheism, because it left no room for anything beside the world.) God must be separate from the world, able to intervene in its affairs whenever He chooses.[17] The avowed atheist who knowingly denies the existence of God does not commit an injustice, because he does not violate

---

[14] Alexander Ross, *Leviathan Drawn Out with a Hook* (London, 1653).
[15] *Leviathan*, 193–4.
[16] See also *De Cive*, 192, and *Leviathan*, 54–6.   [17] *Leviathan*, 193.

natural law by denying the existence of the legislator of that law. Hobbes wavers on the question of whether he none the less commits treason against God. Hobbes acknowledges the force of the argument that God says 'believe in me', but the injunction cannot bind the man who does not believe in Him in the first place. If the atheist is not a traitor or unjust, he is still an enemy, and he is certainly a fool, just as the Old Testament says he is. He is a fool because he is imprudent. Imprudence can be represented as a sin if it is seen as a breach of natural law, and Hobbes had taken a sterner view of imprudence in *De Cive* than he later took in *Leviathan*. In *De Cive*, the fool is reproached with breaking the natural law injunction to take proper care of ourselves, whereas in *Leviathan*, the fact that the law is no law to him leaves him sinlessly imprudent.[18]

This naturalistic account of why we are disposed to believe in God, coming as it does on top of Hobbes's naturalistic and sceptical account of how we come to believe in ghosts, spirits, and fairies seems to blur the distinction between a belief in fairy tales and genuine religion. The next quesiton, then, is what the difference is between *superstition* and *religion*. Hobbes's reply is that all mankind is vulnerable to superstition, and that true religion is believed in by those who believe rightly because they have had the 'speciall assistance of God'.[19] The mark of superstition is idolatry. Right reason steers men away from superstition, because right reason tells us that all we can know of God is that He exists and is omnipotent. Omnipotence is not a positive attribute of God – Hobbes knew better than to leave the gate open to the usual paralogisms; like other terms expressing infinitude, 'omnipotence' expresses an incapacity of the mind, in this case an incapacity to set limits to divine power. Unlike medieval theologians who argued that we ascribed attributes to God on the basis of analogy, Hobbes thought that the ascription was meaningless. Again, this was much deplored: 'it is the good pleasure of God that we should really believe him to be such as we have spoken him to be . . . we ought also to believe that he really in his own Nature and Essence is such, because the same faculties reasonably judge that he is no deceiver, for that is an Attribute inconsistent with the former perfections that constitute his Nature'.[20] Like Hume after him, however, he was not wholly hostile to meaninglessness in a good cause; to call God a 'body incorporeal' was strictly self-contradictory, for our conception of

---

[18] *De Cive*, 184, but see 199; *Leviathan*, 190 repeats *De Cive*, 184.   [19] *De Cive*, 200.
[20] *Great Law of Nature*, 33.

body is the same thing as our conception of the corporeal. Yet if it was meant for praise, that was acceptable.

Who, then, is the true God? He is the God of Abraham and Isaac. The Israelites were commanded to worship Him and no other God, and otherwise to do whatever Abraham and his heirs should command. Hobbes does not suggest that anything other than revelation could have led men to Abraham's God, nor does he try to palliate the arbitrariness of God's behaviour – here or anywhere else.[21] God's revelation of Himself to the Israelites and covenant with Abraham and again with Moses make one important difference to Hobbes's discussion of God's kingdom; the Israelites were actually, not metaphorically, ruled by God through the mouths of His prophets. His kingship over the Israelites was not His natural kingship over all mankind, but a special kingship by covenant.

When Israel chose a king for itself, wanting to be like all other nations, this amounted to the deposition of God with God's own consent, and thereafter there was no special kingdom. It is under the special kingdom of God that the one case arises where obedience to our earthly rulers might be unlawful. For once God had commanded the Israelites to worship Him in the particular ways Abraham laid down, they would have been wrong to worship Him in other ways, even where they were commanded to do so by their earthly governors subsequent to Abraham. This, and this only, is an exception to Hobbes's general insistence that there can be no conflict between the demands of religion and the commands of the sovereign. In God's natural kingdom there is no such conflict. God reigns by natural law over all who believe in Him; the kingdom of Christ, established by the 'new covenant', is neither an earthly kingdom, nor part of God's kingdom by nature, for it refers forward to the kingdom which will be established on earth at the Second Coming.[22]

What Hobbes was eager to establish was that what men were obliged to do was *worship* God; worshipping is defined as praising someone from an opinion we have of their power. Since we are of the opinion that the power of God is overwhelming, there is no limit to the extent to which we should be ready to honour God. There is little else we ought to do – there is little scope for natural theology in Hobbes's system. We know that God is to be worshipped and we know what worship is. We know that the natural rules for worship are that we should do and say whatever

[21] *Leviathan*, 56–7.   [22] *Ibid.*, 261.

expresses a desire to honour His power, and that what is honourable is otherwise a matter of local convention which the sovereign lays down, just as he lays down all other rules of honour. So, if it is a sign of honour to remove your hat in the presence of your superiors, praying bareheaded is the obvious rule to adopt; the crucial non-conventional principle is that nothing may be done which treats God with levity, familiarity, or contempt.[23] There is, to repeat, no point in enquiring into the attributes and qualities of God – and negatively, all we can know is that it must be a sort of insult to Him to suggest that He wants, desires, lusts, or hungers after anything, as it must be to give him a body of any particular shape, size, duration, or motion. All these attributes are privative, and therefore inconsistent with the being of God. It then becomes apparent why there is no room for conflict between the commands of the earthly sovereign and our duties towards God. The sovereign who knows his task will require only that we do what by reason and as a matter of local convention *counts as* doing honour to an essentially unknowable God.

That God is a 'hidden God' Hobbes takes for granted. God no longer appears to prophets; miracles cease and with them true prophecy; all we have to go on is the Bible and its interpretation. Given the inscrutability of God, the interpretation of the Bible cannot be a matter of truth in the usual sense, but a matter of law.[24] It belongs to the office of the sovereign to say how men shall understand the Bible. Hobbes was ambivalent about the effects of the translation of the Bible. At times, he seems to be hostile to its having been translated, complaining bitterly of the way people read it through a couple of times and then think themselves qualified to know just what God intends. On the other hand, he also says that it contains the simplest and most appealing summary there is of men's moral duties, and therefore that it should be made available to everyone – suitably interpreted, no doubt.[25]

Men in civil society have given up the right to use their independent judgement in interpretation; it follows that if there are sins committed in that interpretation, we are innocent of them, and our rulers alone are guilty. We cannot be blamed for the sins of others and can safely give up the right of interpretation to the civil sovereign.[26] The right of interpretation must rest with the civil sovereign and not with the church – or, to put it better, the church

---

[23] *Ibid.*, 193–6.   [24] Leslie Stephen, *Hobbes* (Ann Arbor, 1964), 231.
[25] *Behemoth*, 190–1.   [26] *Leviathan*, 172.

must be one with the city and the spiritual power part of the civil power. Hobbes anticipated Locke in arguing that a church was by its nature, and in the absence of rules established by the civil sovereign, only a body of men agreed in matters of faith. Its authority over its members and its claim on the attention of non-members did not rest on power but on the arguments of its teachers and the goodness of their lives.[27] Once a civil sovereign declared which church people might or might not belong to, that was the end of the matter, but only for the sake of keeping the peace. It was no part of the state's duty to enforce a conception of heresy put about by a church, and heresy in a legal sense was no more than the persistence of a private person in asserting doctrines the sovereign had forbidden him to preach in public.[28]

Most of the argument is avowedly directed towards quelling the pretensions of the Catholic Church and the Puritan sectaries, though all friends of the clergy found it obnoxious. It worked against the Catholic Church by shutting off all possibility that a sovereign might be heretical – if heresy was defined in legalistic terms, it followed that no sovereign was heretical, since he decided what heresy was, and if heresy was defined in doctrinal terms, all a church could do was refuse to take communion with him; and even this was out of the question for the sovereign's own subjects, since their obligation to obey him in externals trumped every other obligation. What they thought of the sovereign's doctrinal attachments was another matter and their business.[29] The argument is intended to secure the supremacy of the civil authority; it also implies something in which Hobbes and Locke are agreed, that doctrinal agreement considered as genuine intellectual agreement is a private matter which ought to be left to individuals. Hobbes seems to have thought that the contentiousness of his contemporaries would make it exceedingly difficult to put this into practice, and therefore that for the foreseeable future there would have to be a large measure of public regulation. The principle of the thing fairly obviously points in the direction of toleration. Uniformity in matters of worship is about manners in public rather than about anything deeper; just as obscenity is in itself no offence but only so when brought to notice, so is eccentricity of worship. Hence, Hobbes sees no cause to curtail individuals' rights to worship *privately* in whatever way they choose.[30] This is one way in which Hobbes would have been a useful prop to the odd alliance of

---

[27] *Ibid.*, 268ff.   [28] *Ibid.*, 316.   [29] *De Cive*, 243–4.   [30] *Leviathan*, 193.

Catholics and freethinkers who aroused so much indignation after the Restoration.

Hobbes wrote to secure the peace. He was not writing about toleration but about the right of the civil sovereign to control the squabbling clergy. Still, the intellectual who wants to get on with his own subject unthreatened is one natural beneficiary of Hobbes's sharp distinctions between the public and the private and between matters of doctrine and matters of philosophical and scientific enquiry. We must not exaggerate. Hobbes's views on the relations of science and philosophy have never been satisfactorily straightened out, nor can we extract any particular view of the social conditions under which science would flourish. We cannot link Hobbes's picture of science to a theory of toleration as we can Popper's or Mill's.[31] None the less, the enquiry into how the world is constructed and how it may be altered for human benefit can only advance if its limits are set and defended against encroachment by religious enthusiasts. Hobbes's views certainly set out these limits.

III

I will end with a short justification of this view of a 'more tolerant' Hobbes and a defence of my taking up a modern audience's time with it. In this section, I turn to Hobbes's critics to show how far it was the 'freethinking' implications of Hobbes's position that infuriated them. The critics of Hobbes were united in two things: they deplored the way his principles justified the subjects of Charles I in deserting him as soon as the Parliamentarians were firmly in control, and they deplored his views on religion, the authority of the clergy, and the role of the state in relation to religion. The first point does not much concern us and may anyway have been factitious; Hobbes insists in his *Letter to Dr Wallis*[32] that his argument was always that 'whosoever had done as much as in him did lye to protect the King in War, had liberty afterwards to provide themselves of such Protection as they could get', which was absolutely not an argument which entitled anyone to transfer his allegiance whenever he could get away with it. For all that, Clarendon repeated the charge in his *Brief View of Leviathan*; writing in exile himself, he also took (or professed to take) exception to Hobbes's

---

[31] See my 'Popper and Liberalism', in G. Currie and A. Musgrave (eds.), *Popper and the Human Sciences* (Mouton, 1985), 89–104.

[32] *Mr Hobbes Considered in his Reputation, Loyalty, Manners and Religion: A Letter to Dr Wallis* (London, 1662), 24.

view that a man under sentence of banishment was no longer a subject but an enemy.[33]

The second point concerns us more. Hobbes's critics held that Hobbes's views were heretical, and that heresy was a crime at common law. This is the whole burden of John Dowel's *Leviathan Heretical* of 1683; Hobbes had argued that heresy originally and properly meant no more than a private opinion contrary to that of other men, and therefore that heresy did not deserve any sort of punishment– it was no more to be punished than any other form of intellectual eccentricity. It is plain that a powerful motive for producing this historical account of heresy (though it could not be published in his lifetime) was to clear himself of the charge of heresy, and to save his skin when the bishops made their motion to have the old man burned as a heretic.[34] Arguments from origins were powerful arguments in the seventeenth century; to seize the 'original' meaning of heresy was to chalk up a victory. Once government laid down what doctrines might be professed in public, then heresy meant any private opinion obstinately expressed against the command of the sovereign. Hobbes always tried to drag the term back to its original meaning, and to insist that when the state first took over authority to require religious conformity, it only exercised this authority over the clergy. Even then the penalty for nonconformity was simply separation. This, obviously, was what Hobbes would have preferred still, even though he confessed that as a penalty it held no terror for the unbeliever.[35]

Dowel and Clarendon insisted that Hobbes was wrong as to history, theology, and law, and Clarendon had predated Dowel in claiming that almost all of the doctrines of *Leviathan* were 'contrary to all the laws established in this country'.[36] Both held that the Romans – whom Hobbes had praised for tolerating any religion which did not threaten the peace – were more uniformitarian than Hobbes said, and deplored Hobbes's claim that the Romans rightly regarded religion as a civil matter. Both attacked at great length Hobbes's (admittedly extraordinary) account of the doctrine of the Trinity as manifestly heretical. Tenison remarked, 'You surprize me here with such an explication of the Trinity as has not been invented by any Heretick of the unluckiest wit, for these sixteen hundred years', and one cannot but sympathise with him.[37] In any

---

[33] Edward Hyde, Earl of Clarendon, *A Brief View and Survey of the Dangerous and pernicious Errors to Church and State, in Mr Hobbes's Book Entitled Leviathan* (Oxford, 1676), Preface.
[34] *Leviathan Heretical*, pp. 110–32; John Aubrey, *Brief Lives* (Harmondsworth, 1964), 316–17. [35] *Hobbes*, 229–32. [36] *A Brief View*, 130–1. [37] *Mr Hobbes's Creed*, 38.

event, Hobbes's attempt to make sense of trinitarian dogma by supposing that Moses 'personified' the Father, Christ the Son and the church the Holy Spirit was heroic but in the circumstances pointless. His opponents were mostly at pains to insist that it was heretical *in terms of English law*; Englishmen were required to adhere to the Creed, and the Creed said plainly that God was three in one, not one represented by three.

Hobbes's attempt to wriggle out of the charge by pointing out that when he wrote *Leviathan* there was no licensing system in operation and that private men might then write what they chose was strenuously resisted by Dowel, who insisted that the writ *de heretico comburendo* was still good in English law.[38] So it went with all Hobbes's theological views. He was accused of treating God as if he had parts – if everything in the universe was corporeal, then God must be a body, and if a body, He must have parts, which was heretical. More subtly, Archbishop Tenison pointed out that Hobbes must believe in a bodily God, but a bodily God had to be part of the universe, and Hobbes himself had insisted that a non-separate deity was no deity at all. Hence, Hobbesian materialism led irresistibly to athcism.[39] This, indeed, was the general consensus, although what remains philosophically interesting is the residual argument whether there can be such a thing as 'thinking matter'.

For our purposes, however, there is a different argument to attend to. All Hobbes's critics deplored his subordination of the church to the state; sometimes they attacked small corners of his argument – such as the claim that the sovereign without ordination could administer the sacraments; generally, they attacked the whole edifice. The result is intellectually interesting in the following way. Hobbes's contemporaries understood him as arguing that once there was a civil society, all moral distinctions were simply what the sovereign said.[40] But, they replied, nobody could really believe anything of the sort – this is particularly well argued by John Shafto; moreover, Hobbes's view is incoherent, because the reason men have for taking any notice of what the sovereign says must be some belief that what he says is right by some standard independent of his merely saying it. This, again, is well put by Shafto. The law of nature must be an eternal law, accessible to individual

---

[38] *Leviathan Heretical*, 125.
[39] *The Creed of Mr Hobbes* 8 ('The Hobbist's Creed': see Appendix); *Great Law of Nature*, 22.   [40] *The Creed of Mr Hobbes*, 76.

reason, directing men to their best interests, and not to be super-seded by the sovereign's say-so.

Now comes the twist. While Hobbes seems to contend for the absolute authority of the sovereign and his ability to lay down rules of right and wrong for his subjects, he makes each individual the judge of what conduces to his own safety, and allows everyone a large measure of self-help in procuring it. Clarendon, for one, becomes extremely heated at Hobbes's suggestion that the criminal who has broken the law commits no further crime by attempting to get away with it. In the sphere of religion and intellectual toleration, the result is that those who defend such constitutionalist views as that the king is 'obliged to assume no greater liberty of command over his Subjects' Persons and Estates than is necessary for the accomplishing those ends for which he is constituted their Prince', that he is bound by law, that law only binds with the people's con-sent, and so on, and who defend Aristotle's view that sovereigns only have such power as is necessary to their function then turn round and argue, first, that this licenses no resistance to the sovereign's commands, and second, that the logical upshot of the rights of individual conscience is not toleration but uniformity.[41]

Shafto travels this unlikely route in three short pages; partly, he argues from the fact that if we all rely on our own consciences there will be chaos to the conclusion that an intellectual equality implies that we must all let ourselves be guided by the consensus, but mostly he argues that if the sovereign is guided by his conscience, he must try to make us all subscribe to the true religion. For him not to do so would be like letting us all drive over a cliff.[42] So, paradoxically, the Aristotelian, functionalist and natural law apparatus which in Locke is turned to the defence of toleration is here turned to just the reverse.

As for who ought to lay down what we are to believe, Hobbes's view that it is up to the sovereign, who alone possesses the authority to do so, and who ought to lay down as little as possible, is denied. His critics agreed that the sovereign ought to lend his power to the decisions of the church on the nature of the true faith, but they do not doubt that 'the Learned' and the clergy must lay down the doc-trine which the sovereign enforces.[43] The moral law possessed authority independently of the sovereign's coercive power; he lent it his power but did not give it authority. Constantine 'rather gave outward air and succour then true Authority and right to the Doc-

---

[41] Ibid., 26, 80ff.   [42] Ibid., 80.   [43] Ibid., 76.

trines and commandments of his Soveraign Jesus'. To suppose otherwise, Tenison told Hobbes, was 'the chief ground of your irreverent and false doctrines against the Power of the Christian Church'.[44] Nor does Hobbes's desire that the sovereign ought to be as sparing as possible in what he lays down for dogma receive any better a hearing. Since the whole of our future salvation depends on good doctrine, the sovereign's duty is to enforce the best doctrine he can find, and he can only find it by making a sincere attempt to listen to 'the Learned' and the clergy. All Hobbes's critics denounced him as an enemy to the clergy, and quite rightly– Hobbes had once again played the seventeenth century's game of going back to origins for justification, and had pointed out that the only authority the clergy originally possessed was such as they could command by the goodness of their lives and the intellectual quality of their arguments. Nor did Hobbes doubt that this was how things ought to continue. His opponents saw it as a thinly disguised attack on the Church of England.[45]

This universal condemnation of Hobbes's theological, philosophical, and political doctrines amounts to an attack on toleration in the following way. Hobbes was seen by all his enemies as allowing an independence to private judgement that none of them thought safe. Hobbes's boasting about his own abilities is to us faintly comic, but to his contemporaries it was all of a piece with his repudiation of the very principle of intellectual authority.[46] It is clear that his arguments from the origins of the church and religion have an ironic thrust and are very much *ad hominem* – it is his opponents who believe in the independent authority of tradition, and Hobbes everywhere else who insists that arguments from what once happened are of no independent value; only if ancient practice conforms to good sense well snuffed by philosophy ought we to take any notice of it.

Hobbes teased his enemies by drawing arguments down from history, since they thought them independently compelling. They responded, of course, by denying his history; both Clarendon and Dowel seized on his claim that Constantine had imposed a purely verbal agreement on the nature of the Trinity as a peace-keeping formula: 'Constantine did desire the Uniformity in Doctrine, but not in an evil Doctrine, and the Peace of his people, but he would not build this upon the foundation of sin and *Heresy*.'[47] Hobbes

---

[44] *Leviathan Drawn Out with a Hook*, pp. 56–7; *Mr Hobbes's Creed*, 185.   [45] Op. cit., 185.
[46] *Leviathan Drawn Out with a Hook*, 15–30.   [47] *Leviathan Heretical*, 34–5.

glossed ancient practice in a thoroughly secular fashion – Roman statecraft was good, because it looked consistently to things the state could control and took no notice of what it could not. Since belief could not be compelled, the Romans never tried to control it, only public utterances and behaviour. Hobbes thus gave maximum offence. Moreover, he was accused of encouraging others to think as he did, and 'smart witts' about the Court were widely thought to share both his opinions and his appalling self-confidence. They prided themselves on their modernity and independence, and it was this (almost as much as their professed 'atheism') that gave particular offence to the friends of the clergy. The inference Hobbes's critics drew was simple; if Hobbes wished to control only that behaviour which threatened the peace, and cared nothing for what men thought in their hearts, the only stopping-place was the abolition of the national church and the toleration of all creeds that did not threaten the peace. This was tantamount to thinking it did not matter whether Britain was a Christian country or not. Hobbes may well have thought it did not, though it did matter that the body politique, being one person, should exhibit one public form of worship. In effect, this is once more to side with the Romans.

IV

Why should anyone take an interest in these squabbles now? It is commonplace that few writers on Hobbes have bothered with Books III and IV of *Leviathan*, and writers who have complained of this – for instance John Pocock[48] – find themselves buried in the more intriguing aspects of Hobbes's theology, such as his mortalism. Those who have argued, as Hood and Warrender[49] both argued, that God plays a serious role in Hobbes's political system, have tried to show the indispensability of a belief in God to the obligatoriness of the law of nature and thus to the obligatoriness of the commands of the sovereign. His views on religion as a social and political force are not their main concern. Indeed, Dr Springborg is almost alone among contemporary political theorists in being interested in Hobbes's views on the authority of churches and priests.[50] My view is one which was adumbrated by Leslie

[48] J. G. A. Pocock, 'Time, History and Eschatology in the Thought of Thomas Hobbes', in *Politics, Language and Time* (London, 1971), 148–201.
[49] F. R. Hood, *The Divine Politics of Thomas Hobbes* (Oxford, 1964); Howard Warrender, *The Political Philosophy of Hobbes* (Oxford, 1967).
[50] Patricia Springborg, '*Leviathan*, The Christian Commonwealth Incorporated', *Political Studies*, 24 (1976), 171–83.

Stephen and Croom Robertson,[51] but has rather dropped out of sight of late. That view is that Hobbes contributes to the growth of toleration by making religious uniformity no more than a 'police matter'. The expression of heretical beliefs in public may be suppressed for much the same reasons as walking naked in the streets or swearing loudly in public; it is an argument which in different ways would be at home in Kant or in Bentham.

None of Hobbes's contemporary critics quite goes as far as to say that Hobbes's defence of freethinking is simply an expression of the self-interest of ambitious practitioners of the new science and this interest is one which ought not to be promoted. It is noticeable, however, that most of his critics defend Aristotle and scholasticism against him, and one objects to the doctrine of the rotation of the earth along with everything else in Hobbes.[52] Hobbes's great achievement was to separate out the realm of the factually and logically ascertainable from the realm of the unknowable, and so to allow freedom to the former. The spirit of scientific enquiry goes on to the attack with Hobbes, and his arguments to show that religion has nothing to fear from science are as offensive as if they had been arguments to the opposite conclusion. None the less, it seems to me that Hobbes stands as a precursor of Kant – that is of the political Kant – in arguing that the philosophical inscrutability of religion and the limited external purposes of the state allowed the state to secure a sort of public politeness but no more, though, of course, for Kant this is a proposition about right, and for Hobbes a proposition about natural duty resting on prudence.

If that is correct, Hobbes's arguments contribute to various strands that have made up modern doctrines of toleration. There is a flanking attack with philosophical scepticism on the one side weakening the belief that there is any particular doctrine with a stronger than average claim to be enforced, and individualism on the other suggesting that it is each man's business what he believes about his own salvation, and none of anyone else's. I can repel attacks from my neighbour; I cannot aggress upon him in the name of my own conception of his salvation. Wolin and others, who see the rise of liberalism as the destruction of the public realm, see all this as part of Hobbes's privatisation of all social goods, and his systematic playing down of the public and political realm celebrated by Aristotle before him and Hannah Arendt after.[53] They go too far.

---

[51] *Hobbes*; Croom Robertson, *Hobbes* (London, 1886).
[52] *Leviathan Drawn Out with a Hook*, 25.
[53] Sheldon Wolin, *Politics and Vision* (London, 1961), ch. 6.

For in this one area, as I have said, it is the classical conception of civic virtue which receives courteous handling from Hobbes and the fanaticism of Puritan individualism which receives the reverse.

Still, there is no certainly no suggestion that a man might follow Machiavelli in loving his city more than his own soul; the argument is always and everywhere premised on the assumption that a man is bound to love himself and his own soul better than his city. That being so, what Hobbes had to show, and tried to show, was that the city could not, and need not, and therefore ought not, to do anything which by threatening our souls would weaken our allegiance. Toleration is not argued for on principle, but as a utilitarian measure; if toleration is unsafe, it must be dropped – public order trumps any notion of a right to free speech. Among rational men toleration would be safe, and when safe a very good thing. This may not be the most inspiring defence ever offered, but it is a good one.

Appendix: 'The Hobbist's Creed'

Croom Robertson could not resist the temptation to print Thomas Tenison's 'The Hobbist's Creed' as perhaps the most engaging example of an intelligent controversialist at work:

I believe that God is Almighty matter; that in him there are three Persons, he having been thrice represented on earth; that it is to be decided by the Civil Power whether he created all things else; that Angels are not Incorporeal substances (those words implying a contradiction) but pretenatural impressions on the brain of man; that the soul of man is the temperament of his Body; that the Liberty of the Will, in that soul, is physically necessary; that the prime law of nature in the soul of man is self-love; that the Law of the Civil Sovereign is the obliging rule of good and evil, just and unjust; that the Books of the Old and New Testament are made Canon and Law by the Civil Powers; that whatsoever is written in those Books may lawfully be denied, even upon oath (after the laudable doctrine and practice of the *Gnosticks*) in time of persecution, when men shall be urged by the menaces of Authority; that Hell is a tolerable condition of life, for a few years upon earth, to begin at the general Resurrection; and that Heaven is a blessed estate of good men, like that of Adam before his fall, beginning at the general resurrection, to be from thenceforth eternal upon Earth in the Holy-Land.

While it cannot be said to be a fair representation of Hobbes's views, it is firmly anchored in what he wrote at various times and in various contexts.

3

Locke: toleration and the rationality of persecution

JEREMY WALDRON

I

This is a paper about John Locke's argument for toleration, or, more accurately, it is a paper about the main line of argument which appears in Locke's work *A Letter on Toleration*.[1] It is *not* intended – as so many papers on Locke's political philosophy are these days – as a historical analysis of his position. I am not going to say very much at all about the development (in some ways the quite remarkable development) of Locke's views on the subject, or about the contemporary debate on religious toleration in which Locke, first as an academic then as a political agitator, was involved, or about the historical circumstances of the *Letter*'s composition.[2] No doubt these are worthy subjects for a paper, but not, I think, for a volume devoted to toleration as an issue in modern political philosophy. Rather, I want to consider the Lockian case as a political argument – that is as a practical intellectual resource that can be abstracted from the antiquity of its context and deployed in the modern debate about liberal theories of justice and political morality.[3] To put it bluntly, I want to consider whether Locke's case

[1] All page references in the text are to John Locke, *Epistola de Tolerantia: A Letter on Toleration*, edited by R. Klibansky and translated by J. W. Gough (Oxford, 1968).
[2] For the development of Locke's views on toleration, see M. Cranston, *John Locke: A Biography* (London, 1957), 44 ff, 59–67, 111–13, 125–33, 314–21, and 331 ff. See also J. D. Mabbott, *John Locke* (London, 1973), 171–5; and J. W. Gough, Introduction to the Klibansky and Gough edition of the *Letter*, 1 ff. For detailed accounts of the historical circumstances of the *Letter*'s composition, see R. Klibansky, Preface to the Klibansky and Gough edition, and M. Montuori, Introduction to John Locke, *A Letter concerning Toleration*, ed. M. Montuori (The Hague, 1963).
[3] It is of course controversial whether Locke's political arguments can be abstracted and deployed in this way. For the suggestion that there may be dangers here, see Q. Skinner, 'Meaning and Understanding in the History of Ideas', *History and Theory*, 8 (1969), and J. Dunn, *The Political Thought of John Locke: An Historical Account of the 'Two Treatises of Government'* (Cambridge, 1969), chs. 1 and 19. For a less pessimistic view, see D. Boucher, 'New Histories of Political Thought for Old', *Political Studies*, 31 (1983).

is worth anything as an argument which might dissuade someone here and now from actions of intolerance and persecution.[4]

There is a further somewhat more abstract reason for examining the Lockian argument. In its content and structure the Lockian case is quite different from the more familiar and more commonly cited arguments of John Stuart Mill.[5] Even if, as I shall claim, it turns out to be an inadequate and unconvincing argument, one that in the last resort radically underestimates the complexity of the problem it addresses, still its distinctive structure and content tell us a lot about the possibilities and limits of liberal argumentation in this area. Those insights and the contrast with the more familiar arguments of Mill may well contribute considerably to our understanding of modern liberal theories of toleration and the 'neutral' state.[6]

II

I have said that I am going to concentrate on the main line of argument in the *Letter on Toleration*. But perhaps it is worth saying a word or two about one subordinate line of argument that I will largely overlook in the rest of my discussion.

At the beginning of the *Letter*, Locke takes some pains to emphasise the peculiarly Christian character of toleration. 'The toleration of those that differ from others in matters of religion', he maintains, is not only consistent with and 'agreeable to' the Gospel of Jesus Christ (p. 65), but actually required by Christian teaching. Persecution, he points out, with the denial of love and charity which it involves, is repugnant to the Christian faith (pp. 59–65.).

Historically, there is no doubting the importance of this aspect of Locke's case. As an *ad hominem* argument addressed to the Christian authorities, it is of course devastating, for it exposes an evident and embarrassing inconsistency between the content of their theory and their practice in propagating it. It is significant that much of the

---

[4] I use 'persecute' in its dictionary sense of 'to harass, afflict, hunt down, put to death, esp. for religious . . . opinions' (*Chambers Twentieth Century Dictionary*, ed. A. M. MacDonald (London, 1977), 994) as a general term to cover all acts at variance with toleration. Jonathan Harrison pointed out to me that the word also has emotive and evaluative connotations. Clearly it would be wrong to *rely* on these for the purposes of argument: I do not intend to and I hope I have not done so.

[5] J. S. Mill, *On Liberty* (1859), ed. C. V. Shields (Indianapolis & New York, 1956).

[6] For modern theories of this kind, see especially: J. Rawls, *A Theory of Justice* (Oxford, 1971), 201–34 and 325–32; R. M. Dworkin, 'Liberalism', in *Public and Private Morality*, ed. S. Hampshire (Cambridge, 1978); and B. Ackerman, *Social Justice in the Liberal State* (New Haven & London, 1980).

immediate reaction to the publication of the *Letter* concerned this part of the Lockian case and that many of the issues taken up in Locke's boring and inordinately repetitive *Second, Third,* and (mercifully) uncompleted *Fourth Letters on Toleration* had to do with the argument from Christian premisses.[7]

But, however effective and historically important this line of argument might have been, it is uninteresting from a philosophical point of view. We are interested in the question of whether the state *as such* is under a duty of toleration and we want an argument addressed to state officials in their capacity as wielders of the means of coercion, repression, and persecution. An argument which addresses them instead in their capacity as members of a Christian congregation is insufficiently general to be philosophically interesting because it leaves us wondering what if anything we would have to say to someone who proposed persecution in the name of a more militant and less squeamish faith. Certainly, it would be an untidy and unsatisfactory state of affairs if we had to construct a fresh line of argument for toleration to match each different orthodoxy that was under consideration.

Locke, I think, recognises this, and the bulk of the *Letter* is devoted to considerations which proceed on a more general front and which purport to show the *irrationality* of intolerance and not just its uncongeniality to a particular religious point of view. It is this argument— the argument by which Locke attempts to show that religious persecution is irrational – that I want to examine in this chapter.

III

An argument for toleration is an argument which gives a reason for not interfering with a person's beliefs or practices even when we have reason to hold that those beliefs or practices are mistaken, heretical, or depraved. (Questions of toleration do not arise in relation to beliefs or practices which are regarded as good or true.[8])

I take it that this is *not* achieved simply by announcing that the enforcement of correct religious belief or practice is not the *function* of the state, or by saying, in the famous terms of the Wolfenden Report, that matters of religion, like personal morality and

---

[7] For the reception of the *Letter*, see Cranston, *John Locke*, 331ff. For the *Second, Third,* and *Fourth Letters concerning Toleration*, see *The Works of John Locke*, 11th edn (London, 1812), VI, 59–274.   [8] Joseph Raz's chapter in this volume provides a contrary view.

immorality, are 'not the law's business'.[9] That sort of talk just begs the question. At most it gives us the *conclusion* we want to reach, but it does not help us to discharge the obligation to argue for that conclusion. But Locke, I am afraid, is often interpreted as having said little more than this. For example, in the entry under 'Toleration' in his recent *Dictionary of Political Thought*, Roger Scruton gives us the following account of Locke's argument:

it is not within the competence of the state to discern the truth of religious doctrines, nor is it the function of the state to save men's souls; rather the state exists to protect men's rights and may use force to that end alone. *Hence*, there ought to be toleration in matters of religion.[10]

When this sort of functionalist talk is in the air, we do well to remember Max Weber's observation that it is impossible to define the state in terms of its functions and that historically 'there is scarcely any task that some political association has not taken in hand'.[11] Among all the tasks that states have undertaken, the question of which fall into the class of the *proper* functions of government is an important one; but it has to be a matter of argument, not of essentialist definition.

Since the state cannot be defined in terms of its functions, the best way of defining it, Weber suggested, was in terms of its characteristic *means*: the means, such as the organised monopoly of legitimate force in a given territory, which are deployed to carry out whatever ends a state may happen to undertake.[12] Now if we can give such a *modal* definition of the state – if we can define it in terms of its distinctive and characteristic means – then we may have the basis for an argument about its proper ends or functions along the following lines:

A state by definition is an organization which uses means of type M. But means of type M are ill-fitted for producing ends of type E. They never produce E-type effects (but perhaps at best mockeries or travesties of them). Therefore it is irrational to use M-type means in order to produce (genuine) E-type effects – and irrational in one of the most straightforward and least contestable instrumental

---

[9] *Report of the Committee on Homosexual Offences and Prostitution*, 1957, Cmnd. 247, paragraph 62.

[10] R. Scruton, *A Dictionary of Political Thought* (London, 1982), 464 (my italics).

[11] M. Weber, 'Politics as a Vocation' (1918), in *From Max Weber: Essays in Sociology*, ed. H. Gerth and C. Wright Mills (London, 1970), 77; see also M. Weber, *Economy and Society*, ed. G. Roth and C. Wittich (Berkeley, Los Angeles & London, 1978), I, 55.

[12] Weber, 'Politics as a Vocation', 78; Weber, *Economy and Society*, I, 55–6.

senses. Therefore, given the type of means that it uses, it is irrational for the state to pursue E-type ends. Therefore – and in this sense – the pursuit of E-type ends cannot be one of the proper functions of government.

That, it seems to me, is the form of an interesting and evidently acceptable line of argument. It is an argument from available means to possible ends – from a modal definition to a (negative) functionalist conclusion. And, in a very compressed form, it captures the structure of the main line of argument in the *Letter on Toleration* that I want to examine.

Locke, like Weber, defines the state in terms of the characteristic means at its disposal. In the *Second Treatise*, he tells us: 'Political power . . . I take to be a right of making laws with penalties of death.'[13] Similarly, in the *Letter on Toleration* he distinguishes the means available to the magistrate from those available to the ordinary man of good will in civil society: 'Every man is entitled to admonish, exhort, and convince another of error, and lead him by reasoning to accept his own opinions. But it is the magistrate's province to give orders by decree and compel with the sword' (p. 69). Looking at the matter in more detail, Locke characterises the power of the magistrate at three levels. Sometimes it is described symbolically in terms of the paraphernalia of force and terror: 'fire and the sword' (pp. 61, 63, 89, 115 etc.), 'rods and axes' (p. 89), and 'force and blood' (p. 113). Sometimes it is described (along Weberian lines) in terms of the way in which force is organised in a political community: 'the magistrate is armed with force, namely with all the strength of his subjects' (p. 67).[14] And sometimes it is characterised in legalistic terms – 'impartially enacted laws' (p. 67), 'laying down laws' (p. 91), and 'legal censure' (p. 115) – and in terms of punishments such as the deprivation of property (pp. 61, 69, 87 etc.), imprisonment (p. 69), mutilation and torture (pp. 61 and 69), and execution (p. 61). But the emphasis is everywhere on *force*: that is, on the coercive nature of penalties – 'if no penalties are attached to them, the force of laws vanishes' (p. 69) – and, somewhat less importantly, on the possibility of direct physical compulsion. The fact that governments and their officials work by coercive force while other organisations do not is the fundamen-

[13] John Locke, *Two Treatises of Government* (1689), ed. P. Laslett (Cambridge, 1960), II, section 3.
[14] See also Locke, *Two Treatises*, II, section 86, and – for the organisation of force – II, section 137.

tal premiss of Locke's argument and the basis of his distinction between church and state.[15]

It is true that Locke says a number of things which might lead a careless reader to believe that he wants to define government in functional terms. For example, early in the *Letter on Toleration*, he says in an apparently definitional tone: 'The commonwealth seems to me to be a society of men constituted only for preserving and advancing their civil goods' (p. 66), where civil goods are defined as 'life, liberty, bodily health, ... and the possession of outward things' etc. (p. 67). But he makes it absolutely clear in the *Letter* that he regards this as something to be established, as a task to be fulfilled (p. 65). He takes it as the conclusion, not a premiss, of his argument:

that the whole jurisdiction of the magistrate is concerned only with those civil goods, and that all the right and dominion of the civil power is bounded and confined solely to the care and advancement of these goods; and that it neither can nor ought in any way to be extended to the salvation of souls, the following considerations seem to me to prove. (p. 67)

And then he gives the arguments that I shall examine in a moment. Elsewhere in the *Letter* the functional theory of government is described explicitly as a *conclusion* (p. 71) and as something which in the course of his argument he has *proved* (p. 91). Those like Scruton and also J. D. Mabbott (in his summary of Locke's arguments) who represent it as a premiss are therefore doing Locke a grave disservice.[16]

Having defined government in terms of its means, Locke then argues that those means – laws, threats, the sword – are not capable of producing genuine religious belief in the minds of the citizens who are subjected to them. Sincere and genuine (as opposed to feigned or counterfeited) belief cannot be produced by these means; so it is irrational for the authorities to use them for that purpose. Thus, from a rational point of view, the state, defined in the way Locke wants to define it, cannot have among its functions that of promoting genuine religion. And since, on Locke's definition,

---

[15] This incidentally undermines John Dunn's view that force and violence are presented in Locke's works as the ways of beasts and the solvents of society and civilisation (Dunn, *Political Thought of John Locke*, 165). A more accurate view is that Locke's account of force is profoundly ambiguous; rightful force is the essence of politics, while force without right is the epitome of bestiality.

[16] For Scruton's account, see n. 10 above and the text thereto; see also Mabbott, *John Locke*, 176 (first premiss of Mabbott's argument ii).

toleration is nothing but the absence of force deployed for religious ends,[17] it follows that the state is rationally required to be tolerant.

That is a preliminary summary of a sophisticated argument. It gives us an idea of the lie of the land; and it has the great heuristic merit of indicating by inequitable exaggeration the extent of the argument's defects and limitations. Let me now discuss it in a little more detail.

IV

The crux of the argument – the step which dominates it and on which everything else depends – is the claim that religious belief cannot be secured by the coercive means characteristic of state action. This is the essence of Locke's challenge to the rationality of religious persecution: that what the persecutors purport to be up to is something that, in the nature of the case, they cannot hope to achieve.

To make this case, he needs to show that this is true *in principle*. It is not enough to show that coercion is *inefficient* as a means of religious discipline or that it is less efficient than the citizens' means of argument and persuasion. For that would leave open the possibility of using coercion as a last resort, and it would also make the case for toleration vulnerable to a reassessment of the relative values of the various effects of coercive action. Locke needs to show impossibility here. He must show that there is a gap between political means and religious ends which cannot in principle be bridged.

On Locke's account, that causal gap between political coercion and religious belief is framed, as it were, by two important propositions: (1) that coercion works by operating on a person's will, that is by pressurising his decision-making with the threat of penalties; and (2) that belief and understanding are not subject to the human will, and that one cannot acquire a belief simply by intending or deciding to believe. If I do not believe in the truth of the Resurrection, for example, there is nothing I can do, no act of will that I can perform, to *make* myself believe it. (There is no way of holding my mouth or concentrating which is going to get me into the state of having this belief.) Of course, I may change my mind about the Resurrection, and people often do. But there is a sense in which

---

[17] Locke defines it explicitly in these terms in the *Second Letter*, in *Works*, VI, 62.

even if that happens it is not my doing: it happens rather as a result of the work of what Locke calls 'light and evidence' on the understanding and not as the upshot of *my* conscious decision-making.

The effect of these two claims then – that coercion works through the will and that belief is not subject to the will – if they are true, is to render religious belief or unbelief effectively immune from coercive manipulation. Laws, Locke says, are of no force without penalties (p. 69), and the whole point of penalties is to bring pressure to bear on people's decision-making by altering the pay-offs for various courses of action, so that willing one particular course of action (the act required or prohibited by law) becomes more or less attractive to the agent than it would otherwise be. But this sort of pressurising is crazy in cases of actions which men are incapable of performing no matter how attractive the pay-off or unattractive the consequences. Sincerely believing a proposition that one takes to be false (like the proposition that one can jump 20 feet into the air) is an action in this category. As Locke puts it: 'what is gained in enjoining by law what a man cannot do, however much he may wish to do it? To believe this or that to be true is not within the scope of our will' (p. 121). The imposition of belief, then, by civil law has been shown to be an absurdity. Intolerance and persecution, at least for religious reasons, have been shown to be irrational.

This is the sort of conclusion that every moral philosopher dreams of when he starts out making an argument. To justify his belief that a certain practice is wrong, he does not want to have to appeal in a Humean fashion to contingent desires and attitudes: he can never be certain that his audience share them, and even if they do this sort of argument often appears to establish nothing more than the undesirability of the practice. Rather he wants to be able to show (if he can) that the wrong practice is also an irrational practice – that it involves in itself the sort of inconsistency or rational absurdity which every philosopher wants to avoid in his life as well as in his arguments.[18] Everyone in his audience – or at least everyone in his philosophical audience – accepts standards of rationality; they are part of the tools of the trade, even for one who is, in other respects, the most rabid of moral sceptics. So the possibility of appealing to those standards to establish substantive moral conclusions has been one of the recurring dreams of Western moral philosophers, at least since Kant. (It finds its latest manifestation in

[18] For some interesting questions about this assumption, see Robert Nozick, *Philosophical Explanations* (Cambridge, Mass., 1981), 405–9.

the work of Alan Gewirth.[19]). And here, in the *Letter on Toleration*, we find John Locke engaged in an early attempt to do the same sort of thing.

V

That is the crux of Locke's argument for toleration. Before going on to indicate some of the difficulties in the argument, I want to make two or three general observations.

The first point to notice is that this argument for toleration does not rest on any religious doubt, religious scepticism, or epistemic misgivings in relation either to the orthodox position Locke is considering or to the beliefs and practices that are being tolerated. It is sometimes said that toleration is the child of doubt, and that there is a philosophical as well as a historical connection between the rise of secular liberalism and the decline of religious certainty. Similarly, it is often said that there is a philosophical as well as a historical connection between liberal doctrine and doubts about the objectivity of ethics.[20] I have to confess that these conceptual connections escape me; and that the view that moral non-cognitivism generates a principle of ethical *laissez-faire* seems to me simply incoherent.[21] Be that as it may, Locke (like most of the great thinkers in the early liberal tradition) has little truck with arguments of this sort. He is adamant that there is a God, that his existence can be established very readily,[22] that this God requires certain things of us in the way of ethical practice, belief, and worship, and 'that man is obliged above all else to observe these things, and he must exercise his utmost care, application and diligence in seeking out and performing them' (pp. 123–5). We should, however, note that although Locke believed that there is 'only one way to heaven', he did suggest at one point that the case for toleration might be even stronger if there were more than one right answer to questions about religious practice: 'if there were several ways, not even a single pretext for compulsion could be found' (p. 91). But this is a mistake. The truth of something like religious pluralism (analogous to the moral

[19] Alan Gewirth, *Reason and Morality* (Chicago and London, 1978), especially 22 ff.
[20] See, for example, R. M. Unger, *Knowledge and Politics* (New York & London, 1976), 76: 'From the start, liberal political thought has been in revolt against the concept of objective value.' (Historically, of course, such a claim is utterly groundless.)
[21] See the excellent argument by G. Harrison, 'Relativism and Tolerance', in *Philosophy, Politics and Society*, 5th Series, ed. P. Laslett and J. Fishkin (Oxford, 1979), 273.
[22] See John Locke, *An Essay concerning Human Understanding* (1690), ed. J. Yolton (London, 1961), Book IV, chs. 3 (section 21) and 10.

pluralism that Joseph Raz discusses [23]) would still leave open the question of what to do about those heretics who, faced with a whole array of different routes to salvation, *still* persist in choosing a deviant and mistaken path. Just as faced with a variety of goods, men may still choose evil, so faced with a variety of true religions men may still choose error and blasphemy.

Certainly, Locke was confidently of the opinion that most of the groups and sects he proposed to tolerate (such as Jews who disbelieved the New Testament and heathens who denied most of the Old as well) had got these matters objectively and evidently wrong. He was prepared to 'readily grant that these opinions are false and absurd' (p. 123). His argument, then, did not depend on any misgivings about contemporary orthodoxy (though in fact he did not support contemporary Anglicanism in all the details of its faith and liturgy); nor was it based on any suspicion, however slight, that at the last trump the sects that he proposed to tolerate might turn out to have been right all along. His position was rather that a false belief, even if it is objectively and demonstrably false, cannot be changed by a mere act of will on the part of its believer, and that it is therefore irrational to threaten penalties against the believer no matter how convinced we are of the falsity of his beliefs. Locke's view, then, is not like the main theme in J. S. Mill's essay *On Liberty* that persecution is irrational because it tends to suppress doctrines which may turn out to have been worth preserving (for one reason or another).[24] It is more like Mill's subordinate argument that the state of mind produced by coercive indoctrination is so far from genuine belief as to call in question the rationality of one who is trying to inculcate it.[25]

There is one line of argument present in the *Letter* which may make us think that Locke was taking a sceptical position on religious matters. Locke was very concerned by the fact that if a magistrate or a ruler were to require certain religious beliefs or practices of us, there would be no guarantee that the religion he favoured would be correct.

Princes are born superior in power, but in nature equal to other mortals. Neither the right nor the art of ruling carries with it the certain knowledge of other things, and least of all true religion. For if it were so, how does it

---

[23] See Joseph Raz's chapter in this volume.
[24] Mill, *On Liberty*, ch. 2.
[25] *Ibid.*, 43 and 49–50.

come about that the lords of the earth differ so vastly in religious matters?

(p. 95)

But at most this is scepticism about the religious discernment of princes, not scepticism about religious matters as such. Locke maintains that 'a private man's study' is every bit as capable of revealing religious truth to him as the edicts of a magistrate (p. 93). He insists that each man is *individually* responsible for finding 'the narrow way and the strait gate that leads to heaven' (p. 71) and that God will excuse no man for a failure to discharge this responsibility on grounds of duress or obedience to orders. If the magistrate makes a mistake and I obey him, then *I* bear the responsibility and the cost I face may be everlasting perdition: 'What security can be given for the kingdom of heaven?' (p. 95) Locke adds one further point which, in his view, 'absolutely determines this controversy' (p. 99) by distinguishing religious from other forms of paternalism:

even if the magistrate's opinion in religion is sound, . . . yet, if I am not thoroughly convinced of it in my own mind, it will not bring me salvation . . . I may grow rich by an art that I dislike, I may be cured of a disease by remedies I distrust; but I cannot be saved by a religion I distrust, or by a worship I dislike. It is useless for an unbeliever to assume the outward appearance of morality; to please God he needs faith and inward sincerity. However likely and generally approved a medicine may be, it is administered in vain if the stomach rejects it as soon as it is taken, and it is wrong to force a remedy on an unwilling patient when his particular constitution will turn it to poison.

(pp. 99–101)

One may be forced to be free, to be healthy or to be rich, but 'a man cannot be forced to be saved' (p. 101). Religious truth must be left to individual conscience and individual discernment alone. So there are here certainly individualistic doubts about the abilities of princes; but none of these points is consistent with any more far-reaching doubts about truth or knowledge in matters of religion.

There is one further line of argument, connected with this, which does have a slightly stronger sceptical content. This is the worry at the back of Locke's mind that an argument for the imposition of Christian beliefs and practices by a Christian magistrate would

---

[26] I am grateful to David Edwards and Tom Baldwin for impressing on me the need to treat this as a separate and important line of argument for toleration.

71

seem to yield, by universalisation, an argument for the imposition of pagan beliefs and practices by a pagan magistrate:

For you must remember that the civil power is the same everywhere, and the religion of every prince is orthodox to himself. If, therefore, such a power be granted to the civil magistrate in religious matters, as that at Geneva he may extirpate by force and blood the religion which there is regarded as false or idolatrous, by the same right another magistrate, in some neighbouring country may oppress the orthodox religion, and in the Indies the Christian.

(p. 113)[26]

Notice that this is a good argument only against the following rather silly principle: (P1) that the magistrate may enforce *his own* religion or whatever religion *he thinks* is correct. It is not a good argument against the somewhat more sensible position (P2) that a magistrate may enforce the religion, whatever it may be, which is *in fact* objectively correct. It may, of course, be difficult to tell, and perhaps impossible to secure social agreement about, whether the view that the magistrate believes is correct is in fact the correct view. (P2 is what Gerald Dworkin has called a 'non-neutral' principle, and the social implementation of non-neutral principles is always problematic.[27]) But opposition to intolerance based on awareness of these difficulties is not opposition to intolerance as such, but only opposition to particular cases of it. Like the argument discussed in section II above, this is not an argument for toleration in general. Suppose, however, that the notion of objective truth in religious matters were a chimera. Would we then be able to make any distinction between P1 and P2? It may be thought that the answer is 'No' and therefore (working backwards) that Locke, who saw no difference between them, must have been sceptical about the objectivity of religious belief. And one does get a sense, especially in the *Third Letter concerning Toleration*, that Locke may be inclined to move in this direction.[28] Be that as it may, we should note that a rigorous sceptic could still draw a distinction between P1 and P2. If there were no objective truth, P1 could be implemented as before (perhaps on Hobbesian grounds of public order[29]); but P2 would not now license the enforcement of any religious belief at all.

[27] G. Dworkin, 'Non-Neutral Principles', in *Reading Rawls: Critical Studies of 'A Theory of Justice'*, ed. Norman Daniels (Oxford, 1975), 124.

[28] See Locke, *Third Letter*, in *Works*, VI, 143 ff.

[29] For Hobbes's views on toleration, see T. Hobbes, *Leviathan* (1651), ed. C. B. Macpherson (Harmondsworth, 1968), chs. 18 and 31.

VI

The second general point I want to make concerns the way in which the case for toleration fits into the general structure of Locke's political philosophy.

I am not sure whether we ought to attach any significance to the fact that the subject of religious toleration is not mentioned at all in the *Two Treatises of Government*. There may be a historical explanation: if we take the *Letter on Toleration* to have been drafted after 1685[30] and we accept something like Peter Laslett's dating of the composition of the *Two Treatises*,[31] then we can say that Locke may well not have formulated his final tolerationist position sufficiently clearly at the time the *Treatises* were drafted to include reference to it there. Even so, it is surprising. Religious toleration was one of Locke's abiding preoccupations and one of the most contested political issues of the age. It is odd that he should make no reference to it in a treatise concerned with the functions and limits of government.

Indeed, the occasional references to religion in the *Second Treatise* indicate, if anything, that the legitimate Lockian state need not be a secular one at all. In the chapters on resistance and revolution, Locke suggests that a people may be entitled to rise up against their Prince if he has by his actions or negligence endangered 'their estates, liberties, lives . . . and perhaps their religion too'.[32] He implies throughout that the failure of the later Stuarts to prosecute and enforce the laws against Catholicism amounted to subversion of the constitution.[33] (This, however, is complicated by the fact that even in the *Letter on Toleration* Locke indicated that he was disposed to exclude Catholics, as he excluded atheists, from the scope of the toleration that he was arguing for (pp. 131–5). We cannot go into the grounds for this here; but it had to do mainly with his suspicion that members of both classes would make bad citizens.) The indications in the *Second Treatise* seem to be that a legitimate state may have an established and constitutionally sanctioned religion and an established pattern of religious discrimination; and that it would be permissible for Lockian individuals to agree on such arrangements when the moved out of the state of nature.

However, I am inclined to regard these indications as superficial:

---

[30] See Klibansky, Preface to the Klibansky and Gough edition of the *Letter*, ix ff.; also Montuori's Introduction to his edition, xv–xxii.
[31] P. Laslett, Introduction to his edition of Locke, *Two Treatises*, Part III.
[32] Locke, *Two Treatises*, II, section 209.   [33] *Ibid.*, II, sections 210, 214, and 225.

arguably they have more to do with the political events of the 1670s than with Locke's deepest convictions in political philosophy. I want to see now whether it is possible to accommodate the argument for toleration within the framework of the political theory of the *Second Treatise*.

The view in the *Second Treatise* is that a state has no greater power than that delegated to it by its citizens. Specifically, what the magistrate has at his disposal is the executive power which everyone previously had in the state of nature to prosecute and punish transgressions of natural law.[34] This power is resigned into the hands of the community and entrusted to the magistrate on entry to civil society. No doubt the magistrate will organise that power efficiently, making it much more effective than the sum of the dispersed powers of the same individuals in the state of nature.[35] (That, after all, is the whole point of the shift to civil society.) But the substance of the power is exactly the same as the individuals' natural right to punish.

The question about toleration, then, is a question not just about the limits of *state* force but about the limits of the use of force by any agency or any individual at all. (It is significant that in Locke's discussion of excommunication (p. 79), he insists that, while it is permissible for a church (like any private club) to expel a recalcitrant member, nevertheless 'care must be taken that the sentence of excommunication carry with it no insulting words or rough treatment, whereby the ejected person may be injured in any way, in body and estate'.) So since the doctrine applies to individual force, let us consider its application to individuals in the state of nature who have retained their natural right to punish: do they have a right to punish heretics and persecute religious deviance? If they do, there seems no reason why that power should not be vested in the community as a whole when civil society is set up. Let us assume for the sake of argument (what Locke certainly believed, as we saw in section V above) that the heresy whose toleration is in question really *is* heresy and that the deviant religious sect really *are* acting in defiance of God's commands so far as their beliefs and practices are concerned. If a heretic is defying God's law (and remember that the law of nature, for Locke, derives all its normative force from the fact that it is God's law), do the rest of us have a natural right to punish him? On Locke's view the natural right to punish has two purposes –

---

[34] *Ibid.*, II, sections 8–12, 86, and 126.   [35] *Ibid.*, II, section 137.

reparation for wrongful injury done, and *restraint* in the sense of coercive deterrence.[36] Clearly, reparation is out of the question in the religious case. Locke takes the Protestant view that a heretic does no injury to anyone but himself and God (pp. 123–5) – and, of course, it is not for us to collect compensation on behalf of the Almighty. That leaves the function of restraint. But if the argument of the *Letter* goes through, then restraint is also out of the question, since coercive deterrence can have no effect on the formation or maintenance of heretical beliefs. The right to punish may not be exercised in these cases, then, because it would serve no useful purpose, and punishment when it serves no useful purpose is wrong on the Lockian account.[37] So, since individuals have no right to punish heretics, governments cannot acquire any such right either, for '[n]obody can transfer to another more power than he has himself'.[38] It follows that it is wrong to set up any sort of confessional state or established church when we move out of the state of nature, if this is going to involve the use of political power for religious purposes.

This argument would not work were Locke to countenance any sort of retributive justification for punishment. For we might then be justified in using force and inflicting pain and loss on heretics simply in order to punish them for their (undoubted) sins without any further purpose of deterrence, reform, or reparation in mind. Force used in this way could not be conceived as a means to any end apart from the immediate infliction of suffering; its employment, therefore, could not be criticised as irrational in the sense of being incapable of attaining the ends at which it was aimed. In a recent book, W. von Leyden has argued that Locke's theory of punishment *is* (partly) retributive.[39] If he is correct, then there is an enormous gap in the argument for toleration. But the passages cited by von Leyden do not support his view. It is true that Locke says that punishment should be such as to make the criminal 'repent' of his crime.[40] But since repentance involves, among other things, forming the belief that one's criminal conduct was wrong, the same argument can be used to establish that force is inapposite to this end as Locke used to establish that it was inapposite to more direct coercion and deterrence. Von Leyden notes that Locke makes

---

[36] *Ibid.*, II, sections 7–12.
[37] For the doctrine that punishment should be waived when it does not serve these aims, see Locke, *Two Treatises*, II, section 159.   [38] *Ibid.*, II, section 135.
[39] W. von Leyden, *Hobbes and Locke: The Politics of Freedom and Obligation* (London, 1982), 115 ff.   [40] See Locke, *Two Treatises*, Ii, section 8 (lines 21–3).

occasional use of the language of retribution and desert: but when 'retribute' is used early in the *Second Treatise* Locke immediately links it in a definitional way to reparation and restraint;[41] moreover he uses 'desert' only in the sense of proportionality[42] and he is adamant elsewhere in the *Treatise* that proportionality of punishment is strictly determined by the damage that has been suffered and thus by the reparation that is to be recouped.[43]

VII

The third general point I want to make about Locke's argument concerns its structure and the sort of toleration it entails.

Locke's position is a *negative* one: toleration, as he says in his *Second Letter* on the subject, is nothing but the absence or 'removing' of force in matters of religion.[44] The argument is about the irrationality of coercive persecution and it entails nothing more than that that sort of activity ought not to be undertaken. Nothing is entailed about the positive value of religious or moral diversity. Unlike Mill, Locke does not see anything to be gained from the existence of a plurality of views, or anything that might be lost in monolithic unanimity, in these matters. There is nothing in his argument to justify a policy of fostering religious pluralism or of providing people with a meaningful array of choices.

Even more important, we need to see that Locke's negative argument is directed not against coercion *as such*, but only against *coercion undertaken for certain reasons* and with certain ends in mind. The argument concerns the rationality of the would-be persecutor and his purposes; it is concerned about what happens to his rationality when he selects means evidently unfitted to his ends. Coercion, as we know, is on Locke's view unfitted to religious ends. But if it is being used for other ends to which it is not so unfitted (such as Hobbesian ends of public order), then there can be no objection on the basis of this argument, even if *incidentally* some church or religious sect is harmed. The religious liberty for which Locke argues is defined *not* by the actions permitted on the part of the person whose liberty is in question, but by the motivations it prohibits on the part of the person who is in a position to threaten the liberty. It is what Joseph Raz has called elsewhere 'a principle of

---

[41] *Ibid.*, II, section 8 (lines 5 ff.).   [42] *Ibid.*, II, section 87 (lines 8–10).
[43] *Ibid.*, II, section 184.   [44] See n. 17 above.

restraint'.[45] Thus it is not a right to freedom of worship as such, but rather, and at most, a right not to have one's worship interfered with for religious ends.

This point is emphasised quite nicely by an example that Locke uses towards the end of the *Letter on Toleration*. In the course of considering various practices that heathen sects may engage in, Locke takes up the case of animal sacrifice. He begins by saying that if people want to get together and sacrifice a calf, 'I deny that that should be forbidden by law' (p. 109). The owner of the calf is perfectly entitled to slaughter the animal at home and burn any bit of it he pleases. The magistrate cannot object when the slaughter takes on a religious character – for the element that makes it a religious *sacrifice* (and therefore an affront to God in the eyes of decent Anglicans) is precisely the internal aspect of belief which political power can never reach. *However*, Locke goes on, suppose the magistrate wants to prohibit the killing and burning of animals for non-religious reasons:

if the state of affairs were such that the interest of the commonwealth required all slaughter of beasts to be forborne for a while, in order to increase the stock of cattle destroyed by some murrain; who does not see that in such a case the magistrate may forbid all his subjects to kill any calves for any use whatever? But in this case the law is made not about a religious but a political matter, and it is not the sacrifice but the slaughter of a calf that is prohibited.

(p. 111)

But, of course, the *effect* of the economic ban on animal slaughter may be exactly the same as a ban that was religiously inspired. Perhaps in both cases the religious sect in question will wither and die out as its congregation, deprived of their favourite ceremony, drift off to other faiths. But what matters for Locke's purposes is not coercion as such or its effects, but the reasons that motivate it. If the reasons are religious, the coercion is irrational. But if the reasons are economic or political, then the argument for toleration gets no grip whatsoever despite the fact that the coercion may discriminate unequally in its consequences against a particular group. There may, of course, be other arguments against this sort of inequity, but they are not based on a Lockian principle of toleration.

---

[45] J. Raz, 'Liberalism, Autonomy and the Politics of Neutral Concern', in *Midwest Studies in Philosophy VII: Social and Political Philosophy*, ed. P. French, T. Uehling, and H. Wettstein (Minneapolis, 1982), 90–1; see also C. L. Ten, *Mill on Liberty* (Oxford, 1980), 40.

I have emphasised this point because it seems to be relevant to some of the modern formulations of the liberal position on religion, personal morality and conceptions of the good life. Recently, philosophers like Ronald Dworkin and Bruce Ackerman have formulated that position in terms of a requirement of *neutrality*: the state and its officials are required to be *neutral* as between the various moral conceptions of the good life that various citizens may hold.[46] But the question arises: what does neutrality involve? Is it just a requirement of impartiality or is it some stronger constraint of equal treatment? Does it involve, as Alan Montefiore has claimed, an effort to help and hinder the contending parties in equal degree?[47] And if it does require such evenhandedness, is it in practical terms *possible* for a government to be neutral in that sense?

In Locke's account of toleration, we have the basis for a conception of neutrality which is very narrow indeed and quite light in the burden that it places on the liberal state. The government and its officials are required to be neutral only in the *reasons* for which they take political actions. They must not act *in order to* promote particular religious objectives. Beyond that no wider neutrality is required. They need pay no attention to the evenness of the impact of their actions on those with whom they are dealing.

Compare now the conceptions of neutrality generated by some of the other familiar lines of liberal argument. If we wanted to use John Stuart Mill's argument about the dialectical value of religious, philosophical, and ethical diversity, then our conception of neutrality would be somewhat more strenuous. For if a sect, such as the animal sacrifice cult, dies out as a result of government action, that is a loss to religious and cultural diversity, and therefore a loss to the enterprise of seeking the truth, no matter what the reason for the action was. *Mill's* liberal government, then, unlike Locke's, must take care to see that diversity is not threatened even incidentally by its actions; and if it is threatened, it must weigh up carefully the value of the loss against the other ends it hopes to achieve by the coercion.[48] Similarly, if our argument for liberal neutrality has to do with the respect that a government owes to the autonomous moral and religious development of its citizens, then again a more strenuous requirement than Locke's will be generated. The govern-

---

[46] See n. 6 above; Dworkin, 'Liberalism', 127; Ackerman, *Social Justice*, 11.
[47] A. Montefiore, *Neutrality and Impartiality: The University and Political Commitment* (Cambridge, 1975), 5. For a useful discussion, see Raz, 'Liberalism' (see n. 45 above).
[48] See, for example, Mill, *On Liberty*, 53–4, 58, and 63–4.

ment will be obliged not merely to refrain from religiously or morally inspired persecution, but to avoid any action which, in its effects, may frustrate or undermine individuals' choices and their self-constitution in these areas.

An important point emerges from all this. The idea of liberal neutrality, like that of toleration, is an abstract concept in political theory of which various conceptions are possible.[49] These conceptions differ considerably in the practical requirements they generate and the burdens they impose on governments. Which conception we opt for is not a matter of preference – it is not a matter of which we find more congenial to our political 'intuitions'. Rather it is a matter of the *line of argument* that we want to put forward. Locke's argument yields one conception of liberal neutrality, Mill's another, and so on. It follows, therefore, that an enterprise like that of Bruce Ackerman, in his recent book *Social Justice in the Liberal State*, is completely misguided. Ackerman puts forward a principle of liberal neutrality which he claims can be defended by any one of at least four distinct lines of argument. (Both Mill's argument and something like Locke's feature on his menu.[50]) He professes indifference as to which line of justification is adopted, claiming that the liberal ought to be as tolerant about that issue as he is about conceptions of the good life.[51] But if I am right, this promiscuity about justification may have disastrous consequences. The different lines of argument do not converge on a single destination: each argument yields a distinct conception which in turn generates distinct and practically quite different principles of political morality and social justice. So the liberal cannot afford to be indifferent or offhand about the justificatory task. The line of justification that is taken *matters* for the articulation of the position he wants to adopt.

VIII

Let us return now, finally, to the details of the Lockian argument. The nub of the case, you will recall, was his claim that there is an

---

[49] For the distinction between concept and conceptions, see Rawls, *Theory of Justice*, 9–10, and R. M. Dworkin, *Taking Rights Seriously*, revised edn (London, 1978), 134–6 and 226. This idea is indirectly linked to the views of Gallie on conceptual disagreement: see W. B. Gallie, 'Essentially Contested Concepts', *Proceedings of the Aristotelian Society*, 56 (1955–6), 167. For discussions of this idea, see William Connolly, *The Terms of Political Discourse*, 2nd edn (Oxford, 1983), chs. 1 and 5–6, and J. N. Gray, 'Political Power, Social Theory and Essential Contestability', in *The Nature of Political Theory*, ed. D. Miller and L. Siedentop (Oxford, 1983). [50] Ackerman, *Social Justice*, 11–12.[[51] *Ibid.*, 359.

unbridgeable causal gap between coercive means and religious ends – the gap which, as I put it, is framed by these two propositions that 'Coercion works on the will' and 'Belief cannot be affected by the will.' So long as these two frames remain in place, the irrationality of using coercive means for religious ends is evident.

We have already seen one reason for questioning the first of these propositions. Coercion, or more generally force, may be applied to a person not in order to put pressure on his will but simply in order to punish him, retributively, for the wrong he has done. But it is with the second of the two propositions that I am now chiefly concerned.

The second proposition is not argued for by Locke at any length in the *Letter on Toleration*. All Locke says is that '[l]ight is needed to change men's opinions, and light can by no means accrue from corporeal suffering' (pp. 69–71). One looks naturally to the *Essay concerning Human Understanding* for further elaboration, for the claim is primarily epistemological in character. We find there very little in the way of argument either. Locke does touch on the point in Book IV of the *Essay*,[52] but what he says is not entirely congenial to the argument put forward in the *Letter*.

The basic position that Locke defends in this part of the *Essay* is that '[o]ur knowledge is *neither wholly necessary, nor wholly voluntary*'. He explains two senses in which knowledge is not voluntary. First, '[m]en that have senses cannot choose but have some *ideas* by them', and what a man sees (for example) 'he cannot see otherwise than he does': 'It depends not on his will to see that *black* which appears *yellow*, nor to persuade himself that what actually *scalds* him feels *cold*; the earth will not appear painted with flowers, nor the fields covered in verdure, whenever he has a mind to it: in the cold winter, he cannot help seeing it cold and hoary. . .'

Secondly, once ideas have been received, the processes of the understanding go to work on them more or less automatically. Once men have received ideas from their senses, 'if they have memory, they cannot but retain some of them; and if they have any distinguishing faculty, cannot but perceive the agreement or disagreement of some of them with one another. And if men have in their minds names for these ideas, then propositions expressing the agreement or disagreement which their understanding has discerned will necessarily be accepted as true.[53]

None of this is subject to the will so none of it can be coerced.

[52] Locke, *Essay*, Book IV, ch. 13.   [53] *Ibid.*, sections 1–2.

Thus far the toleration argument is supported. What, then, according to the *Essay* is *voluntary* in the formation of beliefs? Locke answers: 'all that is *voluntary* in our knowledge is the *employing* or witholding any of our faculties from this or that sort of object, and a more or less accurate survey of them'.[54]

Though a man with his eyes open cannot help but see, he can decide which objects to look at, which books to read, and more generally which arguments to listen to, which people to take notice of and so on. In this sense, if not his beliefs then at least the sources of his beliefs are partly under his control.

All this is familiar and evidently true. But it opens up a first and fatal crack in the framework of Locke's argument for toleration. Suppose there are books and catechisms, gospels and treatises, capable of instructing men in the path of the true religion, if only they will read them. Then although the law cannot compel men coercively to believe this or that because it cannot compel the processes of the understanding, it can at least lead them to water and compel them to turn their attention in the direction of this material. A man may be compelled to learn a catechism on pain of death or to read the gospels every day to avoid discrimination. The effect of such threats and such discrimination may be to increase the number of people who eventually end up believing the orthodox faith. Since coercion may therefore be applied to religious ends by this indirect means, it can no longer be condemned as in all circumstances irrational.

The case is even stronger when we put it the other way round. Suppose the religious authorities know that there are certain books that would be sufficient, if read, to shake the faith of an otherwise orthodox population. Then, although again people's beliefs cannot be controlled directly by coercive means, those who wield political power can put it to work indirectly to reinforce belief by banning everyone on pain of death from reading or obtaining copies of these heretical tomes. Such means may well be efficacious even though they are intolerant and oppressive; and Locke, who is concerned only with the rationality of persecution, provides no argument against them.

Once we catch the drift of this criticism, we begin to see how the rest of Locke's case falls apart. His case depended on the Protestant importance he attached to sincere belief: 'all the life and power of true religion consists in the inward and full persuasion of the mind;

---

[54] *Ibid.*, section 2.

and faith is not faith without believing'. So long as our attention is focused on the state of belief itself and *its* immunity from interference, Locke's argument is safe. But now we are starting to look at the epistemic apparatus that surrounds and supports belief – the apparatus of selection, attention, concentration, and so on – which, although it does not generate belief directly, nevertheless plays a sufficient role in its genesis to provide a point of leverage. Even if belief is not under the control of one's will, the surrounding apparatus may be; and that will be the obvious point for a rational persecutor to apply his pressure.

Perhaps the following sort of response may be made on Locke's behalf.[55] What matters for the purposes of true religion is genuine belief. But belief to be genuine must be based on the free and autonomous activity of the mind, choosing and selecting its own materials and its own evidence, uncoerced and undetermined by outside factors. Belief-like states generated in the mind of an individual on the basis of a coerced input of ideas are not genuine in this sense; they are more like the states of mind of an individual who has been brainwashed or subjected incessantly to propaganda. Such an individual may look like a believer from the outside – and he may even feel like a believer from the inside (he is not merely mouthing formulas to evade punishment) – but nevertheless, in virtue of the history of their causation, his beliefs do not count as genuine.[56] Since it is genuine belief that the religious authorities are interested in securing, it will therefore be irrational for them to resort even to the sort of indirect coercion I have been describing.

I have two worries about this line of argument. First, it is difficult to see why the 'free' input of ideas should *matter* so much in determining what counts as genuine belief. We have said already that it is not a phenomenonological matter of whether beliefs generated in this way *feel* more genuine than beliefs generated on the basis of coercively determined input. So is the point rather that belief-like states which are not 'genuine' in this sense cannot perform some or all of the *functions* we expect beliefs to perform? Are they functionally deficient in some way? Are they, for example, like brainwashed 'beliefs', peculiarly resistant to logical pressure and to requirements of consistency? That, I suppose, is a possibility. But I find it hard to imagine what sort of epistemology or philosophy of mind could possibly connect the *external* conditions under which

---

[55] I am grateful to Joseph Raz for suggesting this line of argument to me. He is not responsible for any inadequacies in its formulation here.

[56] For an interesting discussion, see D. Dennett, 'Mechanism and Responsibility', in *Essays on Freedom of Action*, ed. Ted Honderich (London, 1973).

sensory input was acquired with the functional efficacy of the beliefs generated on the basis of that input. If I am forced at the point of a bayonet to look at the colour of snow, is my consequent belief that snow is white likely to function differently from the corresponding belief of someone who did not need to be forced to take notice of this fact?

Secondly, this approach appears to place such great demands on the notion of *genuine belief* as to lead us to doubt the genuineness of everything we normally count as a belief in ordinary life. In *most* cases (not just a few), the selection of sensory input for our understanding is a matter of upbringing, influence, accident, or constraint; freedom (in any sense that might plausibly be important) and autonomy seem to play only minor roles. But if this yields the conclusion that most religious 'belief is not 'genuine' anyway then we have offered the persecutors an easily defensible position: they can now say that their intention is not to inculcate 'genuine' belief (since that is impossible for most people anyway), but simply to generate in would-be heretics beliefs which are the same in content and status as those of the ordinary members of orthodox congregations. Against this proposal, it would seem, Locke has nothing to say.

We may attack the question of the relation between belief and *practice* in the constitution of religious faith in a similar sort of way. Locke is relying on the view that practice – outward conformity to certain forms of worship – by itself without genuine belief is nothing but empty hypocrisy which is likely to imperil further rather than promote the salvation of the souls of those forced into it. But this is to ignore the possibility that practice may stand in some sort of generative and supportive relation to belief – that it too may be part of the apparatus which surrounds, nurtures, and sustains the sort of intellectual conviction of which true religion, in Locke's opinion, is composed. So here we have another point of leverage for the theocrat. A law requiring attendance at Matins every morning may, despite its inefficacy in the immediate coercion of belief, nevertheless be the best and most rational indirect way of avoiding a decline in genuine religious faith.

Some of these points were raised by Jonas Proast in a critique of Locke's *Letter*, to which the latter responded in his *Second* and subsequent *Letters concerning Toleration.*[57] Proast had conceded Locke's

---

[57] J. Proast, *The Argument of the Letter concerning Toleration Briefly Considered and Answered* (Oxford, 1690). See Introduction to the Klibansky and Gough edition of the *Letter*, 32 ff.; also Mabbott, *John Locke*, 180–2.

point that beliefs could not be imposed or modified directly by coercive means, but he insisted that force applied 'indirectly and at a distance' might be of some service in concentrating the minds of recalcitrants and getting religious deviants to reflect on the content of the orthodox faith.[58] Force may be unable to inculcate truth directly, but it may remove the main obstacles to the reception of the truth, namely 'negligence' and 'prejudice'.[59]

Despite the enormous amount of ink that he devoted to his response, Locke failed to provide any adequate answer to this point. He said that it would be difficult to distinguish sincere and reflective dissenters from those whose religious dissent was negligent, slothful, or based on removable prejudice; and he insisted that it would certainly be wrong to use force indiscriminately on all dissenters when its proper object could only be a certain subset of them. That is undoubtedly correct. But now the case in principle against the use of force in religious matters has collapsed into a purely pragmatic argument: force *may* be serviceable, only it is likely to be difficult to tell *in which cases* it will be serviceable. In place of the knock-down argument against the use of political means for religious ends, we have now an argument to the effect that political means must not be used indiscriminately and without great care for religious ends. Because the in-principle argument has collapsed, the sharp functional distinction between church and state that Locke was arguing for goes with it. We can no longer say that the magistrate's power is *rationally inappropriate* in the service of true religion. Everything now depends on how sure the magistrate is that the deviants he is dealing with have prejudiced and negligent minds. It is impossible, therefore, to agree with J. D. Mabbott that Locke provides a 'complete and effective' response to Proast's critique.[60] On the contrary, the response he provides completely and effectively demolishes the substance of his position.

IX

I do not see any other way of reconstructing Locke's argument to meet the criticisms that I have outlined. Religious faith, and more generally moral commitment, are complex phenomena. Yet Locke has relied, for his indictment of the rationality of persecution, on a

---

[58] Proast is quoted in these terms by Locke in the *Second Letter*, in *Works*, VI, 69.
[59] *Ibid.*, 74.   [60] Mabbott, *John Locke*, 182.

radical and distorted simplification of that complexity. A charge of irrationality based on that sort of simplification is likely to be returned with interest!

It is possible that the gist of Locke's position is correct. Perhaps at a very deep level, there *is* something irrational about intolerance and persecution; perhaps ultimately reason and liberal commitment do converge in this respect. But, on the face of it, it seems unlikely that this convergence is going to take place at the level of *instrumental* rationality. Censors, inquisitors, and persecutors have usually known exactly what they were doing, and have had a fair and calculating idea of what they could hope to achieve. If our only charge against them is that their enterprise was hopeless and instrumentally irrational from the start, then we perhaps betray only our ignorance of their methods and objectives, and the irrelevance of our liberalism to their concerns. If by their persistence they indicate that they *do* have a viable enterprise in mind, then there comes a point when the charge of instrumental irrationality must be dropped (on pain of misunderstanding) and a more direct challenge to their actions taken up.

At this point, what one misses above all in Locke's argument is a sense that there is anything *morally* wrong with intolerance, or a sense of any deep concern for the *victims* of persecution or the moral insult that is involved in the attempt to manipulate their faith. What gives Locke's argument its peculiar structure and narrowness is that it is, in the end, an argument about agency rather than an argument about consequences. It appeals to and is concerned with the interests of the persecutors and with the danger that, in undertaking intolerant action, they may exhibit a less than perfect rationality. Addressed as it is to the persecutors in *their* interests, the argument has nothing to do with the interests of the victims of persecution as such; rather those interests are addressed and protected only incidentally as a result of what is, in the last resort, prudential advice offered to those who are disposed to oppress them.

We have already seen that an argument based on a concern for the moral interests of the potential victims of intolerance would differ considerably from Locke's argument. Not being an argument about rational agency, it would not merely be a principle of restraint on reasons, but would generate more strenuous and consequentially more sensitive requirements for political morality. Perhaps this is why Locke avoided that line. But one cannot help feeling too that part of the explanation lies in the fatal attraction of ethical rationalism: that if only we can show that intolerance is irrational we may be excused from the messy business of indicating the reasons why it is *wrong*.[61]

---

[61] This paper was first presented at the Morrell Conference on Toleration organised in the Politics Department of the University of York in September 1983. I am grateful to Tom Baldwin, David Edwards, Judy Evans, Peter Jones, Onora O'Neill, Albert Weale, and especially Joseph Raz, for their comments, questions, and criticisms.

4

Toleration and Mill's liberty of thought and discussion

DAVID EDWARDS

I grant that an earnest person, being no more infallible than other men, is liable to dislike people on account of opinions which do not merit dislike; but if he neither himself does them any ill office, nor connives at its being done by others, he is not intolerant: and the forbearance, which flows from a conscientious sense of the importance to mankind of the equal freedom of all opinion, is the only tolerance which is commendable, or, to the highest moral order of minds, possible.[1]

This passage from Mill's *Autobiography* seems, at first glance, to be a typical and unproblematic characterisation of his views on toleration. But, on closer inspection, it seems rather to be a slip, for the 'only commendable', indeed 'possible' toleration which Mill here mentions is that of opinion. Mill is, of course, equally celebrated for his arguments concerning toleration of all manner of individual conduct in the category which he styled that of self-regarding action. Even the two spheres of liberty of opinion and self-regarding action taken together do not exhaust the types of freedom and toleration which he championed, and regarded as analytically distinct.

Perhaps Mill wished to emphasise the *grounds* of the forbearance shown in observing liberty of opinion; the 'conscientious sense of the importance to mankind' might implicitly be supposed the *same* as that which requires the respect and toleration shown to individual diversity. If the grounds are the same, this stress on liberty of opinion is simply revealing of Mill's native inclination to the cerebral and intellectual, his natural tendency to give pride of place to the sphere in which he was most at home. But are we to infer from Mill's statement that it was his considered view that the toleration of opinions constitutes the paradigm case of toleration, and that it is thereby the clue to everything else?

[1] J. S. Mill, *Autobiography* (London, 1971), 32.

That considered view is, of course, expounded in the complex of arguments that go to make up the essay *On Liberty*, which, Mill tells us, was the most carefully composed of all his works. No doubt much of his labour of composition went to ensure that he expressed his thoughts with felicity and exactness. But an even more daunting task must have been to organise the sheer fecundity of his ideas into an elaborate doctrine which also squared with, and drew upon, other doctrines which he maintained. Yet Mill insisted on the unity and integration of the arguments used in *On Liberty*. All the various ideas are supposed by Mill to converge and cohere into 'a kind of philosophic text-book of a single truth'.[2]

The text-book is Mill's mature and definitive account of toleration. Its second chapter is devoted to the question of toleration of opinion. Its title is 'Of the Liberty of Thought and Discussion', and my purpose is to consider the place and significance of that theme in the general account. On the surface this involves no more than an investigation of a self-contained portion of Mill's doctrine, but his assertion of the unity and harmony of his doctrine requires that this part of his work be related in some integrated manner to the overall scheme. It must be assimilated to the doctrine of liberty in such a way that the integrity of that doctrine is enhanced, not impaired. This is especially so if the toleration of opinion is the paradigm case of toleration, and its grounds are those of toleration in general.

However, there are two aspects of the argument for the toleration of opinion which seem to be incongruous in the context of the general argument for liberty. The first aspect, which I do not believe to be a real anomaly or menace to the unity of Mill's work, is the absence from the argument of this second chapter of categories and distinctions which Mill regarded as essential to defining the area of individual liberty. These are the famous concepts of harm to others, self-regarding actions, and the legitimate spheres of influence of individual and society. Yet Mill had stated that 'the object of this essay is to assert one very simple principle',[3] namely that which requires that the sole warrant for the coercion of the individual be the protection from harm of others.

With this statement of the object of the essay freshly stamped on his memory the reader may reasonably expect that Mill will either proceed to show that all discussion is harmless, or that he will insist

[2] *Ibid.*, 150.
[3] J. S. Mill, *Utilitarianism, On Liberty and Considerations on Representative Government* (London, 1972), 72 (hereafter *OL*).

on the satisfaction of a strict onus of proof of some future harm before some instance of the expression of opinion is curtailed. This would seem in keeping with Mill's declared 'object' since the liberty of discussion, though not of thought, lies in the sphere which his commentators have styled the 'other-regarding'. However, what Mill contends for in the second chapter of *On Liberty* is not freedom in the self-regarding sphere, or the toleration of a harmless activity, but 'the fullest liberty of professing and discussing, as a matter of ethical conviction, any doctrine, however immoral it may be considered'.[4] That is, Mill believes the conclusion of his argument to be that there should prevail a complete and unqualified toleration concerning the profession of 'doctrines' (or 'ideas', 'opinions', 'convictions'). Mill's contention is that the reader who has rightly weighed his argument must hold that conclusion 'as a matter of ethical conviction', meaning that such toleration should be extended as a moral right.

Mill in no way palliates this doctrine by recourse to any feeble plea that opinions cannot be harmful. For apologetic reasons he is not anxious to stress this fact, but he allows that they can have 'pernicious consequences',[5] or be 'altogether an evil'.[6] Mill's argument certainly cannot be charged with underestimating the potency of opinions; he says of those benefactors to mankind, the expositors of 'new truths':

To discover to the world something which deeply concerns it, and of which it was previously ignorant; to prove to it that it had been mistaken on some vital point of temporal or spiritual interest, is as important a service as a human being can render to his fellow-creatures, and in certain cases . . . (is perhaps) the most precious gift which could be bestowed on mankind.[7]

This potency for good must similarly be a potency for evil. We must surely infer that those who knowingly, or unwittingly, propagate errors might do disservice to mankind of equal, and staggering, proportions. Mill's view, of course, is that such evils 'must be regarded as the price paid for inestimable good',[8] but the point is that he believes that they are evils none the less, and their pernicious effects might be of the greatest imaginable consequence.

Mill's argument for freedom of opinion and discussion is emphatically an argument for tolerance and not indifference. He represents the history of the field of opinions as that of an intermittent combat zone, divided between partisans with powerful rival

---

[4] *OL*, 78n. [5] *Ibid.*, 85. [6] *Ibid.*, 110. [7] *Ibid.*, 89. [8] *Ibid.*, 110.

convictions and antipathies. Even in the anticipated society of mass conformity which he dreads he expects that the received opinions (no matter how vaguely understood) will be defended by spontaneous hostility towards dissidents. Moreover he expects that a regime of free debate will not only be more tolerant (towards the propagators of opinions) but also be more antagonistic (as between the disputed opinions). The conformist and dissident, the enlightened and obscurantist, the tolerant person and the bigot may all perceive, in their different ways, the importance of opinion in giving direction and significance to life.

Mill sees opinions, then, as having a meaning and potency of the greatest consequence. Since this is common ground, he does not labour the point with imaginary adversaries and doubters of his doctrine of toleration. Opinions properly engage the emotions, and being liable to feel hostility is an unavoidable consequence of holding an opinion in earnest. Tolerance of the free expression of the opinions of others arises not from indifference or a belief that opinions are harmless or from a careless agnosticism, but from being persuaded of the decisive force of considerations that override the spontaneous impulse to the suppression of opinions which we feel to be wrong and pernicious.

What Mill takes these decisive considerations to be will be examined later, but for him they involve the entire stake the human race has in knowing the truth. They are of such weight that they establish tolerance in the sphere of debate as a right and duty, not an indulgence or discretionary latitude. In a fully civilised state, Mill contends, dissent is to be recognised as a right, and although the expression of such dissent is bound to be offensive to others, it is incumbent on them to recognise its toleration as a duty. No matter how obnoxious an opinion, or how pernicious its possible consequences, Mill argues that this duty of toleration should be held as an ethical conviction. The toleration of the free expression of opinion is, then, neither indifference nor indulgence, but the conscientious bridling of our spontaneous inclination to stifle opinions to which we are hostile.

The forbearance involved in the liberty of thought and discussion is therefore an authentic instance of toleration. Indeed, as we have seen, Mill goes so far as to say that it is the only commendable tolerance. Presumably this means that the grounds of the tolerance of the expression of opinions are the same as those which justify the toleration of individual diversity. However, the concepts of self-regarding actions, of 'harm', of the distinctive spheres of individual and society (which Mill stated it was the 'object' of his essay to assert) play no part in the argument of the second chapter of the essay *On Liberty*. The toleration of the expression of opinion is in the sphere which Mill's commentators have styled the 'other-regarding'. Though opinions may be pernicious and have harmful consequences, Mill none the less argues for an unqualified, rather than a limited toleration. Though Mill's specification of the object of his essay and the arguments of the second chapter (which contain the grounds of the only commendable toleration) may seem inconsistent, the incongruity is superficial and deceptive. The sphere of expression of opinion is no more free from harm than any other in human conduct, but as we shall see Mill believes that it has special features incident to it which always preclude the use of the self-protecting coercion which is justified in other spheres of conduct.

There is, however, a second singularity about the second chapter which distinguishes it (at least in degree) from the rest of Mill's argument for toleration, and poses considerable difficulty if the case for free expression of opinion is to be taken as characteristic of the case for toleration in general. This is the apparent dominance of a teleological argument as the justifying ground of toleration. This aspect has been pithily summed up by Herbert Marcuse: 'The telos of tolerance is truth.'[9] The tolerance of the second chapter is subservient to a specific substantive end – the revelation and completion of truth. As Margaret Canovan has pointed out,[10] Mill is here affiliated to an old tradition of argumentative strategy, a rhetorical tour de force which steals the clothes of the orthodox (who wish to persecute to promote the truth) through his claim that the toleration of diversity, instead of coercive enforcement of an orthodoxy, is the royal road to truth. Mill adapts and improves on this tour de force, for he opposes no particular orthodoxy, but rather the moral intolerance of mass societies, and his argument for truth places the right of dissent in a solitary dissentient from the whole human race.

The drawbacks to this understanding of tolerance are clear. If the preceding sketch is taken to be the whole of the argument, toleration is merely a prudent strategy instrumental to the desired end (truth). Persecutors of belief are not so much wicked and brutal as stupid and ineffectual; toleration is the continuance of the war for truth by other means. Further, the raison d'être of this tolerance is uniformity, though it is necessarily uniformity on the instalment

[9] Herbert Marcuse, 'Repressive Tolerance', in *A Critique of Pure Tolerance* (London, 1971), 104.   [10] In Chapter 8 below.

plan. 'Tolerance' here is simply the sagacity to perceive that variety in opinion is ultimately suicidal.

The logic of this grounding of the case for toleration would appear to lead inexorably to an outcome of consolidation and uniformity. This is not merely an implicit tendency in the argument of the second chapter, for Mill recognises with a gratification tempered by reserve the necessity of the gradual narrowing of the bounds of diversity of opinion. For him this is the ineluctable, but highest and best, result of improved intelligence:

As mankind improve, the number of doctrines which are no longer disputed or doubted will be constantly on the increase: and the well-being of mankind may almost be measured by the number and gravity of the truths which have reached the point of being uncontested. The cessation, on one question after another, of serious controversy, is one of the necessary incidents of the consolidation of opinion; a consolidation as salutary in the case of true opinions, as it is dangerous and noxious when the opinions are erroneous. [11]

The grounding of the case for toleration on a logic which must issue in such uniformity would appear to menace the integrity and coherence of the whole argument of *On Liberty*. As we have seen, Mill regarded the work as a systematic unity, as 'a kind of philosophic text-book of a single truth'. [12] Presumably Mill thought the essence of that single truth was condensed in the quotation from von Humbolt which he used as the opening motto to *On Liberty*: 'The grand, leading principle, towards which every argument unfolded in these pages directly converges, is the absolute and essential importance of human development in its richest diversity.' [13] This, we take it, was appropriated as Mill's own promise that all the arguments would converge, and they would do so in order to demonstrate the paramount importance of human diversity. In his *Autobiography* Mill reflected that his essay was animated by the conviction of 'the importance, to man and society, of a large variety in types of character, and of giving full freedom to human nature to expand itself in innumerable and conflicting directions'. Here the value of toleration is not that it is a legitimate instrument of consolidation, but that it frustrates the 'noxious power' of 'compression'. [14]

The third chapter of *On Liberty* appears entirely consistent with the motto of the essay. It is a paean to individuality, energy of character, and originality; the cultivation and unfolding of talents

[11] *OL*, 103.   [12] Mill, *Autobiography*, 150.   [13] *OL*, 63.   [14] Mill, *Autobiography*, 150, 151.

and proclivities, the owning (both possessing and recognising) of our desires and impulses. The logic of the argument might, perhaps, be interpreted as another teleological argument for toleration: 'the telos of tolerance is individuality'. But such an interpretation would be a mistake. There is no anticipated substantive end; for Mill individual spontaneity is of intrinsic worth, and deserves regard on its own account. Since the manifestations of spontaneity are obviously unpredictable, its free play could not yield a substantive end to be appraised. Human nature is like a tree 'which requires to grow and develop itself on all sides, according to the tendency of the inward forces which make it a living thing'. [15] The 'end' of the developmental process – the individual – is an unpredictable self-creation. An undiscovered truth may be 'unpredictable', but, unlike the individual agent's selfhood, it is not disclosed and defined by acts of sovereign designation. The toleration of individuality which Mill here advocates cannot be a prudential stage towards an imagined, wished-for outcome, for the play of spontaneity will result in a myriad different forms, all to be respected. Least of all could the chapter on individuality, with its vision of indefinite patterns of human self-transmutation, be thought a plan for phased uniformity.

Mill would seem to be in a very serious dilemma. The logic of his case for the toleration of opinion appears to lead to an eventual uniformity of thought and belief. Moreover, he was capable of saying of 'the forbearance, which flows from a conscientious sense of the importance to mankind of the equal freedom of all opinion' that it is 'the only tolerance which is commendable, or, to the highest moral order of minds, possible'. This at least suggests that such a logic is the paradigm of any fundamental case for toleration. Yet Mill's typical characterisation of the argument of *On Liberty* is that it rests on the recognition of the incomparable worth of diversity in human thought and conduct and that it is a statement of the paramount importance of variety in character and the need for the expansion of human nature in innumerable and conflicting directions.

Does Mill have two views of toleration, one of a provisional and instrumental character, the other involving a recognition of the intrinsic value of human diversity that will never lose its force as long as the species lasts? If so, he is guilty of a remarkable oversight in stressing the unity of his doctrine, and failing to perceive how the

[15] *OL*, 117.

logic of one account does much to impair (even if it does not nullify) the cogency of the other. This is a much more serious problem than that of the relation of the argument for the toleration of opinion to the concepts that Mill uses to define the sphere of individual liberty.

On the face of it, the consolidation of opinion seems a melancholy prospect for individuality and variety, for energy, originality, and strangeness. Mill attached the greatest importance to the intellectual life of mankind, not only on its own (very considerable) account, but also because he regarded it as inextricably connected with the whole moral and spiritual condition of the species. He was well aware that only a tiny fraction of humanity resembled him in the extraordinary predominance of his intellectual faculty, but this in no way lessened his estimation of the profound importance of beliefs and sentiments (derived, no matter how imperfectly, from reasonings) for conduct and feeling. If 'opinions' have such vastly significant implications, then so does the prospect of the inevitable narrowing of the bounds of their diversity. So Mill's anticipation of the eventual 'consolidation of opinion' would seem to bear an ominous aspect for human diversity in all its forms. If this really is the heart of Mill's doctrine of toleration, he is a tragic figure indeed. In a devastating footnote, Fitzjames Stephen observes:

I must own that the nervous fear that a time may possibly come when there will be nothing left to argue about appears to me about as reasonable as the 'thought of the exhaustibility of musical combinations of the seven notes and semitones which make up the octave', by which Mr Mill tells us ... he was 'seriously tormented' at one time of his life.[16]

One resolution of Mill's dilemma restores his intellectual (at whatever cost to his moral) integrity. This solution follows from being persuaded of a particular line in the interpretation of Mill's works, of which Maurice Cowling's *Mill and Liberalism* is the most remarkable exemplar. The following quotations from that book will suggest how the problem might be resolved: '*On Liberty*, contrary to common opinion was not so much a plea for individual freedom, as a means of ensuring that Christianity would be superseded by the form of liberal, rationalistic, utilitarianism which went by the name of the Religion of Humanity. . . Mill's object was not to free men, but to convert them to a peculiarly exclusive, peculiarly insinuating moral doctrine.'[17] For Mill, 'Individual freedom must

---

[16] James Fitzjames Stephen, *Liberty, Equality, Fraternity* (Cambridge, 1967), 93, 94 n.
[17] Maurice Cowling, *Mill and Liberalism* (Cambridge, 1963), xiii.

be maximised, not because diversity of opinion is desirable in itself, but because, without diversity of opinion, men are unlikely to approach nearer to truth than they have done hitherto.'[18] That truth, Mill supposes, will be homogeneous, and 'if only men will submit their actions to critical examination, a moral, social and intellectual consensus will eventually supersede the miscellaneity of the age in which he lived'. 'All avenues at first are to be opened, but only because that is the best way, in the long run, of ensuring that some of them are closed.'[19]

This sort of account at least acquits Mill of confusion. He is indeed the advocate of an instrumental, prudential toleration, and that alone. Such a policy of toleration Mill adopted as the most appropriate (perhaps solely appropriate) means to a substantive end. That end *is* the 'consolidation of opinion' which, far from being an embarrassment to Mill's general view of toleration, is its justifying purpose. (Whether this 'consolidation of opinion' is equivalent to the 'Religion of Humanity' does not, for our purpose, matter.) The toleration of individual diversity in self-regarding conduct is either an unimportant mode of satisfying hedonism or part of a consolidation of conduct that is the counterpart of that of opinion. The high-flown Humboltian talk is merely that; perhaps it is part of the tactics of 'insinuation'. Even on this interpretation, the imputation to Mill of 'something resembling moral totalitarianism'[21] or a 'carefully disguised intolerance'[22] might seem a shade excessive, but, by its light, his doctrine of toleration is shown to be somewhat meagre, but also straightforward and consistent.

Another way of resolving the problem is implied by a remark of Paul Feyerabend. Unlike the solution implied by Cowling's work this is not derived from a general interpretation of Mill, for it occurs in a footnote to a short article on Mill's 'model of epistemic change'. It is none the less suggestive: 'For Mill the (material and spiritual) welfare of the individual, the full development of his capabilities, is the primary aim. The fact that the methods used for achieving this aim also yield a scientific philosophy, a book of rules concerning the "search for truth", is a side effect, though a pleasant one.'[23] Feyerabend commends Mill for holding the view that whatever the importance of the search for truth, it should never outrank the interests of the individual.

On this interpretation, the integrity of Mill's work again seems to

---

[18] *Ibid.*, 41.   [19] *Ibid.*, 34.   [20] *Ibid.*, 159.   [21] *Ibid.*, xii.   [22] *Ibid.*, xiii.
[23] Paul K. Feyerabend, *Problems of Empiricism* (Philosophical Papers, 2) (Cambridge, 1981), 68 n.

be restored. [In contradiction to the previous interpretation the 'search for truth' is not the central concern of Mill's toleration, it is, so to speak, a parenthesis in the doctrine. The philosophic text-book is indeed unitary; its arguments do converge on the welfare of the individual and on the development of the individual diversity. But there is a beneficial side-effect; the conditions for development of individuality providentially coincide with the conditions which prosper the search for truth.] The relation between the two (the development of individuality, the search for truth) would seem to be a contingent one. To interpret Mill correctly it is essential to understand that [the welfare of the individual outranks the search for truth]and therefore(despite evidence to the contrary) his case for toleration is grounded on the former consideration rather than the latter.

Neither of these contrasting interpretations of the significance of Mill's second chapter seems plausible. In what follows, I will examine more closely the relation between the argument for freedom of thought and discussion and the general argument of *On Liberty*. Particular attention must be paid to the question whether this part of Mill's argument is indeed a teleological argument in which toleration is expected to issue in a unified, substantive end, the achievement of truth in a general consolidation of opinion.

Mill's argument is avowedly utilitarian in character. 'I regard utility', he states, 'as the ultimate appeal on all ethical questions; but it must be utility in the largest sense, grounded on the permanent interests of man as a progressive being.'[24] [As he has warned us, the term 'utilitarian' will tell us little unless we understand by it Mill's own version of utilitarianism. One distinctive part of his doctrine is what John Gray[25] has termed Mill's 'indirect utilitarianism', which denotes the theorem that the direct pursuit of general utility is self-defeating.] It follows from this theorem that all attempts to promote welfare should be oblique, for they must observe the 'terms of social cooperation'[26] which are the subject of a theory of justice (chapter 5 of the essay *Utilitarianism* being the most complete account of such a theory). [For Mill, there are certain 'interests' that are of pre-eminent importance in any social theory of justice, and Gray styles them the interests in autonomy and security.] Gray believes, and I think argues convincingly, [that this line of inter-pretation is the clue to elucidating the grounds of Mill's doctrines of

---

[24] *OL*, 74. [25] In John Gray, *Mill on Liberty: A Defence* (London, 1983).
[26] See, for example, *ibid.*, 116.

'harm' and the spheres of self- and other-regarding conduct, themes that run through *On Liberty.*]

However, Mill has warned us that 'utility' is to be used in the largest sense, and he is by no means precluded from advancing arguments which are 'utilitarian' in a far more direct and conventional manner than that indicated above. Now, *On Liberty* is both a philosophical and an apologetic work. It is a philosophical interpretation and explanation of a vast area of human affairs, and it is also a reasoned defence (and attempted vindication) of a course of policy. Like the author of any apologetic work, Mill has to appeal to his audience in terms of things that they already acknowledge as good. He must persuade them that implicit in this acknowledgement is a further acknowledgement of the good of things they doubt to be good or mistakenly regard as bad.

To take one instance of such reasoning, we find Mill asking his readers to recollect 'that nothing was ever yet done which some one was not the first to do, and that all good things which exist are the fruits of originality', therefore, 'let them be modest enough to believe that there is something still left for it to accomplish, and assure themselves that they are more in need of originality, the less they are conscious of the want'.[27] The argument is as straightforward as it is effective; it is an apologetic argument using simple notions of progress and utility. To those who are indifferent towards originality, or even jealous of it, Mill says: since all those good things contrived by fellow humans which you enjoy and acknowledge to be good are the fruits of originality, you should (even if you can't muster more enthusiasm) at least be tolerant of originality.

There are more elaborate instances of this type of argument. The most bizarre (or farsighted?) is that which reminds the reader that stationary, ossified societies, like the Byzantine or Chinese empires, are fated to an ignominious and wretched end. Mill asks his audience to draw the inference that, unless they place more value on individuality, the nations of Europe and North America must share this fate. At any rate, the ideas of progress and utility are used impressively; whatever might be the misgivings about the plausibility of Mill's diagnosis, of the prognosis few would deny that this was a state of affairs to be avoided.[28]

---

[27] *OL,* 123.

[28] The theme of 'decline and fall' runs through *On Liberty.* Mill tells us that *OL* was conceived on the steps of the Capitol in Rome (*Autobiography,* 144). He makes no reference to the fact that this was the case with Gibbon's work, and has made a mistake about his own. Actually

One of the things that Mill is confident that his audience will approve is that mankind be in possession of the bodies of knowledge labelled 'truths'. Since it will be granted that these bodies of knowledge are in constant change (in the direction of augmentation, it is hoped), it follows that 'there is always need of persons . . . to discover new Truths, and point out when what were once truths are true no longer . . . This cannot well be gainsaid by anybody who does not believe that the world has already attained perfection in all its ways and practices.'[29] This modest opening is the logical start of Mill's apologetic plea for liberty of thought and discussion. It is common ground with anyone who will grant that knowledge is of value, perhaps for its own sake, and certainly for the prosperity of all human affairs.[30]

This is certainly common ground with many of those not otherwise sympathetic to Mill's argument. In his critical review of Mill's doctrine on this subject, James Fitzjames Stephen writes:

Few persons would be found, I suppose, in these days to deny the paramount expediency, the utility in the highest sense, of having true opinions; and by true I mean not merely honest, but correct opinions. To believe true statements, to disbelieve false statements, to give to probable or improbable statements a degree of credit proportioned to their apparent probability or improbability, would be the greatest of intellectual blessings.[31]

Here of course, the stress is on having 'correct' opinions, and having the informed knowledge necessary to make an educated estimate of probability.[32]

Mill does not merely agree with the conventional view that truth, in the sense of 'correct opinion', is eminently desirable, he agrees with Stephen that it is a 'paramount expediency' and 'utility in the

---

it was conceived some days before (see *Collected Works of John Stuart Mill*, XIII (Toronto, 1977), lxxxi. Gibbon's work was familiar to Mill from childhood. H. B. Acton thinks 'Mill has a strange idea of the Byzantine Empire', (*OL*, 427), but it is entirely faithful to Gibbon. At the end of the second chapter of *Decline and Fall* two paragraphs occur that could easily be placed in *OL*. It is strange that Gibbon's title is so often used as an anti-libertarian catchphrase. Perhaps those who use it thus, unlike Mill, haven't read the book.

[29] *OL*, 122.

[30] R. P. Wolff sketches an ingenious argument against 'the premise, unmentioned by Mill, but clearly essential for the argument, that knowledge makes men happy' in pp. 9–11 of his *The Poverty of Liberalism* (Boston, 1968).

[31] Stephen, 86.

[32] Stephen is certainly not oblivious of the general desirability of strong and vividly held convictions. But he tends to sunder this from any intellectual mode of confirmation of the 'truth' of the conviction at issue: 'If you want zealous belief, set people to fight' (p. 79).

highest sense'. He believes, moreover, that intellectual activity is the predominant agent of all human progress:

Now, the evidence of history and that of human nature combine, by a striking instance of consilience, to show that there really is one social element which is thus predominant, and almost paramount, among the agents of the social progression. This is, the state of the speculative faculties of mankind; including the nature of the beliefs which by any means they have arrived at, concerning themselves and the world by which they are surrounded.

It would be a great error, and one very little likely to be committed, to assert that speculation, intellectual activity, the pursuit of truth, is among the more powerful propensities of human nature, or holds a predominating place in the lives of any, save decidedly exceptional individuals. But, notwithstanding the relative weakness of this principle among other sociological agents, its influence is the main determining cause of the social progress; all the other dispositions of our nature which contribute to that progress, being dependent on it for the means of accomplishing their share of the work.[33]

Thus, the advances in industrial processes (that are necessary to gratify the desire for increased comfort) depend on improved knowledge of the properties of physical objects. Since (at least in a backward state of human living together) the social union depends on subordination to some common system of opinions, the improvement of that union depends on a modification of those opinions. So, although among the whole ensemble of human motives those of enquiry and speculation are comparatively weak, this weakness 'has not, therefore, prevented the progress of speculation from governing that of society at large; it has only, and too often, prevented progress altogether, where the intellectual progression has come to an early stand for want of sufficiently favourable circumstances'.[34]

According to Mill's account, then, mankind possess beliefs concerning themselves and the world by which they are surrounded which are the products of their speculative faculties, which may 'arrive at' conclusions by various modes.[35] But such beliefs are of immense importance, conditioning as they do every sphere of mankind's social existence. This importance is in no way diminished

---

[33] J. S. Mill, *A System of Logic*, Book VI, in *Collected Works of John Stuart Mill*, VIII (Toronto, 1974), 926.

[34] *Ibid.*, 927.

[35] *OL* contains a vivid example of how various are the means by which beliefs have been arrived at. See 69, 70 for the 'multifarious causes' of past beliefs about the 'fitting adjustment between individual independence and social control'.

by the comparative feebleness of speculative activity as an engrossing pursuit among the mass of mankind, because the other dispositions are ultimately dependent upon it for all the benefits currently enjoyed, and all prospects of future advance. The degree to which mankind can prosper depends, however, on the degree to which these beliefs are correct interpretations of their nature and circumstances. The modes by which mankind derive their beliefs must therefore be of the kind which yield true knowledge and the social 'circumstances' must be favourable to 'intellectual progression'.

This sketch hints at the philosophical theory by which Mill so far agrees with the popular opinion that truth is eminently desirable that he regards it (other virtues apart) as the predominant agent of social progress. The ascertainment of truth, the gaining of correct opinions, has pre-eminent utility for man as a progressive being. Naturally, Mill exploits this common ground that he shares with his audience by giving it a part in the apologetic strategy of *On Liberty*. He proceeds beyond this common ground by the contentions that the mode of arriving at certifiably true beliefs is that of reason, and that the social circumstances favourable to intellectual progression are those which accord complete toleration to thought and discussion.

Towards the end of the chapter on the liberty of thought and discussion, Mill summarises the four distinct grounds by which he holds the doctrine of the complete toleration of opinions.[36] In abridged form these are:

1. If any opinion is compelled to silence, that opinion may, for ought we can certainly know, be true.
2. Though the silenced opinion be an error, it may, and very commonly does, contain a portion of truth.
3. Even if the received opinion be the whole truth, unless it is vigorously contested, it will tend to be held as a prejudice, with little comprehension or feeling of its rational grounds.
4. Indeed, the very meaning of the doctrine will be in danger of being lost, deprived of its vital effect on character and conduct.

Of these four grounds, the first two are clearly conducive to the ascertainment of a body of well-founded knowledge and correct opinion. From this viewpoint, the third and fourth grounds may be

---

[36] *Ibid.*, 111, 112.

regarded as supplementary considerations, encouraging the growth and maintenance of the rationality by which truth is discovered and correctly estimated and our apprehension of it is modified and supplemented.

Mill's argument is not merely that well-founded knowledge must presuppose the fullest liberty of professing and discussing opinion, but that the suppression of any opinion (to use James Fitzjames Stephen's phrase) 'proceeds on a theory involving distinct intellectual error'.[37] The argument shows that in so far as correct opinion is desirable, toleration is necessary and suppression is incoherent and irrational. To the degree that his argument is valid, Mill will have demonstrated (to the satisfaction of those who agree with him that knowledge is pre-eminently desirable) that there should be complete liberty in the sphere of thought and discussion.

The relevant part of the argument runs along the following lines[38]: the whole strength and value of human judgement depends on one property, that it can be set right when it is wrong. The foundation of all knowledge is experience and understanding. But the whole history of beliefs testifies that both depend upon the help of criticism. Experience is not self-interpreting, and the correctness of interpretation is a matter of critical evaluation. The inherent force of human understanding, unaided by criticism, is shown as woefully inadequate even in the greatest thinkers. The sole rational ground for holding an opinion is, therefore, that it is proof against criticism. To hold that an opinion is true and consequently to be *protected* against all dissent is an incoherent and irrational contention. It follows that no silencing of dissent is justified on rational grounds, and that a complete toleration of opinions should prevail.

The whole intellectual and moral achievement of mankind depends on the power of rectification of errors. At the moment of their first belief, humanity became the prey of a Pandora's boxfull of error and false belief, but they can be saved by their only source of intellectual hope: corrigibility. The false caution that would keep this boxed in is ultimately suicidal, but if criticism is allowed to do its work, there are potentially as many sources of mutual correction as there are intelligences. The same power of rectification not only saves from error, but is also the only firm ground of confidence and certainty:

---

[37] Stephen, 78.
[38] See *OL*, 81–3. C. L. Ten makes some valuable distinctions between Mill's arguments in ch. 8 of his *Mill on Liberty* (Oxford, 1980).

If even the Newtonian philosophy were not permitted to be questioned, mankind could not feel as complete assurance of its truth as they now do. The beliefs which we have most warrant for have no safeguard to rest on but a standing invitation to the whole world to prove them unfounded. If the challenge is not accepted, or is accepted and the attempt fails, we are far enough from certainty still; but we have done the best that the existing state of human reason admits of; we have neglected nothing that could give the truth a chance of reaching us: if the lists are kept open, we may hope that if there is a better truth, it will be found when the human mind is capable of receiving it; and in the meantime we may rely on having attained such approach to truth as is possible in our own day. This is the sole amount of certainty attainable by a fallible being, and this is the sole way of attaining it.[39]

Truth does indeed have a warrant and safeguard, and that is the standing invitation to the world to prove an opinion unfounded. Fallible beings are 'far from certainty' in so far as an unassailable belief is plainly precluded from such a warrant. Any such conception of a definitive because incontrovertible truth is an incoherent illusion. But the standing invitation does give the sole amount of certainty of which we are capable, and the only rational assurance and confidence in our beliefs.[40] Toleration is the social condition of certainty.

We may conclude that a line of argument does indeed run through *On Liberty* in which the telos of tolerance is truth. Tolerance alone permits the emergence of new truths, the eclipse of super-annuated truths, the transformation of knowledge that comes from the critical synthesis of partially true opinions; and tolerance is the condition of whatever certification of truth is possible. The development of opinion is of prime importance in all ages, but Mill is here specifically concerned with its development under his reading of modern circumstances. Under these circumstances knowledge, as an agent of social progress, has power in proportion to the breadth and strength of the dissemination of true opinions throughout the population, and the degree to which their rational and critical faculties have been cultivated. People are no longer inclined to implicit trust in beliefs on the credit of their supposed

[39] *OL*, 83.
[40] One wonders whether Paul Feyerabend's admiration for *OL* is in spite of, or because of, some peculiarities of interpretation. Feyerabend rightly praises Mill's stress on 'negative logic', but then states of Mill's theory 'This theory takes the bull by the horns: theories *cannot* be justified, and they *need not* be justified' (*Problems of Empiricism*, 194). But Mill believes that the withstanding of the assault of negative logic *is* a warrant, safeguard, complete assurance. It is true that this can never be definitive in the sense that further criticism is ever prejudged as futile, but what is this if not the language of 'justification'?

superiors; indeed the chief intellectual menace of the modern age is the collective mediocrity of opinion. However, the progress of education and equality has made that tolerance possible which modern circumstances render indispensable. 'Liberty, as a principle, has no application to any state of things anterior to the time when mankind have become capable of being improved by free and equal discussion.'[41] Mankind have now, however, attained the capacity of being guided to their own improvement by conviction or persuasion, an incomparably more congenial climate to the promotion of true opinions and their clear apprehension than any in the past. Mill concludes that the time is ripe, and the need is pressing for 'absolute freedom of opinion and sentiment on all subjects, practical or speculative, scientific, moral or theological'.[42]

The logical result of this line of argument is the prospect of a consolidation of opinion, the constant increase of the number of doctrines no longer disputed or doubted, a state of affairs where 'the well-being of mankind may almost be measured by the number and gravity of the truths which have reached the point of being uncontested'.[43] Of course, free debate and dissent will always be permitted, indeed welcomed. But the essence of this case for toleration must have this conclusion implicit within it. The corrigibility of opinion implies that there is indeed a 'correct' solution, no matter how many subtle transmutations the original rough conjectures go through. The antagonism of opinions is only possible because they are putative solutions to the same problem. The challenge which supplies the warrant of truth to opinion must issue in victory or defeat. The transformation of partially true opinions by mutual criticism ultimately results in synthesis. The ascertainment of truth is a systematic and exclusionary process that is tolerant towards holders of opinions, but coercive towards the opinions themselves. Needless to say for Mill there is loss in this process of consolidation. He has the keenest awareness of the need for contradiction in order to give a lively apprehension of the nature, implications, and grounds of our opinion. Dissident critics of the reigning opinion should be not only tolerated, but thanked; educators will have to exercise ingenuity in showing it in a problematic light. But the outcome of these disputes will be to enhance the consolidation.

The line of argument which we have been considering is a utilitarian argument derived from the importance to human progress of the discovery of truths. Tolerance is the social condition of

41 *OL*, 73.　42 *Ibid.*, 75.　43 *Ibid.*, 103.

the discovery of truth, its diffusion, and its clear, vigorous apprehension. Mill, in unfolding this argument, is expounding his own sincere belief, but it also has great apologetic value. It is not, however, the heart of *On Liberty*, or even what he regards as its utilitarian case. The heart of *On Liberty* is the doctrine of individuality presented in the first half of Chapter 3. The supremely important 'end itself' is the free development of individuality in its proper sphere. Human nature, we are told, requires the free play of native capacities, faculties, susceptibilities. This is the doctrine in which human nature, like a tree, 'requires to grow and develop itself on all sides, according to the tendency of the inward forces which make it a living thing'.[44] Within the legitimate sphere of individuality, desires and impulses should be gratified, according to individual judgement. The release, within this sphere, of latent energies, of the capacity to initiate and originate, is both of social utility and intrinsic value. This intrinsic value of human spontaneity is part of 'utility in the largest sense'. All other desirable things in progress and improvement are measured according to their tendency to promote human welfare. But '[a]mong the works of man, which human life is rightly employed in perfecting and beautifying, the first in importance surely is man himself'.[45] The ultimate criterion of development is not what men do, but what manner of men they are that do it.

For Mill himself, this is the crown of the argument:

Having said that Individuality is the same thing with development, and that it is only the cultivation of individuality which produces, or can produce, well-developed human beings, I might here close the argument: for what more or better can be said of any condition of human affairs than that it brings human beings themselves nearer to the best thing they can be?[46]

However, Mill here faces the same problem as in the 'proof of utility', namely that ultimate ends are not amenable to direct proof, since desirability can only be demonstrated in terms of some further, and acknowledged, good.

This difficulty only becomes fully explicit at the crux of Mill's argument, but has been implicit from the beginning. In his introductory chapter, Mill states as his thesis 'Mankind are greater gainers by suffering each other to live as seems good to themselves, than by compelling each to live as seems good to the rest.'[47] He regards it as an apologetic convenience that before the exposition of

[44] *Ibid.*, 117.　[45] *Ibid.*, 117.　[46] *Ibid.*, 121.　[47] *Ibid.*, 75, 76.

104

the general thesis, he first examines 'a single branch of it, on which the principle here stated is, if not fully, yet to a certain point, recognised by the current opinions'.[48] That branch is the liberty of thought, and after his examination of that subject, he capitalises (by use of analogy) on this partially acknowledged liberty to press his claims for liberty of self-regarding actions. The liberty of thought is already acknowledged in current morality because of the experience of, and respect for, religious toleration and free institutions. Implicit in these practices are sentiments which recognise, in however vague a manner, the intrinsic good of the exercise of individual judgement. It is Mill's strategy to make this explicit by examination of the 'grounds' of the belief in the liberty of thought, and what he contends these imply. The value of individuality as an 'ultimate end' or intrinsic good cannot be demonstrated in terms of something else. But if there already exists a partial recognition of this intrinsic good, Mill may attempt to demonstrate that it should be extended to the whole.

The recognition of the intrinsic good of the exercise of individual judgement is the intellectual aspect of according worth to the whole inner life of heart and mind. Considered from this aspect, Mill's review of the grounds of the liberty of thought and discussion is a survey of the intellectual conditions of individual integrity and human dignity. To see his argument from this standpoint requires a transformed interpretation of the grounds by which Mill holds the doctrine of the complete toleration of opinion. Previously we have followed Mill's argument as a reasoned statement of the tolerant conditions necessary for the ascertainment of a body of well-founded knowledge and correct opinions. These conditions are necessary for the rationality which gives rise to such opinions and for their vindication and further for their clear and lively apprehension. But Mill is concerned not merely with the conclusions of men's thoughts, or the rationality of these conclusions, or the clarity, vividness, and insight with which these conclusions are held. What must be evaluated in conduct is not only what men do, but what manner of men they are that do it. Similarly, for Mill, what is involved in the question of freedom of thought is the very worth of mind and spirit.

Considerations of character, mental vitality, moral buoyancy, and imagination are present at every turn of the argument of Mill's second chapter, structured though it is around the concept of truth. For example Mill shows this relation between the exercise of

[48] *Ibid.*, 77.

105

individual judgement and the moral qualities in his characterisation of the faculties that go to make up a 'thinker'. The first duty of
a thinker, he says, is to follow his intellect to whatever conclusions it
may lead. This is a call not only on the intellectual but also the
moral resources; openness, sensitivity and conscientiousness are
required, together with vigour, tenacity, and courage. Of course,
such qualities are rare, and their harmony is much rarer. But there
is no reason why thought on deep and controversial subjects
should be confined to persons of exceptional abilities. The great
convulsions of modern history have opened up such controversies
to whole populations. When many among these were stirred to
exercise their judgement, so the exercise of their intellectual
faculties went hand-in-hand with their spiritual and moral development. In this manner, says Mill, persons of ordinary capacities have
risen to the dignity of thinking beings.

Even those who deprecate the exercise of individual judgement
hold it desirable that people should subscribe to their preferred
beliefs. But even assent to such beliefs implies understanding what
the belief is, and that is impossible without the exercise of
individual judgement. The whole force of such an understanding
lies in the apprehension of the superiority of the doctrine in question over its competitors, and therefore no such understanding is
possible without permitting the belief to be contradicted. Without
the possibility of such contradiction, assent, even to a true opinion,
'abides in the mind, but abides as a prejudice, a belief independent
of, and proof against, argument – this is not the way in which truth
ought to be held by a rational being. This is not knowing the truth.
Truth, thus held, is but one superstition the more, accidentally
clinging to the words which enunciate a truth.'[49] Mill's protest is a
moral, not simply intellectual, protest. What is involved in this false
doctrine of assent is a profound degradation; Mill hypothesises
assent to a true opinion not to mitigate but to highlight the abjectness of the bondage to superstition.

Without the exercise of individual judgement, not only are the
bearings and implications of the belief assented to lost, but the very
meaning of the belief itself vanishes. '[T]he creed remains as it were
outside the mind, incrusting and petrifying it against all other
influences addressed to the higher parts of our nature; manifesting
its power by not suffering any fresh and living conviction to get in,
but itself doing nothing for the mind or heart, except standing sen-
tinel over them to keep them vacant.'[50] The loss is not merely

[49] *Ibid.*, 96.   [50] *Ibid.*, 100.

intellectual, but moral. The belief is not realised in consciousness, it is not tested by personal experience, nor can it help to interpret real experience; the belief has ceased 'to connect itself at all with the inner life of the human being'.[51] For belief can only connect with the inner life if it is held with comprehension and conviction, which in turn implies liberty of contradiction. Without the exercise of individual judgement, not only is intellectual life paralysed, but the spiritual and moral life connected with it is impaired and ossified.

'Truth', Mill tells us, 'gains more even by the errors of one who, with due study and preparation, thinks for himself, than by the true opinions of those who hold them because they do not suffer themselves to think.'[52] This is partly the Baconian insight that truth comes more easily out of error than confusion, but it is also a tribute to the moral qualities of earnestness, scrupulousness, and honesty that are essential to the proper understanding of any difficult matter. Again, the moral, spiritual, and intellectual virtues are brought together in the quality of wisdom:

the only way in which a human being can make some approach to knowing the whole of a subject, is by hearing what can be said about it by persons of every variety of opinion, and studying all the modes in which it can be looked at by every character of mind. No wise man ever acquired his wisdom in any mode but this; nor is it in the nature of human intellect to become wise in any other manner.[53]

Mill's case for the toleration of opinion is not merely a concern for the correctness of conclusions, but for the whole spiritual, moral, and intellectual health of the inner life. His concern is both for 'the truth' and for individuality. But how are they related? Is the relation between the development of individuality and the search for truth a merely contingent relationship? Is the individual's capacity for independent judgement valuable because it happens to be instrumental to the ascertainment of truth, or is the discovery of truth an incidental, though valuable, by-product of individuality? Perhaps there is a clue in Mill's quotation from von Humbolt: 'the end of man, or that which is prescribed by the eternal or immutable dictates of reason, and not suggested by vague and transient desires, is the highest and most harmonious development of his powers to a complete and consistent whole'.[54] The value of individuality has to do with a conception of wholeness, completeness (whether it is ever achieved, or not), and this in turn has to do

---

[51] *Ibid.*, 100.   [52] *Ibid.*, 94.   [53] *Ibid.*, 82.   [54] *Ibid.*, 115.

with reason. Mill asserts that the source of everything that is respectable in man as an intellectual or moral being is that his errors are corrigible, that his experience may be interpreted and mistakes rectified by reason. Without the discipline of 'truth', judgement would be impossible, and so would be Mill's attribution of dignity, stature, sanity, or wisdom to individual achievements. Is it Mill's doctrine that the welfare of the individual outranks the search for truth? For Mill, since apprehension of the truth can only be the free achievement of an individual intelligence, truth cannot be said to be competitive with individuality; rather it is the condition that gives to individual thought its stature and significance.

In the chapter on the liberty of thought and discussion, Mill has been amplifying what he believes to be the implications of the value placed on the exercise of individual judgement. This value is already latently recognised in current morality, since it is implicit in the practices of religious toleration and free institutions. In his third chapter, Mill endeavours to show that this respect should be extended to the use of individual judgement in the sphere of self-regarding conduct: '[t]o a certain extent it is admitted that our understanding should be our own: but there is not the same willingness to admit that our desires and impulses should be our own likewise'.[55]

The analogy between opinion and self-regarding conduct, between the exercise of judgement in beliefs and that in tastes and patterns of living recalls the unresolved problem of the consolidation of opinion. Given Mill's perception of the spiritual and moral dimensions of the holding of beliefs, the consequences of the necessary 'narrowing of the bounds of diversity of opinion'[56] already seem deeply menacing to human vitality and variety. The analogy between judgement in opinion and judgement in self-regarding conduct appears to make matters infinitely worse. Mill contends that the *same* reasons apply in both cases:

That mankind are not infallible; that their truths, for the most part are only half-truths; that unity of opinion, *unless resulting from the fullest and freest comparison of opposite opinions*, is not desirable, and diversity not an evil, but a good, *until mankind are much more capable than at present of recognising all sides of the truth*, are principles applicable to men's modes of action, not less than to their opinions. *As it is recognised that while mankind are imperfect* there should be different opinions, so it is that there should be different experiments of living; that free scope should be given to varieties of character, short of injury to others.[57]

[55] *Ibid.*, 117, 118.   [56] *Ibid.*, 103.   [57] *Ibid.*, 114, 115 (my italics).

If we suppose a total consolidation of opinion, and that conduct and character are exactly analogous in the grounds of their toleration and the future prospects these grounds imply, the result will be the virtual extinction of human variety. Are we to suppose that 'men's modes of action', after a process of the fullest and freest comparison, are to become uniform in type? That when mankind are more capable than at present of discerning the advantages of such modes of action, a general synthesis of the best forms of conduct will result? As mankind become less imperfect, will 'experiments in living' cease, and will a provisional variety of character be superseded by some more definitive model?

Of course, Mill does not anticipate any consolidation of opinion until 'mankind shall have entered a stage of intellectual advancement which at present seems at an incalculable distance'.[58] This is small consolation. And, needless to say, he insists that judgement in both opinion and conduct should always be freely exercised. The very validity of the best warranted beliefs will always depend upon the standing challenge to contradictory competitors. The judgement that an 'experiment in living' is a success or failure will be as free as that involved in any other interpretation of experience. But does the immanent logic of Mill's doctrine of toleration and liberty tend to the result of a freely chosen, if distant, homogeneity?

In the sphere of conduct, there is no question that Mill does not anticipate any such uniformity. His view is that people differ, and presumably will always differ, in their fundamental physical, temperamental, and psychic constitutions. This variety is not a provisional imperfection; it makes the human race what it is. Whether its variety is innate or the result of the spontaneous, unpredictable mutations of childhood, or the proportion which belongs to either, does not matter. There is a wonderful tendency to variety in the human condition that is beyond exact control or calculation. Mill is also well aware of the mutability of the human race, of how social relations may be congenial towards, or frustrating of, such a diversity of types and propensities: '[D]ifferent persons . . . require different conditions for their spiritual development; and can no more exist healthily in the same moral, than all the variety of plants can in the same physical, atmosphere and climate.'[59] The 'experiments in living' are to provide presumptive evidence, offered to the interpretation and judgement of the individual, of what that healthy atmosphere and climate might be. They are emphatically not

---

[58] *Ibid.*, 105.   [59] *Ibid.*, 125.

expected to usher in a definitive model of conduct. The entire inspiration of *On Liberty* is the inestimable value of individuality, and Mill's purpose was to understand its conditions and make it more abundant.

Mill strongly affirms the relatedness of character and belief, the connection between intellectual development and the inner life, between heart and mind. The efflorescence of individuality, with the resulting intensification of differences of taste, temperament, and character must surely then involve an ever-continued variety of opinions. How can such an inference be compatible with Mill's expectation of a consolidation of opinion? In the second chapter of *On Liberty*, Mill distinguishes between mathematics and science on the one hand and, on the other, morals, religion, politics, social relations, and the business of life. He contrasts these groups in terms of the latter group's being 'infinitely more complicated'.[60] But he also speaks of 'many truths of which the full meaning *cannot* be realised until personal experience has brought it home'.[61] These, no doubt, are the truths about moral and human subjects, where meaning itself may only be interpreted in terms of the whole inner life. Such truths may range from the homely wisdom contained in proverbs to the profound paradoxes of the beatitudes.

Of course, Mill is not saying that truths concerning moral and human subjects are incommunicable; much the reverse. Part of the inner life is a sympathetic interpretative faculty, that draws from personal belief, temperament, and character, but is also pre-eminently 'social', for it construes the experience and utterance of others. Because his view of mental life connects intelligence so closely with empathy, emotion, and imagination, Mill says that the meaning in some moral and human beliefs cannot fully be realised without direct personal experience. But these same qualities of empathy and imagination can make accessible to us experiences, beliefs, and opinions utterly remote from our own. In the sphere of belief this often, perhaps generally, happens in a contest of opinions. Sometimes it is only where there is the earnest, forceful, insistent exposition of a contrary opinion that we make 'real contact'[62] with an entirely different cast of mind.

In the essay *Bentham* Mill tells us that human nature and human life are wide subjects, the only hope of understanding which comes from the breadth of the enquirer's own nature and circumstance

---

[60] *Ibid.*, 96.   [61] *Ibid.*, 103 (italics in the original).   [62] *Ibid.*, 97.

and his 'capacity of deriving light from other minds'.[63] To begin to form such an understanding, there must be

a thoughtful regard . . . for the collective mind of the human race. What has been the opinion of mankind, has been the opinion of persons of all tempers and dispositions, of all partialities and prepossessions, of all varieties in position, in education, in opportunities of observation and inquiry. No one inquirer is all this: every inquirer is either young or old, rich or poor, sickly or healthy, married or unmarried, meditative or active, a poet or a logician, an ancient or a modern, a man or a woman; and if a thinking person, has, in addition, the accidental peculiarities of his individual modes of thought. Every circumstance which gives a character to the life of a human being, carries with it its peculiar biases; its peculiar facilities for perceiving some things, and for missing or forgetting others. But, from points of view different from his, different things are perceptible; and none are more likely to have seen what he does not see, than those who do not see what he sees. The general opinion of mankind is the average of the conclusions of all minds, stripped indeed of their choicest and most recondite thoughts, but freed from their twists and partialities.

Opinion on human and moral subjects is, then, interfused with our distinctive features of character and personal experience. Opinion and character react upon each other in an intimate symbiosis. If we are tolerant and open, we may, through our faculties of empathy and imagination, understand what is seen from the point of view of those whose character and opinions are entirely foreign to us. We can not only make 'real contact' with such minds, but also be persuaded that their insight is superior or supplementary to our own. This form of corrigibility involves a modification, slight or deep, of our own opinions and character. Further, Mill holds that the very meaning of our opinions, and the significance of our character, are only truly realised in the recognition of what is foreign to us.

On human and moral subjects there is indeed an 'opinion of mankind', an average of conclusions of all minds. This lacks depth, but sees all that is on the surface. Such a 'collective mind' is therefore entitled to a thoughtful regard as a likely source of correction of our own peculiarities. But the distinctive beliefs which make individuals what they are are not 'accidental peculiarities', or a deviation from some definitive, universal understanding of the human condition. They can offer a deeper insight into some aspects

---

[63] The quotations from the essay *Bentham* are to be found on 90, 91 of *Collected Works of John Stuart Mill*, X (Toronto, 1969).

of that condition than can ever be the result of an easily accessible general opinion.

Our fundamental beliefs are part of what we are, and are related to the travails of the formation of our identity. These are, in principle, always open to modification. But if the modification is to be of any depth, it must derive from an interpretation of experience which is of similar formation; from the singular experience of individual intelligences. In Mill's account of opinion on human, moral subjects the relation of intelligence and character is such that all significant achievement is so much part of individuality that the collective opinion must be only superficially comprehensive.

The collective opinion is still a valuable average since it supplements my opinion and experience with an average of the experiences of others of all conditions. But because it is an average, it is necessarily a surface interpretation of human existence. For a deeper form of 'corrigibility' we must 'derive light from other minds' by evaluating what is said on a subject by 'all modes in which it can be looked at by every character of mind'.

This is an attention to the singularity of the different modes which does not average, but rather retains exactly what we find to be 'choice' or 'recondite' *because* singular. If this is so, then whatever his hopes for consolidation of demonstrably correct opinions in other forms of knowledge, Mill could not expect from a regime of free debate that any body of received opinion could arise concerning the most significant human and moral subjects. He could not expect, much less welcome, a prospect of the cessation of serious controversy on such matters, or a narrowing of the bounds of diversity of opinion and the creation of a voluntary unanimity.

The argument for the liberty of thought and discussion occupies a central place in Mill's view of toleration – as we have seen, he was capable of calling it the only commendable, even the only possible, source of tolerance. I have sought to indicate the internal complexity of that argument and its complicated relation to Mill's doctrine of liberty as a whole, especially the value to be placed on human diversity. Mill gave the clearest testimony to the crucial importance he placed on the case for the toleration of opinion in his philosophical understanding of the nature of liberty. There is equally emphatic evidence that the inspiration and purpose of *On Liberty* was to attest the value of human development in its richest diversity and its expansion in innumerable and conflicting directions, and to combat the noxious power of compression. Mill was confident that his arguments cohered in this 'single truth'. Yet the most conspicuous element in the case for the toleration of opinion (where the telos of tolerance is truth) has a remorseless immanent logic that seems inimical to this inspiration and purpose. Mill advances other powerful doctrines and arguments – concerning the intrinsic value of the exercise of individual judgement; the spontaneous tendency to diversification in personality and identity; the need for tolerance as the condition of conviction, vitality of spirit, intellectual and moral health; the relatedness of belief and interpretation of meaning to character and personal experience.

I have tried to trace the coherence of these arguments and doctrines as sympathetically to Mill as possible, well aware of the philosophical difficulties that remain even if this conjectural interpretation is faithful to Mill's thought. We are compelled to conjecture because in the argument of *On Liberty* Mill hardly seems to perceive that the essential problem raised above *is* a problem for him. In the essay *Bentham* Mill says 'The first question in regard to any man of speculation is, what is his theory of human life?' The problems arising from his case for the toleration of opinion take us, I think, quite deep into Mill's own 'theory', for better or worse. As he says, 'In the minds of many philosophers, whatever theory they have of this sort is latent, and it would be a revelation to themselves to have it pointed out to them in their writings as others can see it, unconsciously moulding everything to its own likeness.'[64]

[64] *Ibid.*, 94.

Unlike the other contributions to this collection, this paper was not presented at one of the Morrell Conferences on Toleration. An earlier form of it was, however, discussed by the Political Theory Workshop, a gathering of some members of the Politics, Philosophy and Economics Departments of the University of York, together with postgraduate students sponsored by the Morrell Studies in Toleration. I am glad to record my obligation to all of them.

5

Rousseau and respect for others

NICHOLAS DENT

PREAMBLE

It would widely be agreed that the question of the significance and value of tolerance can usefully be considered by seeing tolerance as one central aspect or component of affording due respect to others. Of course being tolerant of others and rendering due respect to them are not equivalent. The latter comprehends a far wider range of attitudes and actions towards others than the former does, but I am inclined to think that all that having a tolerant regard towards others involves will be part of granting them the respect which is their due. That is, all failures in tolerance will be failures in respect, but not vice versa. I am not able to say clearly what subclass of, loosely, attitudes and actions constitutive of respect for others comprises being tolerant of them. Tolerance appears largely to take as its target beliefs and attitudes of others which form their conception of the great ends and proper conduct of life, and actions so far as these are exhibitive of or consequent upon these beliefs and attitudes. Respect clearly extends additionally to cover for instance respect for the physical integrity of another as such. This indicated demarcation is, of course, extremely vague, but, fortunately, nothing in what I want to go on to consider depends upon getting this more precise.

We are familiar with cases where the requirement to afford others the respect due from us to them, in one of its shapes or forms, becomes problematic. Either this requirement may be overridden by some more weighty demand, or it may be unclear whether acceptance of the requirement really does entail, say, non-interference, in the case in point. A very familiar case is this. The duty of non-interference in others' execution of their projects – which I take to be part of respecting them as centres of autonomous conduct – is properly overridden if the other is about to commit murder. Or perhaps one may say that one does not at all fail in showing the respect due to another if one violently intervenes to stop them acting like this. It never was part of what respect for them implied that one should honour their murderous projects. Similarly, one may be faced with a signal instance or a general habit of intolerance and it is certainly not clear that one is obliged to show tolerance towards this, for example by way of non-interference with the expression of intolerant views or with the carrying out of actions consequent on that intolerance. In some cases, indeed, one is surely clearly obliged not to tolerate intolerance; for instance all forms of racial intolerance should not be borne with.

Rousseau, I shall argue, was almost before all else concerned with the harmfulness and wrongness of a system of social and personal relations of which each person having contempt for the person and life of others was the dominant characteristic and in which, as an immediate corollary, intolerance was wholly pervasive. Equally he was concerned to try to display the good and rightness of a system of social and personal relations in which respect for and honour of the person and life of each by each was the most fundamental ordering principle, and in which, as an immediate corollary, tolerance would be a leading characteristic. In the course of his treatment of these matters he makes suggestions about what would be necessary to achieve the social order he thinks best which are, at first glance, quite inimical to tolerance in their nature and implications. Consider, for instance, his claim that those who do not believe in the dogmas of civil religion should be banished, or his only too well-known thoughts about 'forcing' people to be free. I shall argue, however, that nothing Rousseau says in connection with these matters can properly be seen as a failure on his part to hold to the main tenets of his position. In them he is facing the issue of how it is fit to contend with attitudes and actions which are themselves intolerant or will lead to intolerance, cases of a kind I glanced at above. It is for the sake of ensuring the possibility and reality of tolerance and respect for persons more generally that he makes the proposals he does on these points. No moral, social, or political thinker can neglect the issue of how it is proper to respond to the sources and actuality of intolerance. Any adequate response is bound to involve the circumscription of some beliefs and actions, and this may then appear, superficially, to be an expression of intolerance. But the appearance is superficial merely (or rather, it *may* be merely superficial; the account may go astray here). Along the lines I indicated earlier it will be appropriate to say that it never was part of what tolerance required that one should bear with the kind and degree of intolerance the need to avoid which Rousseau has identified. Of course, it is always possible that Rousseau's specific proposals are not altogether appropriate to their intended task. But that is a mistake in practice, not of principle, in what he is attempting to do here.

My discussion will take the following form. I shall first present Rousseau's vision of a society, an order of personal and social relations, of which contempt for the person and life of each by each is the dominant feature. I shall then set against this his conception of an alternative, and in his view much better, form for social and personal relations to take, and try to show how his account of the nature of respect for others sits with this second conception. I shall conclude by examining in a little detail Rousseau's views on civil religion as a test case both to provide an assessment of the cogency of the account of Rousseau's views on the matter of tolerance and respect I have been offering and also to provide an appraisal of the effectiveness of Rousseau's own commitment to the importance of tolerance and respect for others.

AMOUR-PROPRE

Although the notion of *amour-propre* (hereafter *a-p*) has little visible place in the arguments of *The Social Contract*, it plays a very important role in Rousseau's earlier discussions, which form the essential background to any proper understanding of *The Social Contract*.[1] It is principally because *a-p* is the dominant motive in people that there arises that order of social relations to which contempt for and intolerance of others are central, indeed are essential (as we shall see).

This paper was presented at the Morrell Conference on Toleration, University of York, 24–6 September 1985. Pressures of time and space have prevented me from giving as full and detailed a set of references to, let alone quotations from and discussions of, Rousseau's texts as would be necessary to provide proper support for the interpretation of his ideas I offer here. I accept, of course, the obligation to provide this kind of support; I would hope in due time to be able to discharge this obligation. I hope that despite this very evident defect (and others no doubt equally evident to all but me) a reasonably cogent reading has been offered.

[1] References to *A Discourse on the Origin of Inequality* (*DI*) and to *The Social Contract* (*SC*) are to the translation by G. D. H. Cole (revised J. H. Brumfitt and J. C. Hall), *The Social Contract and Discourses* (London, 1973). References to *Emile* (*E*) are to the translation by Barbara Foxley, *Emile* (London, 1969). This translation is in parts quite unsatisfactory, but it remains the only readily available one, so I have used it.

It is not easy to find a good translation for the term *amour-propre*, particularly because theorising about the phenomenon tends to colour the original characterisation of the phenomenon. But it means something like vain-glory, a good conceit of oneself, a strong and prickly sense of one's own importance, an insistent concern for priority to be given to oneself. It is Rousseau's view that when *a-p* is the predominant sort of regard for themselves that people have this will result in relations between them coming to be vindictive, cruel, malicious, contemptuous, dismissive, intolerant. Let us consider why this might be so.

A person possessed by *a-p* assigns an importance to himself and expects (demands almost as his right) that others acknowledge, defer to, this self-assessment by affording him the kind and degree of deferential regard and esteem which is owed (in his eyes) to one of such importance as himself. But, or so Rousseau argues, this self-assessment of one's importance is not so secure, so well established, as to survive in the face of contempt, derision, or indifference from others. Quite the contrary, in fact. One whose sense of the value of his own person takes the form of *a-p* will find it impossible to continue to bear a good regard towards himself if others are scornful of him. He will be no Socrates capable of continuing to have a quiet assurance of his own worth and the good in what he is doing in the face of ridicule and dismissal.[2] He will be devastated by this, annihilated (made to be as nothing) by it,[3] for his sense of his own importance requires constant confirmation by his enjoying prestigious distinction in the eyes of others. His self-appraisal is made through the appraisal others make of him; he takes the measure of his worth by the measure made of him by others.[4]

This means that so far from such a person in reality enjoying the dominance over others which his sense of his own importance causes him to demand, he is in actual fact enslaved by the opinions

---

[2] Rousseau makes many references to Plato's dialogues in *Emile*, and it is certain that he was much influenced by certain ideas in Plato. Of particular relevance is a passage in the *Gorgias* where Socrates contrasts his subservience to the 'caprices' of 'the son of Clenias', who 'never keeps to the same line for two minutes together', with his subservience to 'philosophy', which never varies in its demands and is not wilful and capricious (*Gorgias* 481e–482b). There is also a passage where Socrates speaks, ironically, of 'refutation by laughter'. See also G. Vlastos: 'The Paradox of Socrates', in G. Vlastos, ed., *The Philosophy of Socrates* (New York, 1971). Compare too *A Discourse on the Moral Effects of the Arts and Sciences* (in Cole), 10–13. I shall return to the (idealised) figure of Socrates which was, I think, of great importance to Rousseau.

[3] Compare Shakespeare, Sonnet 29: 'When in disgrace with fortune and men's eyes' . . .

[4] See *DI*, 104, for instance: 'social man lives constantly outside himself, and only knows how to live in the opinion of others, so that he seems to receive the consciousness of his own existence merely from the judgment of others concerning him'.

of others, for it is only by currying favour with them according to what they pay out regard to that he can draw any attention upon himself.[5] This will lead in time to the adoption of a 'false self', a persona – a dramatic mask – which is moulded according to whatever prove to be the requirements for securing esteem and consideration from others and which will be mistaken for his real face even by the wearer himself.[6] Thus even the self which one can think well of, the self which enjoys the desired acknowledged importance (if one is successful in winning others' acclaim) is a self-estranged self, the self which is created to further the paramount need to be the recipient of others' approval.

This speaks only of the deleterious effects on the individual himself of the dominance in him of *a–p*. What are the effects of this motive in connection with someone's relation to others? Rousseau maintains that the demand for consideration to be given to one which *a-p* contains is not sufficiently satisfied if one enjoys some degree of deferential regard, perhaps more than that enjoyed by some, equal to that enjoyed by others and less perhaps than that enjoyed by yet others. This demand will be satisfied only by standing foremost in others' eyes, only by enjoying a unique, exclusive supremacy in securing prestigious distinction. *A-p* incorporates a jealous exclusive desire to achieve invidious singularity in relation to each and every one who also seeks prestigious distinction.[7]

Because the desire for others' regard is of this jealous exclusive kind it will include an element of vindictive ill will towards anyone who may threaten to remove, or even partially to divert, deferential attention away from oneself. Now, *anyone* else whose self-regard takes the form of *a-p* constitutes such a threat, for they will be trying to secure for themselves just what you are trying to secure for yourself and only one person can enjoy.[8] The consequence will be ra-

---

[5] See, for example, *E*, 47: 'Power itself is servile when it depends upon public opinion; for you are dependent on the prejudices of others when you rule them by means of those prejudices. To lead them as you will, they must be led as they will. They have only to change their way of thinking and you are forced to change your course of action.' Compare Plato, *Republic* 578e–579a on the tyrant's need to 'curry favour' if he is to remain secure; and elsewhere.

[6] See *DI*, 86–7; 104: 'society offers to us only an assembly of artificial men and factitious passions, which are the work of all these new relations, and without any real foundation in nature'. Compare *E*, 191; 282.   [7] See *DI*, 81, 101, and elsewhere.

[8] A query very naturally arises here. If everyone is intent upon gaining precedence, who is there left to pay out deferential regard, on the plausible assumption that deference implies the acceptance of inferiority? There is a familiar social solution to this problem, in the formation of in-groups, cliques, etc. Within the group there is reciprocal paying of court to others and having court paid to one. But the groups as a whole assumes a position of superiority with regard to 'outsiders'.

pacious, unending competitiveness to win a prize which is really
unwinnable and, even if it were won, would only after all reward the
'false' self, as we saw earlier. It is important to note that one can be
first, with everyone else nowhere, in two ways: either by so far
excelling along an accepted socially prestigious path that one's distinction quite overshadows the performance of everyone else;[9] or,
perhaps more subtly, not by surpassing others but just by doing
them down, by undercutting, subverting, denigrating, their
qualities while one so to say 'stands still'. The distinction at issue
here is a purely relative one and may be as well achieved by rendering contemptible the attributes of one's competitors as by coming
out first on a commonly accepted scale of merit. As Rousseau
says[10]: 'rich and powerful men . . . prize what they enjoy only in so
far as others are destitute of it, and . . . without changing their condition, they would cease to be happy the moment the people ceased
to be wretched'.

What is of value to the rich and powerful, what they prize, has
value to them solely because it affords this invidious distinction to
them. It has no other significance than this, than to be the provision
of a factor which can lead to deference and consideration being
taken from some and given to others (or, more favourably, to just
one other, oneself). The very role of the factors, these markers of
social 'merit', is to make it possible for there to be a condition of life
in which there can be superiority and inferiority, prestige and
insignificance, triumph and humiliation, top dogs and underdogs.
The desire for that unique singularity of distinction,[11] which alone
guarantees to one a sense of self-worth when one is governed by a-p,
generates the apparatus of signs and signals which make it possible
for such a thing to be achieved in the relations of men. This
apparatus comprises what Rousseau calls at various places the
whole body of caprice, fashionable, factitious, artificial, conventional, or more generally mere prestige 'merits'.[12] It is fitting to put
'merit' in scare quotes because all that is really involved is the
introduction and holding in place of markers which will provide
watersheds for the differential distribution of invidious esteem.
Calling something whose sole function is to further this purpose a

[9] Compare Shakespeare, *Julius Caesar*, Act 1 Scene 2: Cassius: 'Why, man, he doth bestride
the narrow world like a Colossus; and we petty men walk under his huge legs, and peep
about to find ourselves dishonourable graves . . .' [10] See *DI*, 101; *E*, 149.
[11] See *DI*, 101: 'this unremitting rage of distinguishing ourselves'. Compare *A Discourse on the
Moral Effects of the Arts and Sciences* (in Cole), 16: 'the rage of singularity'.
[12] See, for example, *DI*, 102; *E*, 305–6.

merit at all sounds oddly, for all that those who are on the 'inside' of the competition for distinction (or, better, *mere* distinction) will regard the possession of such differentiating attributes or accomplishments as being one of the most devoutly to be wished for and splendid of things for themselves.

It is in relation to this aspect of the social climate established by the rule of *a-p* that the inescapable pervasiveness of intolerance in such a mode of life can most clearly be seen. As an immediate part of the wish contained in *a-p* to gain ascendancy over others so as to enjoy a superior distinction there will be an obdurate unwillingness to entertain the admissibility of any opinions or styles or modes of life which might constitute any threat to that ascendancy, and a constant desire to suppress the expression of these opinions, to deny the possibility of living these modes of life. For it never can be known whether or not they will gain a greater popularity, secure a greater cachet, than do those things which one professes and by which one lives. In which case one will lose that distinction for which alone one lived. A rigid intolerance of all difference will be bound to mark all personal and social relations. Each and every device by which alternative, potentially prestige-drawing, views, ideas, moral ideals, or whatever, can be suppressed, ridiculed, dimissed, will be constantly utilised by those in whom *a–p* is dominant. Of course, it is not likely that there will be clear awareness that this is what is going on. It will be held for example that such and such an alternative view 'has nothing at all to commend it and hence does not require a hearing' – people all the while being oblivious of, or deceiving themselves about, the self-serving significance of these seemingly dispassionate judgements.

Such, then, is Rousseau's vision of a mode of social life in which *a-p* is the predominant motif. Is there any alternative order for human relations to assume? Rousseau thinks that there is, and it is to an account of this I now turn.

AMOUR DE SOI

The matter must be taken in two stages. First I shall outline some aspects of the beliefs, desires, and valuations made by someone possessed of *amour de soi* (in one of its forms – see below). It will appear from this account that someone whose life is ordered by *amour de soi* does not stand in, and need not stand in, any significant social relations with other men. Indeed Rousseau himself often writes as if this were so.[13] I shall go on to argue in the next section, however, that *amour de soi* does provide a basis for an order of social relations, and comprises the core of Rousseau's account of respect for others.

By *amour de soi* (hereafter *a de s*) Rousseau does not understand just one specific structure of desire, evaluation, and action in a person. It is immaterial here to try to disentangle the different, though importantly related, 'soul states' that he had in view; I shall focus on only one of these, that which stands in the most direct contrast with *a-p*. I shall call this form of *a de s* self-respecting *a de s*, a care for oneself to be and to behave in such a way that one is able to hold what one is and what one does in respect, as at least decent and if possible creditable, worthy of regard.

So put there appears to be no significant difference between self-respecting *a de s* and *a-p*. For in the case of the latter too there is the need or the wish of the individual to be able to think well of themselves, to be able to see what they are and what they do as having some import, some value. The differences between these two forms of self-concern begin to become apparent when one asks what the basis is on which one has some respect for oneself in the case of *a de s*. Although Rousseau's account of this is not wholly clear, the main outline is firmly enough drawn. In the case of *a de s* one has some respect for oneself because what one is and does measures up to some criterion of value, decency, worth, the status of which as such a criterion is – to put the point first negatively – altogether independent of, nothing whatever to do with, its being the sort of thing which draws favour, applause, deference, consideration, or whatever from others upon one. Even if acclaim is given in relation to the attribute, achievement and so on in question, it is not on the ground of acclaim being given that it comes to count as a 'merit', or something of value.[14] Or – now to put the point positively – the status of this or that as a criterion of worth depends upon the intrinsic merit of, for instance, the achievement in question, this being

---

[13] Rousseau, of course, presents 'natural man' as being possessed of *amour de soi* in an altogether presocial condition, i.e. before coming into *any* relations with other men. Although the matter is a complex one, I think it is appropriate to distinguish here the question of the analysis of the notion of *amour de soi* from a genetic story about the conditions in which it arises and flourishes. I would suggest that the 'isolation' of Rousseau's natural man be regarded only as a graphic image for representing the independence of others' opinions which he enjoys.

[14] See *E*, 104–10; and especially *E*, 304–5, echoing Aristotle. Emile will say not ' "I am delighted to gain approval", but "I am delighted because they say I have done right; I am delighted because the men who honour me are worthy of honour; while they judge so wisely, it is a fine thing to win their respect." '

something that the individual can recognise for himself, and because he recognises this he can elect according to his own free judgement to make it his goal to try to achieve in the relevant way.

There is, of course, a great deal in this that would require further eludication if we needed a full and precise account of self-esteeming *a de s*. However, to see the contrast with *a-p* enough has been indicated. In that case it was the aptness of something to draw invidious esteem upon one which constituted its very being as a 'merit'. And the desire to be able to think well of oneself turned into a craving to be an object of good regard in others' eyes. As a result of this one became everywhere enslaved to the opinions of others. But where self-respecting *a de s* is in view none of this applies. One enjoys at the very least freedom from the tyranny of opinion and at best a secure confidence in one's own worth because one's being and life realise qualities of intrinsic and immutable value.[15]

It is useful to recur here to the (real or dramatised) life and conduct of Socrates.[16] He was able to carry on with his life and work in indifference to the mockery, or come to that the praise, of other men because he was no longer dependent upon achieving the prestige merits of his society for his sense of the worth of himself and the decency of his life. What gave meaning to his endeavour was the honour he paid to the truth by giving unstinting service to its demands, this being something intrinsically honourable and fitting to a person.

It is a remarkable fact, and one the conceptual possibility of which I do not properly understand, that (most) adult humans are incapable of happiness unless they are able to look upon themselves and what they do as having something good about them, as being of such a kind that they can feel them to be of some kind of worth or acceptability. To take an extreme case, someone who is chronically lacking in self-respect, someone who perhaps finds all they are and do ridiculous or contemptible or loathsome, will be often incapable of enjoying even the most basic pleasures, let alone of finding contentment in the realisation of their projects – if, that is, they can get as far as conceiving any (which would presumably require that they can see some point in doing something) and if they can get as far as embarking on them (which would presumably

---

[15] It might be appropriate to try to distinguish *amour de soi* from *amour-propre* in terms of a distinction between self-respect and self-importance. I think that there are very significant differences between these notions, but at present I do not understand the matter clearly enough to be able to utilise points drawn from this.   [16] See n. 2 above.

require their thinking that it makes some difference whether they do so or not). Happiness comes to require, as at least a necessary condition for its attainment, that one's character and actions meet some standards of what can be respected, of what can fitly be regarded as worth anything. It is, therefore, not at all a side-issue to consider the nature and basis of different forms of self-regard, of concern for oneself, as Rousseau does. Such matters are central to the viability of human life, to the possibility of living one's life in a potentially rewarding way.

The emphasis in this outline of self-esteeming *a de s* has fallen on the independence of the self-evaluating judgement of a person possessed of *a de s*. No reference to the attitudes of others towards them is made by such a person and, indeed, they seem to measure themselves against standards which do not relate to their conduct towards others. It is easy to have the picture of a wholly self-reliant, self-sufficient person keeping their own counsel pretty well unconcerned with the ways of others, quietly occupied in doing that which recommends itself to them as a fit occupation for mortal life. And it is hard to see how such a structure of concern and action can form a basis for a social order different from that established by *a–p*. The latter binds a person only too tightly to his fellows. *A de s*, on the other hand, seems to entail a self-contained separateness, in which relation to others barely seems to come in at all. The next stage of my discussion will be concerned to try to show that this is not so.

RESPECT FOR OTHERS

Rousseau's account of respect for others comprises one strand in his treatment of the nature and role of pity as a sentiment one is capable of feeling towards others which is such that it will, if duly moulded and encouraged, enable the corrupt and destructive modes of relation between people intrinsic to *a-p* to be replaced by benign and creative relationships. It is not, therefore, out of *a de s* alone that an alternative mode of human relation grows, but out of *a de s* in conjunction with the sentiment of pity, and pity obviously involves some form of relation towards others. But, as we shall see, the place of *a de s* in the kind of regard one has for others in pity remains quite central.[17]

It is out of the question to try to give here a full account of

---

[17] Rousseau's fullest account of pity occurs in *E* Book IV, especially 182–98. See also *DI*, 66–9. Rousseau also regards part of the relation between people established by compassion as dependent upon the confidence in themselves of the pitier, upon the security of their *amour de soi*. See *E*, 182, 190.

Rousseau's investigations into the nature of pity and its role as providing a basis for an alternative order of human relations. I shall try to extract from this account that which is most directly concerned with respect for others. Because this will lack its full setting it may seem a thinner and less convincing view than I believe it to be. But I hope to be able to do enough to avoid this appearance.

Pity is engendered in relation to the sufferings of others. We can divide the suffering of others into two general kinds: suffering 'natural' ills, and suffering 'conventional' ills. By 'natural' ills we are to understand such misfortunes as cuts and abrasions, headaches and toothaches, flu and measles, arthritis and cancer and so on – things which engender pain, discomfort and misery, principally because of some disturbance of bodily integrity or function (though one would want also to include, for example, grief over the death of one's child). By 'conventional' ills we are to understand the distress, the agony sometimes, of shame, humiliation, of being the object of contempt, mockery, derision, and the like (the ills which, as we saw, were centrally involved in relations ordered by *a-p*). It is the latter which are of concern here. These ills comprise the experience of some wound or injury to our self-esteem or good regard for ourselves, comprise the experience of some temporary or permanent loss of the power to feel that we amount to, count for, anything and the coming to feel in ourselves some degree of loathing or scorn for ourselves and what we do.

Clearly, suffering a natural ill can at the same time involve suffering a conventional ill. A man who trips as he enters a room full of distinguished persons, by whom he is anxious to be accepted as very much one of their kind, may hurt his ankle. But also, and possibly more painfully, he may have his pride hurt, especially if his mishap is greeted with sniggers, contemptuously raised eyebrows and the like.[18] We may observe this sort of co-occurrence in young children. Often the howls that greet falling over are more to do with affronted dignity ('how can the world insult *me* so?') than to do with the pain of a grazed knee. The child is outraged because of the uncouth behaviour of an unruly world.[19]

[18] Compare *DI*: 82, 'every intended injury became an affront; because, besides the hurt which might result from it, the party injured was certain to find in it a contempt for his person, which was often more insupportable than the hurt itself'. See also Rousseau: *Reveries of the Solitary Walker*, tr. P. France (Harmondsworth, 1979), 128.

[19] People may find it absurd to attribute to a young child thoughts about the consideration due to their person and importance. There is no question, of course, of such thoughts being conscious and articulate. But I submit that there is much in the child's behaviour which requires for its explanation the ascription of some such thoughts as these. The issue is too large to pursue further here, however.

Let us simply take it as read here that pity includes an inclination to relieve the suffering person of their distress. How might relief be given to someone suffering a 'conventional' ill? There would seem to be two ways one might proceed here: A: to try to repair, restore, the self-regard that has been damaged; B: to try to relieve the person of the need to have a good regard of themselves *on these terms*, that is sought and held after the fashion of the strategies involved in *a-p*, and to try to enable them instead to have a sense of self-worth upon some other basis which will relieve them from susceptibility to this sort of hurt.

I shall try to indicate how and why the adoption of procedure A would be unsatisfactory, whereas adopting procedure B would be more satisfactory – according to criteria of satisfactoriness which will become clear. By doing this I shall be exhibiting the salient components of Rousseau's theory of respect for others since idea of the fitness of following procedure B comprises the core of this theory.

I think it is pretty plain what the main points of contrast between these two procedures are. It *is* possible to repair someone's damaged pride, to ease the hurt to their sense of their self-importance, though often pretty difficult. Hurts of this kind often linger, and are sometimes dwelt upon in a strange way with an almost masochistic delight in re-enacting in memory the tormenting situation. But suppose one succeeds; suppose one does enable someone to recover their own sense of their proper standing because they once more stand well in the eyes of others. What has been achieved by this? Have they not returned to a condition of life, a mode of relation to others (and, if one may so put it, to themselves), which is ordered by the principles of dominance and servility, arrogance and abjectness, vanity and humiliation, distinction or nothingness? They thus remain bound by the estimations made of them by others according to caprice standards, standards whose sole function is to further the mode of relation between people which is constituted by such principles. They have recovered only their 'false' selves, and have been confirmed in a condition of self-alienation as having only a being-for-others (to use idioms which are not Rousseau's, though their appropriateness to Rousseau's themes is clear enough). This would, it seems, be to do little service for another. To have one's viability as a creature capable of finding any worth in oneself and in one's life thus conditional upon the favour of others who are also living a life thus conditional would appear to be no very good condition of life to find oneself in.

What may be said of procedure B? In this case one endeavours to help someone recover, or perhaps to possess for the first time, some respect for themselves which is not dependent upon their standing in the eyes of others, to enable them to live without always and everywhere competing for an invidious 'edge' over others, and so on. Instead the person may come to bear for themselves a quiet and unassuming self-regard which does not depend upon the approval of them they win from others.

In the terms in which Rousseau frames this issue, we endeavour, if following procedure B, to strengthen someone in, or indeed to afford them for the first time, their self-respect after the manner of *a de s*, a sense that they and their lives amount to something, have merit enough in them, without regard to the deference or esteem which they win from others. Instead, they may come to see that they and their lives have sufficient intrinsic worth and merit in view of which they can properly give honour to themselves. This is not to say that a man possessed of self-respecting *a de s* may not come to hold himself in disesteem or contempt. He may. But this will be because of his failure to keep faith with standards, ideals, or whatever, of intrinsic merit which recommended themselves to him as comprising what becomes, befits, people, makes them creatures with good in them, and not because he has lost the adulation of others. Rousseau is himself inclined to hold that sufficient 'nourishment' to sustain self-respecting *a de s* may be found in some very basic human attributes and competencies if these can be viewed rightly, seen as displaying what is pretty remarkable in the very fact of being human. But of course, such modest qualities will usually be scorned, disclaimed, or ignored because they can contribute nothing to achieving that *singularity* which one possessed of *a-p* so much needs if they are able to see themselves as amounting to anything.[20]

For all the importance Rousseau attached to self-respecting *a de s* as crucial to human well-being and happiness (both directly and because of the alternative 'fate' which awaited those who lacked this) he was profoundly pessimistic about the possibility of showing someone that they have enough about them to give honour to

[20] There are still some unclarities in my mind about aspects of this matter. Does one's power to bear a good regard towards oneself depend upon one's living up to one's independently valued ideals; upon one's recognising and appreciating oneself as being a member of a species 'all round, the most advantageously organised of any' (*DI*, 47); or upon something more basic than this – some kind of fundamental 'belief in oneself'? More investigation of the likenesses and differences between these possibilities is called for than I have made.

themselves in view of, say, their capacity to till a field and grow enough food to keep themselves, once they have become entranced by the hope of enjoying precedence before others. For that hope, once taken root, reduces all else to nothing. In a remarkable and moving passage, Rousseau implies that even the carefully watched and formed Emile will be lost to this delusion. He writes[21]:

my dear Emile, in vain did I dip you in the waters of the Styx, I could not make you everywhere invulnerable; a fresh enemy has appeared, whom you have not yet learned to conquer, and from whom I cannot save you. That enemy is yourself . . . you were dependent on nothing but your position as a human being; now you depend on all the ties you have formed for yourself; you have learnt to desire, and you are now the slave of your desires.

(Emile is, at this point, engaged in thoroughly dispossessing himself of himself in self-contrived subjection to a fantasy Sophie. The real Sophie is not the capricious tormenter that Emile has fabricated for himself in his own self-written drama of enslavement to her[22].) The practicability of offering someone the chance to 'belong to themselves' is not, however, of central concern here. What we need to appreciate is, rather, the nature and significance of that condition in which we do so belong to ourselves after the fashion that Rousseau has tried to explain.

This is, I suggest, the core of Rousseau's account of what it is to give others the respect which is due to them. Starting with the movement of compassionate concern for another who is suffering the pain of self-hate or a sense of worthlessness consequent upon his rejection by others, we are concerned to have that person be well and do well. This concern comprises attempting to help them find for themselves a sufficient sense of their own worth which is untouched by the caprices of others' acclaim or disdain because grounded in qualities of intrinsic worth which they possess and which they can recognise for themselves. By this they are relieved from a servitude which not only controlled their outward comportment but which also shaped their ideas and feelings to a form which was required to become a person of 'distinction'. This does not mean that they will never have occasion to think ill of themselves, but it does mean that their entire lives will not be conducted in terms to which the possibility of thinking ill of themselves is essen-

---

[21] *E*, 406–7.
[22] Is Rousseau consistent in suggesting that Emile is the author of his own enslavement? Elsewhere, of course, enslavement is said to originate in the deleterious effects upon the individual of 'society'. This is not the place to consider this problem.

tial, essential because if there are to be winners in the competition for prestige there *must* be losers – 'masters' require 'slaves' – and it is in these terms that they form any appraisal of their own worth and standing. So although they may very well not live happy lives (nothing can guarantee that), at least the necessity that if any shall be happy many must be unhappy is removed and each may make what they can of their life without its being built into 'making' something of one's life that others should be dispossessed or wretched.

I said that Rousseau was profoundly pessimistic about relieving those in thrall to *a-p* of their delusions about what is worth anything and what would make them worth anything. While in the grip of the idea that only by achieving exclusive, paramount prestigious acclaim will they count for anything, someone will find perfectly ridiculous the idea that greater freedom, a great possibility of happiness, may be found in attachment to things which are basic to human life and common to all. Rousseau speaks often of the 'craving' for distinction, the 'rage' for singularity, as if there were something like an addiction here. So intoxicating are the dreams of prestigious pre-eminence involved that even the inevitably attendant nightmares are insufficient to cause someone, unaided, to want to leave their state behind. It is with this sort of thought in mind, I believe, that Rousseau speaks of the need to 'force' people to be free. Left to themselves, people would not, could not, free themselves, if for no other reason that they cannot see as good that which they are being invited to choose instead. But, as we saw, the condition in which they remain has enslavement at its very heart.[23]

Rousseau's constitutional proposals for a just and humane community are, I suggest, intended to achieve two things: first, so far as possible to preclude the growth and development of the desires and relations intrinsic to *a-p*; and second, to encourage and consolidate that mode of self-respect which *a de s* comprises, that kind of self-respect which is the object of our concern in our pity if we act to help others following procedure B (and, of course, success in this second way will all but guarantee success in the first way). This is why there is such stress, in *The Social Contract*, on the citizens' mutual recognition and honour as persons with the dignity afforded by being part of the sovereign body which administers law to itself. None of them are subject to control by another, and thus do not become dependent for their well-being upon complying with the

---

[23] *SC*, Book I, ch. 7, 177. It is to be noted that Rousseau speaks, in this passage, explicitly of securing people against 'all personal dependence', i.e. dependence upon the favour of other individual people.

requirements imposed on them by that other. The central constitutive bond which unites people as members of one community is the reciprocal acnowledgement of the standing of each as a creature of worth in their very nature. Because this is the basal relation between persons, each person's own recognition and acceptance of themselves as a person of worth in their own right is facilitated; indeed it is almost *insisted* upon against all tendencies someone may show to value themselves only if they make a distinctive mark upon their peers or community at large.[24]

Rousseau's root governing concern is with the psychological ramifications which different modes of relation between people both express and encourage. His political philosophy is, I suggest, an outgrowth of his philosophy of psychology and is continuous with the ideas central to the latter. The 'chains' which men in (ordinary corrupt) society carry are not originally economic or those of a class-ridden society. The differences between men in these regards – which do indeed enslave – are the consequences and not the causes of something more basic, namely whether one's regard for oneself as a person of value turns upon one's own judgement or upon the verdict of others upon one. We have, in his view, two almost categorically different modes of self-evaluation with two categorically different notions of personal good and worth. Yet we can, or Rousseau thinks we can, stand outside each of these and look in upon them, considering the kind of creature exemplary of each and the possibilities for life each contains. From this standpoint we shall, Rousseau holds, give decided preference to a mode of life in which each person holds on their own judgement a secure confidence in their basic goodness and worth, a confidence which is confirmed and reinforced in the mode of recognition and acknowledgement which is afforded to them by others. This is a form of life to which self-respecting *a de s* is central, both in a person's own self-regard and also in what each person honours in others, their fundamental worth as human beings as such.

I hope it will be quite clear, from this, that tolerance towards others will be a major mark of a community basically constituted by that kind of respect for others which Rousseau has argued to be appropriate. The very presence of intolerance would be, as we saw earlier, an immediate symptom of the emergence of relations deter-

---

[24] One might think here of the position of an insecure child who feels that he will only be loved, cherished, if he is good and does well. He may learn in time that love for him is not based on these things but upon what he is in himself, or as such – that he is loved as an individual, not as an achiever.

mined by *a-p*. But the presence of tolerance is not merely the absence of intolerance in Rousseau's ideal community. Rather, tolerance will be a matter of the positive welcoming and prizing of human individuality where that is expression of that integrity of mind and spirit of life which is facilitated by affording to everyone a fundamental confidence in their value and worth as persons with a life to make for themselves. What cannot be tolerated will be all, but only, that which removes, or tends to remove, the possibility of people holding the value of their lives on these terms, for that will lead to a reversion to a mode of personal life, and an order of relation to others, which is as destructive to the self as it is injurious to others.

I want, in conclusion, to consider what Rousseau has to say about the place and importance of 'civil religion' in his ideal community. By doing this we can, I believe, see the justice of the kind of account of Rousseau's concern with self-respect, respect for others and tolerance which I have been suggesting. And we can also see how consistent Rousseau himself is in his commitment to the value of tolerance.

CIVIL RELIGION

Rousseau's discussion of 'Civil Religion' is in the penultimate chapter of *The Social Contract* (Book IV, chapter 8), and comprises, I believe, the longest *explicit* discussion of tolerance (particularly with regard to religious doctrine and practice) in his writing.[25] It serves very well as a target for closer examination in relation to the themes I have made central to my discussion.

As noted right at the start, Rousseau says that any who do not believe the articles of the civil faith can be banished, and any who publicly recognise these dogmas but yet act contrary to them should be put to death. And this seems, at first sight, to comprise an institutionalised form of religious intolerance of the most drastic kind. But yet Rousseau goes on to say that among the dogmas of this civil faith should be the prohibition of intolerance; and earlier, in criticising one of the possible modes of relation between religious faith and practice and society, he lays as an objection that it 'makes a people blood-thirsty and intolerant'. So unless Rousseau is being, in a rather blatant way, inconsistent, we must suppose that he knew what he was about and that there is some material distinc-

---

[25] I may be wrong about this; I have not looked through every possibly relevant text to check this. All quotations in what follows are to this chapter (268–77).

tion to be made between the civil faith he approves of and the other forms of religious faith and practice he examines. What might be the ground of such a distinction?

What Rousseau is concerned to see preserved and consolidated is the 'bond of union' of society, that which concerns the duties to which each man or citizen is bound in relation to the others who comprise the community. He believes that men will be caused to love their duty only if each has a religion, for contained in the religious impulse are powerful sentiments which would make, for example, departure from the laws come to be experienced as impiety, that is the kind of act which brings down the anger of the gods. By harnessing the patterns of thought and feeling implicit in religious conviction to the basic duties each citizen owes to each, commitment to those duties will become if not wholly unwavering at least very firmly seated in the character of each man. Rousseau is very definite, however, in saying that the right of the sovereign over the subjects does not 'exceed the limits of public expediency', that subjects owe the sovereign 'an account of their opinions only to such an extent that they matter to the community'. Anything further that a body of religious thought might contain is not properly subject to control by the sovereign. 'Tolerance', he says, 'should be given to all religions that tolerate others, so long as their dogmas contain nothing contrary to the duties of citizenship.'

Rousseau does not appear seriously to have contemplated the possibility that men might have a sufficient commitment to the primacy of those duties towards their fellows which are constitutive of their common membership of the body politic without recourse to the hopes and fears of religion, whereas we do, perhaps, think this is both possible and desirable.[26] But this, I suggest, reflects the fact that religious practice has become very largely marginal in society in these days and everywhere circumscribes its commitments to remain within the bounds of civil law. Rousseau, on the other hand, was writing in a context where religious commitment could, and very often did, comprise an alternative allegiance to that involved in adherence to the civil law– not that, in every case, it was easy or proper to make the distinction between civil and theological authority, as Rousseau himself makes quite clear. The alternatives were not, for him, between primary allegiance to the bond of society being associated with religious sentiments and its not being

---

[26] But see SC, 273, where Rousseau speaks of the laws having 'the force they have in themselves'. But he goes on immediately to say that religion can make an 'addition to it' and may comprise 'one of the great bonds that unite society considered in severalty'.

so associated, with religious conviction being then thoroughly marginal. Rather the alternatives were between religious sentiments being associated with the basic social bond and their having some different objective either contrary to or in direct conflict with the commitment to the social bond. Given this as the context of the issue, it can hardly be seen as intolerant that Rousseau should recommend a 'civil profession of faith'; to leave religious conviction unregulated was not as he perceived the matter a viable option, since it would result in the subversion of the social bond.

How would this result? Rousseau's argument, very briefly, is this. He distinguishes three 'kinds of religion'. The first is 'confined to the purely internal cult of the supreme God and the eternal obligations of morality'. The second is 'codified in a single country, [and] gives it its Gods, its own tutelary patrons'. The third Rousseau calls 'the religion of the priest', in which there is a 'theological system' separate from the 'political system', where the clergy of some religious denomination comprise a corporate body distinct from, but claiming authority at least equal to, the sovereign in the body politic. To these kinds of religion, he makes objection as follows. To the third, that it destroys social unity and makes men subject to contradictory duties so that they cannot be 'faithful both to religion and to citizenship'. To the second that, although it 'teaches . . . that service done to the State is service done to its tutelary god' (which is a good), it deceives men and becomes tyrannous and exclusive. It 'makes a people blood-thirsty and intolerant . . . and regards as a sacred act the killing of every one who does not believe in its gods'.

To the first kind of religion Rousseau objects that it leads to indifference to the earthly prosperity of the citizenry and the body politic; that it leads to the state's being open to usurpation of public authority since 'in this vale of sorrows, what does it matter whether we are free men or serfs?'; and, finally, that it leads to the state's being easy prey in war, for 'what does it matter whether they win or lose? Does not providence know better than they what is meet for them?'

Obviously some of these claims are not wholly well founded and are principally provocative in intent. But this should not obscure the main intent which is clear in all of them and in Rousseau's own proposal of a 'civil profession of faith'. What Rousseau is everywhere concerned to guard against is the emergence of parties, cults, or whatever which would set people against each other and preclude paramount place being given to that equality of regard and honour which, as I have argued, is the basic constitutive bond between men in Rousseau's ideal community. And what he is everywhere concerned to provide for is the overriding claim upon each and every citizen of the duties they owe to their fellow-citizens, so that the unity of the society shall be maintained. Rousseau says very clearly that 'the Sovereign has no authority in the other world, [so] whatever the lot of its subjects may be in the life to come, that is not its business, provided they are good citizens in this life'. And there is no reason at all to suppose he is insincere in saying this, or that it is inconsistent with any of the principal features of his overall position. Religious belief and practice is to be constrained so far as, but *only* so far as, it impinges upon the priority being given to the law by which each citizen enjoys his equality of right. Any further constraint is not merely unnecessary, but is also actually contrary to the proper ends of law. For it would lead to the emergence of allegiances to creeds which set man against man and invest this differentiation with all the force of religious exclusion, of eternal damnation. It is, Rousseau rightly says, 'impossible to live at peace with those we regard as damned ... we positively must either reclaim or torment them'. So far from there being here any departure from his requirement that equal regard be paid to each and every citizen, Rousseau seems to me clearly to be insisting that the requirements of religion be made not only consistent with this but actually supportive to it.

I believe, then, that Rousseau is consistent in his commitment to tolerance as an essential mark of a properly ordered society. Furthermore we can, I think, see that he regarded distinction and exclusion as inimical to the welfare of and justice in a community, though here considered only in relation to religious distinction and exclusion. And this serves to confirm the overall thesis of my discussion that it is an equality of honour, dignity, and worth which is to be the primary and inviolable regard which is intended to unite men in a good society. The reason why those who will not make the civil profession of faith are to be banished is not because of some sectarian prejudice against them. It is because by their refusal they make known their intent, or their willingness, to override the duties attendant upon giving equal regard to the worth of each member of the body politic. And to do this would be, of course, to make known the intent, or willingness, to break the law. And that a state should act to prevent this is hardly an extravagant doctrine.

I suspect that some may take Rousseau's proposals as more threatening than I take them to be because they suppose that they prescribe a greater unity of religious practice which permits little or no freedom of religious mind or conduct to individuals. But it is only such commonness of practice as is requisite to preserving equal respect for all citizens that is to be prescribed. And this will leave a great deal to the discretion of individuals or sects. Rousseau's views on this matter do not strike me as in any serious way repressive. We do not any longer, as I said earlier, perhaps see religion as such a powerful force as Rousseau did. But, did we do so, I think the position he adopts is one which has much to commend it.

6

The intolerable

D. D. RAPHAEL

The papers in this book were originally written for a conference meeting under the auspices of the C. & J. B. Morrell Trust, which has encouraged the study of toleration. The aim of the Trust has no doubt been to promote the practice of toleration, and it is natural and right that nearly all of the studies supported by the Trust should be designed to serve that end. Nevertheless we ought to remember that the virtue of toleration, like any virtue, has its limits. There are circumstances in which intolerance is right, either in the weaker sense of being morally permissible or in the stronger sense of being morally obligatory. Take the example of the toleration of religion, the issue which gave rise to the first sustained discussion of toleration in Western political thought. We would all nowadays go further than Locke in advocating toleration of religious beliefs and practices that do not conform to established or majority patterns in our country; yet we would not think it right to include a religion which practised human sacrifice. An understanding of the virtue of toleration can be clarified by trying to mark its limits, by asking when it ceases to be a virtue and becomes a weakness or even a vice.

Mr Peter Nicholson has made a couple of valuable suggestions in a recent paper. The subject of his paper is 'Toleration as a Moral Ideal', and after giving a positive account of his views on that topic he ends up with some remarks about the limits which the ideal imposes. He lays down two major limitations. First, since the duty to be tolerant rests, in his opinion, on the basic duty of 'respect for all persons as full moral agents', it follows, he says, that we ought not to tolerate actions or practices which themselves contravene the duty of respect for persons. The second limitation, 'a special case of the first', is that we should reject whatever contravenes the ideal of

137

toleration itself. The suggestion that one ought to tolerate the destruction of toleration is, quite simply, self-contradictory.'[1]

The second limitation recalls J. S. Mill's dictum in the essay *On Liberty*[2] that it is self-contradictory, and therefore irrational and wrong, for a man to use his freedom to end it, by selling himself into slavery. This application of the criterion of self-contradiction is not without difficulty, as we know from discussions of Mill's position. However, my concern here is with the first and more fundamental suggested limitation, namely that we ought not to tolerate acts which contravene the principle of respect for persons.

The idea that the basic principle of morality is a duty to respect all persons as moral agents is a way of expressing Kant's theory of the Categorical Imperative. It is used by a number of modern philosophers who follow a broadly Kantian approach to ethics. I too hold a broadly Kantian theory of ethics, and while I find the expression 'respect for persons' rather vague, I acknowledge that what is intended by it is the essence of the Kantian view. For my own part I prefer to retain Kant's language about acting so as to treat human beings as ends in themselves and never merely as means. (I think that Kant's principle needs to be extended to take in our duties to animals, but let us leave that aside for the time being.) To treat other persons as ends in themselves, Kant explains, is to make their ends your own. I understand this as follows. A person's ends fall into two categories, the objects of desire and the objects of choice. To make the ends of another person your own ends is to feel obliged to act in respect of his ends as you would naturally act in respect of your own ends. The natural action to take, in respect of your own ends, the objects of your desires or choices, is to strive to obtain them, or, if there is no difficulty, simply to allow the causal force of your conations to reach their objective. So the obligation that you have in respect of the ends of another is to help him to reach his objective if he cannot do it by himself, or, if he does not need help, to refrain from hindering him. In either event, whether one is concerned with one's own ends or those of another person, the action described is right only if there are no moral considerations, of greater importance, which go against it.

The weaker form of making the ends of others your own ends, namely refraining from interference, is the duty of allowing other

---

[1] Peter P. Nicholson, 'Toleration as a Moral Ideal', in *Aspects of Toleration*, ed. John Horton and Susan Mendus (London, 1985), 169.

[2] J. S. Mill, *On Liberty*, ch. 5; Fontana edition of *Utilitarianism*, etc. (Glasgow, 1962), 235–6; Everyman edition of *Utilitarianism*, etc. (London, 1972), 157–8.

people liberty to go their own way. This is not quite the same as the duty of toleration. Toleration is a particular species of allowing liberty. The idea of toleration implies that you really disapprove of what you are prepared to leave alone. The simple idea of leaving free does not carry that implication, though perhaps it does imply that you have some sort of inclination to interference; if you had no feelings at all on the matter, the idea of interfering or refraining from interference would not arise. Liberty, then, is a wider notion than toleration.

Toleration is the practice of deliberately allowing or permitting a thing of which one disapproves. One can meaningfully speak of tolerating, i.e. of allowing or permitting, only if one is in a position to disallow. You must have the power to forbid or prevent, if you are to be in a position to permit. Furthermore, you must think that you have a right to exercise your power, if you are to claim any credit for not exercising it, i.e. if your toleration is to count as a virtue.[3] This means that your inclination to disallow must not be the result of mere whim or arbitrary dislike; it has to be reasonably grounded disapproval which you can expect to be shared by others. To disapprove of something is to judge it to be wrong. Such a judgement does not express a purely subjective preference. It claims universality; it claims to be the view of any rational agent. The content of the judgement, that something is wrong, implies that the something may properly be prevented.

But if your disapproval is reasonably grounded, why should you go against it at all? Why should you tolerate? Why, in other words, is toleration a virtue or a duty? Because it respects the freedom of others to do as they choose. You may disapprove of their choice, but they are as much entitled as you are to act as they think fit. Although toleration is not simply identical with respecting liberty, it acquires its value from the value of liberty. The decision to tolerate is a decision that your respect for the exercise of choice by other people should have priority over your opinion that what they have chosen is bad or wrong. Clearly, however, there can be circumstances in which the decision about priority should go the other way. It is not right always to treat liberty of action as more important than the moral quality of the action itself.

Toleration, then, is allowing, leaving undisturbed, something which you think is wrong. I can now state my difficulty with the

---

[3] Cf Steven Lukes, 'Social and Moral Tolerance', *Government and Opposition*, 6 1971, 224–5.

suggestion that the limits of toleration are set by the principle of respect for persons. If all moral duties can be brought under the Kantian principle of respecting persons (or treating persons as ends in themselves), it follows that all wrong actions, all breaches of duty, are wrong because they fail to respect persons (they fail to treat persons as ends). The suggestion about the limits of toleration is that toleration is wrong in those circumstances where the object of the proposed toleration fails to respect persons. This seems to imply that whenever somebody does what is positively wrong (whenever somebody does what breaches the Kantian principle of morality), his action ought not to be tolerated. But does not that confine too narrowly the scope of toleration? To tolerate is not simply to allow; it is to allow despite disapproval. To disapprove is to judge wrong, and so toleration presupposes that what is tolerated is judged to be wrong. However, if we accept the suggestion that one ought not to tolerate what is morally wrong, then toleration will have to be limited to the object of non-moral disapproval.

That is a paradoxical conclusion, but at least it leaves *some* scope for toleration. It may be, however, that the difficulty is greater still. Is there such a thing as non-moral disapproval? If there is not, then no room at all will be left for toleration. Is this additional point a genuine difficulty or not?

At first sight it seems to be groundless. Surely there are intellectual values which call for a form of approval that is not moral approval. I approve of clarity and disapprove of obscurity in philosophical writing; but this is not to say that I think obscurity a moral fault. The distinction becomes more dubious, however, when one thinks of truth as an intellectual value. The unswerving pursuit of truth, even if unpalatable, is a cardinal virtue in any sort of research or scholarship; it receives and should receive unqualified approval. Is it a moral virtue; is the approval a species of moral approval? People who choose not to engage in research or scholarship are not guilty of any moral fault – or of intellectual fault either. People who do choose to engage in such enquiry are guilty of intellectual fault if they blind themselves to the truth or if they fudge their results. Are they also guilty of moral fault? To mislead or deceive others is undoubtedly a moral fault, but there will be difference of opinion whether it is a moral fault to blind oneself to a truth, or a path to truth, which one could have found. But now let us go back to my earlier example of clarity and obscurity. Why is clarity an intellectual virtue and obscurity an intellectual vice? Is it not because clarity is an aid to the discovery of truth, and obscurity a hindrance? If so, I was mistaken in suggesting that the virtue of clarity is not a moral virtue.

What should we say of aesthetic values and defects? Surely in this field there are favourable and unfavourable appraisals which are not moral. Yes, but it is incorrect to call them examples of approval and disapproval. One does not *tolerate* art which one dislikes or fails to admire; for the concept of toleration, as I have noted before, implies that one has the right to suppress. Aesthetics is a matter of taste, in which people differ but are not entitled to call for conformity. By contrast, the intellectual values of truth, proof, and evidence can be expected to command universal assent; and in principle the same claim can be made for moral values.

Where do we now stand with the suggestion that one ought not to tolerate a contravention of the principle of respect for persons? To tolerate is to allow or endure something of which one disapproves. Approval and disapproval must be distinguished from aesthetic admiration and repulsion. Approved virtues and disapproved vices are certainly moral and immoral if they affect, favourably and adversely, other persons. If they affect the agent alone, there is difference of opinion whether they should be counted as moral and immoral. Should we say, then, that the proposed criterion forbids the toleration of that which is disapproved because it adversely affects other people, and allows the toleration of that which is disapproved only because it adversely affects the agent? This would be a virtual repetition of J. S. Mill's criterion for the limits of liberty.[4]

Mill himself would say that his principle makes the limits of liberty coincide with the limits of morality. For Mill took the view that moral duties apply only to the treatment of other persons. Mill's criterion for the limits of liberty allows a man to harm and degrade himself, if he deliberately chooses to do so. Mill's theory of moral and non-moral value implies that such a man acts imprudently (and perhaps also, in the case of degrading himself, ignobly, the 'noble' being an 'aesthetic' category) but not immorally.[5] So if toleration is allowing freedom for what one disapproves as morally wrong, Mill's criterion has scope for liberty but not for toleration.

What is the position of the Kantian theory on this issue? Kant undoubtedly believed that a person has duties to himself as well as

[4] *On Liberty*, ch. 4.
[5] Cf J. S. Mill, *System of Logic*, Book VI, ch. 12, section 6; D. D. Raphael, 'Fallacies in and about Mill's *Utilitarianism*', *Philosophy*, 30 (1955), 345–6 and n.; *On Liberty*, ch. 4; Fontana edn, 209; Everyman edn, 135.

to others. Kant's second formulation of the Categorical Imperative requires that we treat 'humanity', whether in our own person or in that of others, as an end in itself. Kant did distinguish between the character of the duties owed to ourselves and to others: he said that our duty is to pursue perfection for ourselves and happiness for others.[6] Whether or not we follow Kant on that particular point, if the principle of respect for persons is meant to represent the position of Kant, then a breach of duty to oneself is a breach of the principle of respect for persons. So if we ought not to tolerate any contravention of the principle of respect for persons, then we ought not to tolerate any breach of moral duty, even if the action to be suppressed affects no one other than the agent.

However, one can take a broadly Kantian theory of ethics while making a sharper distinction than Kant does between duties to other persons and duties (or so-called duties) to oneself. Quite apart from disputes about the adequacy of one moral theory or another to fit the facts of morality, there appears to be a genuine difference in moral outlook between those who include self-regarding conduct within the scope of moral duty and those who do not. We all know how Mill's opinion on this issue affects his discussion of liberty. The Kantian theory of ethics excludes paternalism no less, despite its acceptance of duties to oneself. Since we ought to treat other persons as ends, to respect their choices as well as their desires, then we ought to leave them free to give effect to their own choices even if we think that those choices are imprudent or liable to degrade. On Mill's view, as I have said before, the allowing of liberty which ought to be allowed is not toleration because we are not entitled to disapprove morally of the conduct concerned. On Kant's view, we are entitled to disapprove morally (of self-degradation, though not of imprudence) and therefore the liberty which we ought to allow can also be toleration.

After these historical remarks let us return to the paradox of the suggested criterion for limiting toleration. If toleration implies moral disapproval of what you tolerate, and if the criterion of moral approval is conformity to the principle of respect for persons, then toleration presupposes that what you tolerate does not conform to the principle of respect for persons. But on the other hand, so it is suggested, we ought not to tolerate whatever contravenes the principle of respect for persons. Then how can there be toleration at all? We cannot, as a matter of logic, tolerate anything unless it goes

[6] I. Kant, Preface to the *Metaphysical Elements of Ethics* (*Tugendlehre*), tr. T. K. Abbott, in *Kant's Theory of Ethics* (London, 1927), 296.

against respect for persons, and yet we ought not to tolerate anything which does that.

The apparent self-contradiction can be removed by distinguishing between more and less stringent categories of moral obligation, the more stringent being both wrong and intolerable, the less stringent being wrong but tolerable. One possible way of drawing the distinction is at the line between acts and omissions. It is wrong to cause pain (unless for moral reasons of greater urgency) and it is wrong to fail to remove or prevent pain when one is able to do so. Both the positive act and the negative omission call for disapproval, but while the first is intolerable the second is not. We could say, then, that toleration implies disapproval for an omission, a failure to live up to the principle of respect for persons, while a positive act of contravening the principle not only calls for (stronger) disapproval but goes beyond the bounds of the tolerable.

Another possible line of distinction is that drawn, in past philosophical tradition, between duties of perfect obligation and duties of imperfect obligation. A third possibility, perhaps coinciding in effect with the second, is the distinction between duties which imply corresponding rights and duties which do not. For example, the duty of promise-keeping is a duty of perfect obligation and implies a right on the part of the promisee that the promise be kept, while the duty of charity is a duty of imperfect obligation and does not imply a right on the part of potential or actual beneficiaries to receive charitable gifts.

What exactly is meant by the distinction between perfect and imperfect obligation? A duty of imperfect obligation leaves the agent with a good deal of discretion in his application of the duty, while a duty of perfect obligation is not discretionary. The duty to be charitable does not specify who shall be benefited, or when. The duty to keep promises or the duty to refrain from giving pain applies to all occasions (unless outweighed by a conflicting and more urgent duty). But how do we know whether a duty is discretionary or not? Is it just by an appeal to intuition? The duty of promise-keeping applies to all occasions as a matter of logic: to promise is to undertake an obligation, and so it is analytically true that one is obliged to fulfil what one has promised. The duty to refrain from inflicting pain, however, does not rest on a basis of simple logic. How do we know that the duty to refrain from giving pain is not discretionary, while the duty to confer positive happiness is discretionary?

Kant offers a different criterion of the distinction between duties of perfect and duties of imperfect obligation. His second formulation of the Categorical Imperative says that we ought to treat humanity as an end and never merely as a means. According to Kant, treating people merely as a means is a breach of a duty of perfect obligation, while simple failure to treat them as ends is a breach of a duty of imperfect obligation.[7] At first sight this seems a promising criterion. It is much clearer than an appeal to intuitions of discretion. Here is an example to illustrate Kant's notion. If I torture someone to make him disclose information which I want to know but which he wants to conceal, then my action treats him as a means to my end and fails to have regard to his end. I breach a duty of perfect obligation. By contrast, if I pass by a starving beggar, I fail to have regard to his end (his desire for help), but I do not treat him as a means to my ends since I do not do anything to him; I do not *use* him. (Not that this second case illustrates a breach of duty of imperfect obligation, since the imperfect obligation to be charitable does not require me to help this particular needy person. For a breach or failure to implement that imperfect obligation, I would have to pass by all the needy people or good causes that come to my attention.)

But does Kant's criterion work for all cases? Suppose I hurt somebody, not in order to obtain information which I want, but just for devilment. Am I treating him as a means? If 'for devilment' means in order to get pleasure for myself, then yes. But it does not always mean that. The action might be purposeless, quite irrational. Some woundings do seem to be of that nature. They are not treating the victim as a means to an end of the agent. Yet they are clearly breaches of duty of perfect obligation – because they infringe the rights of the victim, not because they emanate from a particular attitude of the agent.

Suppose I deceive someone with an untruthful answer to a question. If I do so for my own gain, for example to prevent him from digging up a hoard of gold before I can, or to dissuade him from applying for a job which I want, then my lie serves my ends and fails to serve the ends of my questioner. Does my lie treat *him* as a means to my ends? I cannot see that it does. Suppose I tell him a lie, not in order to further my ends, but simply because I dislike him and do not wish to serve his ends. Do I then treat him as a means to my ends? Yes, if I act in order to obtain for myself the pleasure of doing him down. But usually such an action is not undertaken *in order* to

---

[7] H.J. Paton, *The Categorical Imperative* (London, 1947), 172.

secure malicious pleasure; it is not done as a means to obtain the pleasure. Rather it is an expression of ill will and produces pleasure as a consequence, not as a purpose aimed at.

Suppose I break a promise. If I do so deliberately for gain, for instance having intended at the start to obtain the benefit of one side of a contract without fulfilling my side of the bargain, then certainly I make use of the other party's trust as a means to my end without treating him as an end. But suppose I break a promise because I cannot be bothered to keep it. I have promised the organiser of our conference to write a paper and to attend. I then decide that I am not willing to take the trouble to do as I promised. Do I treat the organiser as a *means* to my end? My end is to avoid bother; so I do nothing. I fail to act as I have promised, and I do not even let the organiser know. This is certainly a breach of a duty of perfect obligation. I fail to have regard to the organiser's ends; but do I treat him as a means? Not so far as I can see.

So Kant's suggestion will not do. The distinction between perfect and imperfect obligations seems to fit together more smoothly with the distinction between duties that imply and duties that do not imply corresponding rights. In one of my examples, purposeless wounding, I said that the act is a breach of perfect obligation because it infringes the rights of the victim, not because it emanates from a particular attitude of the agent. So reference to rights seems a more secure method of determining whether a duty is one of perfect obligation. But, just as with the proposed criterion of discretionary or non-discretionary duty, we have to rely on moral intuition to say whether or not there is a right; and there can be striking differences of opinion, as for example in the ascription of rights to animals or foetuses.

What about my first suggested method of distinguishing between intolerable and tolerable wrongdoing, namely by identifying the first with wrongful acts and the second with wrongful omissions? This distinction does not have to rely on variable intuition. Although deliberate omissions to perform acts are themselves acts of will, it is usually quite clear whether the object of disapproval is a positive action or a negative omission to do what one ought to do. (It is possible to imagine situations in which there might be some doubt, but they are exceptional.) This method of distinction, then, would have an advantage if it could fit the bill. Can it do so? Does it in fact coincide with the distinction between duties of perfect obligation (understood to mean non-discretionary duties, which imply corresponding rights) and duties of imperfect obligation

145

(understood to mean discretionary duties, which do not imply corresponding rights)? Clearly not. A failure to keep a promise is an omission but it is also a breach of a duty of perfect obligation. A failure by a doctor to treat a patient who seeks his aid, or a failure by a motorist to keep a sharp look-out for pedestrians crossing the road, is a breach of a duty of perfect obligation. It is also clear that such omissions go beyond the bounds of the tolerable. So the distinction between acts and omissions is not a suitable method of drawing the line between intolerable and tolerable objects of disapproval.

We are left with the distinction between duties of perfect and imperfect obligation, understood as a distinction between duties that are non-discretionary and imply corresponding rights, and duties that are discretionary and do not imply corresponding rights. If we now ask whether there can be duties of perfect obligation towards oneself, the answer requires a choice between our two criteria. It makes sense to think of non-discretionary duties to oneself; the duty of self-respect seems a worthy candidate. It does not, however, make sense to think that a duty to oneself can imply a right against oneself – unless we try to split a person's self into a higher and a lower self, or into a present and a future self, which I regard as real nonsense. (It is worth noting, incidentally, that Kant's criterion of distinction between perfect and imperfect obligation implies that there cannot be duties of perfect obligation to oneself; for the breach of such a duty would involve the self-contradictory idea of acting so as to use oneself as a means to one's own ends while at the same time failing to respect one's own ends.) It does not matter much how we choose to use the terms 'perfect' and 'imperfect obligation'. What matters for our present purpose is whether the criterion of being non-discretionary or the criterion of implying a corresponding right is the one which will indicate the bounds of the intolerable.

This brings us back to the question of paternalism. If we regard a breach of non-discretionary duty as the criterion of the intolerable, then we imply that some sort of control (not necessarily by law) is proper to discourage a class of actions, most of which adversely affect others but some of which adversely affect only the agent. (This limited measure of paternalism, however, will still require the toleration of a breach of discretionary duties to oneself, such as the duty to improve one's character or to develop one's talents.) If, on the other hand, we regard the infringement of rights as the criterion of the intolerable, then all duties to oneself will be outside its boundaries, since non-discretionary duties to oneself do not imply rights against oneself. It seems to me that our normal concept of toleration and the intolerable requires us to adopt the second alternative. In saying this, I do not mean that paternalism is ruled out by all our common moral intuitions; I mean rather that any paternalism which is supported would not be justified in terms of intolerability. For example, I think it is perfectly proper to control, for paternalistic reasons, the availability of drugs which are both addictive and harmful. Now while it is natural to defend this opinion by saying that freedom to harm oneself by addictive drugs is a freedom which we should forgo, it is less natural to express the view by saying that freedom to harm oneself by addictive drugs is intolerable or should not be tolerated. This is not because 'intolerable' or 'should not be tolerated' is a more emphatic form of condemnation than 'should be forgone'; after all, the taking of some addictive drugs, such as heroin, does call for emphatic condemnation. Rather, it seems to me, the notion of the intolerable tends to carry a reference to concern for others. It would not be odd to say that the freedom of drug-pushers to sell their drugs is intolerable.

My tentative conclusion, then, is that the boundary of the intolerable is fixed by infringement of rights. Acts of which we disapprove but which do not infringe rights may be tolerated despite our belief that they are wrong, and should be tolerated if those who do the acts have deliberately chosen to do them. In the latter event toleration is called for because it shows respect for the ends (the choices) of those who do the acts.

The conclusion is not a mere restatement of J. S. Mill's principle for the limits of liberty, namely the causing of harm to other people. Mill's principle is wider than mine and rightly so, since the area appropriate to liberty is wider than the area appropriate to toleration. The idea of toleration is relevant for non-interference with acts of which one disapproves, but the idea of liberty is relevant also for non-interference with acts of which one does not disapprove. Of course we speak or think of allowing freedom only where there is some suggestion of possible interference, and in general nobody suggests possible interference with things that are morally approved or are regarded as morally neutral. But there certainly can be the suggestion of interference with things that are disliked, even though not disapproved; and in such circumstances it is proper to make a claim of liberty but not accurate to describe the claim as one of toleration.

I come back now to the more troublesome and more serious problem that there is no clear method of applying the distinction between duties of perfect and imperfect obligation. It seems that we have to rely on moral intuition, but moral intuitions can vary from one person to another, from one generation to another, from one society to another. With a great many, indeed the majority, of our moral duties there is a reasonable consensus, at any rate for one's own time, on the question which of them should be regarded as implying corresponding rights and which should not. But there is an area of disagreement, often sharp. Can philosophical reflection give us any guidance on that, with particular reference to the question of toleration?

It seems to me that there has been a gradual widening of our application of the concept of rights, and that this is a mark of widening the scope of duties of perfect obligation, with a consequent demand for legislation or other forms of social control. The process poses a peculiar problem for the issue of toleration, because those who oppose the widening may well do so in a spirit of moral conviction and therefore their attitude has a claim upon toleration. A good example is afforded by disagreement concerning our duties to animals.

It should be noted in the first place that the Kantian formula of the Categorical Imperative is defective in confining our moral duties to the treatment of human beings. Kant made the limitation quite deliberately because, in his conception of ends-in-themselves, he emphasised the capacity for rational choice. There are, however, in some parts of his work, signs of uneasiness with his official doctrine that duties to animals can only be indirect duties to men.[8] It is debatable whether one should ascribe rights to animals, but it is perfectly clear that one should ascribe to human beings duties towards animals which appear capable of feeling pain (if not pleasure also). These duties can be brought within the conception of treating other creatures (rational or sensitive) as ends-in-themselves, that is of making their ends one's own, since ends include the objects of desire as well as the objects of choice.

It is nevertheless proper to say that the status of human beings as ends-in-themselves is superior to that of other animals, because human beings possess more developed capacities of the kind relevant for moral consideration. These are the capacities concerned with ends or purposes. They include the capacity to desire, the capacity to imagine and to think, and the capacity to choose. The notion of an end or conscious goal is of something desired or consciously aimed at. When we think of an animal as capable of feeling

---

[8] See Alexander Broadie and Elizabeth M. Pybus, 'Kant's Treatment of Animals', *Philosophy*, 49 (1974), 375–83.

pain, that idea of pain includes the notion that the animal wants to be rid of the experience. The capacity of thought and imagination makes it possible, among other things, to enlarge the scope and the character of ends, so that they extend into the more distant future, cover a range of experience, and apply to others as well as to oneself. The capacity of choice makes it possible to differentiate between ends, to grade the value attributed to them, and to follow out that grading in one's pursuit of them. We may be mistaken in supposing that human beings are superior to all other species in the degree to which they possess the capacities of thought, imagination, and choice. If we should find good reason to revise our ideas (for example on the capacities of dolphins in relation to those of human beings), we should be rationally obliged to revise our moral priorities. In the light of our present knowledge, or supposed knowledge, we are justified in giving priority to human beings over other animals.

This priority, however, does not imply that other animals do not count, that they are not in any way to be treated as ends-in-themselves. A human being can and should treat other human beings as having ends like those which he himself has, because he can imagine himself in their place. When he thinks of a non-human animal as capable of suffering pain and as wanting to be rid of it, he can do so because here too he can see a similarity with himself and can imagine the animal's experience on the analogy of his own. He has the same sort of evidence, and the same sort of grounds, for feeling a moral obligation towards the animal.

Consequently I consider that Kant's version of the Categorical Imperative is too narrow in declaring that we ought to act so as to treat 'humanity' as an end and not merely as a means. Does the same criticism apply to the phraseology of respect for persons? Since we normally think that only human beings (and any super-human being or beings that we may believe to exist) are persons, this formula too seems to neglect our duties to animals.

How is the concept of the intolerable affected by our moral duties towards animals? There are some debatable issues, to which I shall turn in a moment, but first let us note that there is a much larger class of non-debatable cases. We would all agree that simple cruelty to animals is intolerable and should be punishable by law. There are differences of opinion when we turn from 'sports' which are now outlawed, such as bear-baiting and cock-fighting, to others which are not, like fox-hunting. However, when there is agreement that a practice affecting animals is intolerable, does this fit my suggestion that the intolerable is what contravenes a duty of perfect obligation and therefore breaches a right? Our duties to animals are certainly not discretionary duties; they apply at all times. I have argued in favour of the common view that duties to animals are less important than duties to human beings, but that does not prevent them from being duties of perfect obligation. There is dispute whether it is proper to ascribe rights to animals. It is not true that everyone who would call cruelty to animals intolerable would describe it as an invasion of the rights of animals. On the other hand the growing practice of referring to animal rights is intended to reinforce the moral opinion that the infliction of pain or terror upon animals is intolerable, something that should be outlawed. The history of the concept of rights shows a gradual and continuing extension of its application. It is a way of indicating extension of the area of duties of perfect obligation. I suspect that the idea of animal rights will in time become generally accepted, as the idea of human rights in the social and economic field is now becoming gradually accepted.

Let me now turn to the empirically debatable issues concerning duties to animals. Apologists for fox-hunting claim that the practice is not only a source of pleasure to the hunters but is morally justifiable as the only viable method for keeping down the numbers of foxes, with their nasty habit of killing chickens and other useful livestock on farms. I do not know whether apologists for bull-fighting in the countries where it flourishes are wont to produce moral reasons to justify that practice. But since the main reason for the continuance of such sports is the pleasure of the human participants or spectators, I prefer to consider a different sort of example, in which there is more clearly a disagreement on moral issues.

If you think it is morally wrong to conduct experiments on human beings without their consent, you will, I trust, agree that such experimentation is intolerable. Now suppose you think it is morally wrong to conduct experiments on live animals other than human beings, but you are aware that many people, including a majority of reputable biological scientists and medical practitioners, think it is morally justifiable or even morally necessary: what should your attitude be towards tolerating such research? You may say that since you do not have the power to suppress the research, the question of tolerating it does not arise. You are entitled to campaign against it, since you think it is morally wrong. Meanwhile you are compelled to 'tolerate' it in the sense of putting up with it willy-nilly; but the idea of toleration in the sense of choosing to allow its continuance is not open to you, because you have no choice. Well, suppose that in due course your campaign is success-ful, so that you and those who think as you do are able to promote legislation which would end the present, miserably weak, control of animal experiments and replace it by a complete ban. You now have the power and you have the right. Should you nevertheless tolerate the practice because those who conduct the experiments have a sincere conviction that it is the right thing to do? If you dis-approve of what others do with sincere approval, why should your moral judgement outweigh theirs?

When we ask whether toleration or suppression is the right policy in these and other circumstances, the difficulty arises from the complex character of the basic principle of morality. Respect for the ends of human beings includes a respect for their choices (or decisions) as well as respect for their desires. Other human beings are as capable, and as entitled, as I am to take decisions, including moral decisions, and I ought not to interfere with their following out their decisions, even though I would take a decision contrary to theirs if I were in their shoes. But moral decisions, more often than not, have effects which go beyond the person taking them, and my obligation to respect the ends (in the form of choices or decisions) of another man does not cancel my obligation to respect the ends (in the form of desires) of those who will be affected by his action. What he thinks he ought to do cannot be the sole determinant of what ought to happen to others. If the others who would be affected by his action are adult, sane, human beings, who can speak up for themselves, their voice is decisive in forbidding acts that would breach their rights. But if those affected are infants or imbeciles or animals, someone else must speak up for them. The problem is not so much that the would-be actor and the would-be controller differ in their opinions, so that neither can claim a monopoly of moral wisdom. If that were all, the answer would lie in toleration, and this is why it is easy to preach toleration for dissident opinion. The problem is rather one of weighing up the conflicting claims which arise from the practical consequences of the different opinions. The scientific researcher who thinks it right to perform experiments on animals justifies his action by the hope, or even the reasonable expectation, of consequences beneficial to mankind in general. The critic who thinks it wrong condemns the action because it violates the rights of animals (or the obligations of men towards animals). If it were a question of killing an animal to save the life of a human being, the obligation to the human being would have priority. But when it is a question of using an animal as a means to achieve some general benefit for humanity at large, the case is by no means so clear.

In practice we tend to follow majority opinion. When a majority of articulate people, or a majority of their representatives in Parliament, came to think that the cruelty to animals involved in bear-baiting and cock-fighting was not condoned by the pleasure given to spectators, these sports were outlawed. If a majority comes to think that experiments upon animals cannot be justified by the potential benefit to mankind, the law will be changed. This is not a solution which is clearly satisfactory. We are not content to leave all disputed moral questions (capital punishment, the toleration of sexual practices that deviate from the conventional norm) to decision by a majority of public opinion; we hope to get a more enlightened view from Members of Parliament and we look to the result of a free vote from them. In either event we have to recognise that opinion, among the general public or among members of the legislature, changes from one era to another. So we accept decisions which are plainly relative to time, place, and social background. This seems the best we can do. As with politics generally, the democratic procedure is the least bad method that we know.

I am not happy with this conclusion. It accords with the democratic implications of Kantian ethics: we must acknowledge that others are as capable and as entitled as we are to form moral judgements about the rightness or wrongness of a practice, and therefore we have no business to make them conform to our view unless we can claim to have a general consensus on our side. But the conclusion also involves a cultural relativism with less acceptable implications. It seems to imply that a practice which is approved by a majority (of the population or of the legislature) should not be regarded as intolerable by those who disapprove. As before, it is relevant to recall that dissentient minorities do not have the power to suppress, so that the idea of toleration does not arise. Nevertheless the conclusion seems to suggest that moral justification for suppression of a practice depends solely on having the majority behind you in your disapproval, and not on the intrinsic merits of the disapproval itself. We would surely not be prepared to say this of the treatment of human beings: of Hitler's treatment of 'inferior races', of the policy of apartheid in South Africa, of the custom among the ancient Spartans of leaving weak infants to die on the mountain-side. All three of my examples are practices accompanied by sincere approval on the part of those with political power. Yet we would not hesitate to describe the practices as intolerable because they clearly breach the Kantian principle of respect for persons. The fact is that those who followed (or follow) the practices did not (or do not) accept the Kantian ethic. They regarded (or regard) 'inferior races' or weak infants as of less value than themselves. Nearly all of us take that view of animals as compared with human beings. So it is not possible to say confidently that one opinion about the treatment of animals is morally perverted even if sincere. Unless and until we can say that, we have to allow ethical disagreement to be settled by political methods.[9]

[9] This is a revised version of a paper read at a Morrell Conference on Toleration held at the University of York in September 1984. I am much indebted to members of the Conference for critical discussion of the earlier version.

7

Autonomy, toleration, and the harm principle*

JOSEPH RAZ

This is a paper about the relation between two ideas, autonomy and toleration. Both are deeply rooted in liberal culture, and I shall rely on this fact. I shall say very little to explain the liberal concepts of personal autonomy and of toleration, just enough to make the points on which the argument of the paper depends. I shall say even less on the reasons for valuing personal autonomy. My purpose is to show that a powerful argument in favour of toleration is derivable from the value of personal autonomy. This is not a surprising conclusion. I hope some interest lies in the details of the argument; but the main interest is in what it does *not* establish, in the limits of the autonomy-based principle of toleration.

There are, of course, other powerful arguments for toleration. Their conclusions overlap those of the argument from autonomy, being narrower in some areas and wider in others. This is exactly what one would expect. It shows the strength of the commitment in our culture to toleration that it is supported by different arguments from different points of view. Nor need a single individual be too parsimonious in the arguments on which his faith in toleration rests. Many of them can be subsumed under one moral umbrella. There is, however, a special interest in closely examining the argument from autonomy. It is sometimes thought to be the specifically liberal argument for toleration: the one argument which is not shared by non-liberals, and which displays the spirit of the liberal approach to politics. This paper contributes to an exploration of this view. It does so in two ways.

First, it is sometimes assumed that respect for autonomy requires governments to avoid pursuing any conception of the good life. In

* © Joseph Raz 1987. Reprinted from *Issues in Contemporary Legal Philosophy: The Influence of H.L.A. Hart*, edited by Ruth Gavison (1987) by permission of Oxford University Press.

other words the ideal of autonomy is used to support a principle of toleration reflecting anti-perfectionism, the exclusion of ideals from politics. I shall argue that no such conclusion follows from a concern for personal autonomy. Therefore, if liberalism, or any liberal tradition is wedded to anti-perfectionism then it must find some other roots.

Another well-known liberal argument for toleration is based on the harm principle. This principle, first formulated by J. S. Mill, has found a powerful champion in H. L. A. Hart. The principle asserts that the only purpose for which the law may use its coercive power is to prevent harm. In the last section of this paper I shall argue that the autonomy-based principle of toleration is best regarded as providing the moral foundation for the harm principle. It explains why liberals are sometimes willing to employ coercion to prevent harm, as well as why they refuse to use coercion for other purposes. Thus viewed the principle helps assess the relative seriousness of various harms, as well as to answer potentially damaging criticisms of the harm principle which claim that it reflects the ideology of the night watchman state.

I AUTONOMY AND PLURALISM

The ruling idea behind the ideal of personal autonomy is that people should make their own lives. The autonomous person is a (part) author of his own life. The ideal of personal autonomy is the vision of people controlling, to some degree, their own destiny, fashioning it through successive decisions throughout their lives. Once stated in this way the problems involved in working out a plausible conception of autonomy become only too evident. No one can control all aspects of his life. How much control is required for the life to be autonomous, and what counts as an adequate exercise of control (as opposed to being forced by circumstances, or deceived by one's own ignorance, or governed by one's weaknesses) is an enormously difficult problem. Fortunately for us, although its solution is required in order to formulate policies to implement the autonomy-based principle of toleration, it is not required in order to appreciate the structure of the argument for toleration, which is our sole concern. All that has to be accepted is that to be autonomous a person must not only be given a choice but that he must be given an adequate range of choices. A person whose every decision is extracted from him by coercion is not an autonomous person. Nor is a person autonomous if he is paralysed and therefore cannot take advantage of the options which are offered to him. We will need to examine some of the criteria of adequacy for available options. But, for the purposes of the present argument, we do not require a general doctrine of the adequacy of options.

One other aspect of the problem of adequacy of options has to be noted here in order to avoid a common misunderstanding. People usually control their lives not by deciding once and for all what to do for the rest of their lives. Rather they take successive decisions, with the later ones sometimes reversing earlier decisions, sometimes further implementing them, and often dealing with matters unaffected by the earlier decisions. The question arises, to what extent does autonomy require the continuous possibility of choice throughout one's life. Given that every decision, at least once implemented, closes options previously open to one (it may also open up new options) the question of whether, and when, one's own decisions may limit one's autonomy raises tricky issues.

Autonomy is often confused with self-realization. But the two are distinct moral ideals. Self-realization consists in the development to their full extent of all the valuable capacities a person possesses. The autonomous person is the one who makes his own life and he may choose the path of self-realization or reject it. Nor is autonomy a precondition of self-realization for one can stumble into a life of self-realization or be manipulated into it or reach it in some other way which is inconsistent with autonomy. One cannot deny this last claim on the ground that one of the capacities one has to develop is that of choosing one's own life. For this and any other capacity can be developed by simulation and deceit, that is, by misleading the person to believe that he controls his destiny. In any case autonomy is at best one of many elements which contribute to self-realization and it does not enjoy any special importance compared with many of the others.

It follows that the autonomous person must have options which will enable him to develop all his abilities, as well as to concentrate on some of them. One is not autonomous if one cannot choose a life of self-realization, nor is one autonomous if one cannot reject this ideal. Here lies one clue to a proper understanding of what counts as 'an adequate range of options' necessary to make a person autonomous. Our concern is not to develop this idea but to bring out the point which it illustrates, that is, that a commitment to autonomy entails commitment to moral pluralism.

Let us approach this problem in two stages. Given that it requires an opportunity to concentrate on some and neglect others of one's capacities, it requires that incompatible forms and styles of life be available. Developing this idea will be the subject of the second line of argument. But first let it be noted that autonomy requires that many morally acceptable, though incompatible, forms of life be available to a person. This is an additional aspect of the test of adequacy of the available options. It is of great importance to the connection between autonomy and toleration.

I shall use a rather artificial and extreme example to bring out the point. Imagine a person who can pursue an occupation of his choice but at the price of committing murder for each option he rejects. First he has to choose whether to become an electrician. He can refuse provided he kills one person. Then he is offered a career in dentistry, which again he is free to refuse if he kills another person, and so on. Like the person facing the proverbial gunman demanding 'your money or your life', who is acting freely if he defies the threat and risks his life, the person in our dilemma is acting freely if he agrees to murder in order to become a dentist, rather than an electrician. If he does so then his choice does not tend to show that his life is not autonomous. But if he chooses the right way and agrees to be an electrician in order to avoid becoming a murderer then his choice is forced.

I think it will be generally agreed that in this case the life of the person in my example is not autonomous and that his choice and the nature of his options are enough to show that he is not. That is, our judgement that he is not autonomous is unaffected even if the example is developed to show that his predicament is a result of a series of bizarre accidents and coincidences resulting from the breakdown and freak behaviour of several computers in some futuristic society. Autonomy requires a choice of goods. A choice between good and evil is not enough. (Remember that it is personal, not moral, autonomy we are concerned with. No doubt is cast on the fact that the person in the example is a moral agent and fully responsible for his actions. So are the inmates of concentration camps. But they do not have personal autonomy.)

Autonomy cannot be achieved by a person whose every action and thought must be bent to the task of survival, a person who will die if ever he puts a foot wrong. Similarly, it cannot be obtained by a person who is constantly fighting for moral survival. If he is to be moral then he has no choice, just as the person struggling for physical survival has no choice if he is to stay alive.

Given this conclusion, how is autonomy related to moral, or

value pluralism? Moral pluralism is the view that there are various forms and styles of life which exemplify different virtues and which are incompatible. Forms or styles of life are incompatible if, given reasonable assumptions about human nature, they cannot normally be exemplified in the same life. There is nothing to stop a person from being both an ideal teacher and an ideal family person. But a person cannot normally lead both the life of action and of contemplation, to use one of the traditionally recognized contrasts, nor can one person possess all the virtues of a nun and of a mother.

To establish moral or value pluralism, however, the existence of a plurality of incompatible but morally acceptable forms of life is not enough. Moral pluralism claims not merely that incompatible forms of life are morally acceptable but that they display distinct virtues, each capable of being pursued for its own sake. If the active and contemplative lives are not merely incompatible but also display distinctive virtues then complete moral perfection is unattainable. Whichever form of life one is pursuing there are virtues which elude one because they are available only to people pursuing alternative and incompatible forms of life.

Such descriptions of moral pluralism are often viewed with suspicion, at least in part because of the elusiveness of the notion of a form of life. How much must one life differ from another in order to be an instance of a different form of life? The question seems unanswerable because we lack a suitable test of relevance. Indeed there is no test of relevance which would be suitable for all the purposes for which the expression 'a form of life' was or may be used. But this does not matter as the test of relevance we require is plain. For the purpose of understanding moral or value pluralism forms of life differ in their moral features.

Two lives must differ in the virtues they display, or in the degree that they display them, if they are to count as belonging to different forms of life. A form of life is maximal if, under normal circumstances, a person whose life is of that kind cannot improve it by acquiring additional virtues, nor by enhancing the degree to which he possesses any virtue, without sacrificing another virtue he possesses or the degree to which it is present in his life. Belief in value pluralism is the belief that there are several maximal forms of life.

Moral pluralism thus defined is weak moral pluralism. It can be strengthened by the addition of one or more of the following three claims (and there are further ways of refining and subdividing them). First, the incompatible virtues are not completely ranked relative to each individual. That is, it is not the case that for each person all the incompatible virtues can be strictly ordered according to their moral worth, so that he ought to pursue the one which for him has the highest worth, and his failure to do so tars him with a moral blemish, regardless of his success in pursuing other, incompatible, moral virtues.

Second, the incompatible virtues are not completely ranked by some impersonal criteria of moral worth. Even if the first condition obtains it is still possible to claim that, although there is no moral blemish on me if I am a soldier and excel in courage because I am made of bronze, excellence in dialectics, which is incompatible with courage and is open only to those made of gold, is a superior excellence by some moral standards which are not relative to the character or conditions of life of individuals. The second thesis denies that such impersonal strict ordering of incompatible virtues is possible.

Third, the incompatible virtues exemplify diverse fundamental concerns. They do not derive from a common source, or from common ultimate principles. Some forms of two-level and indirect utilitarianism are morally pluralistic in the weak sense, and may also accept the first two strong forms of moral pluralism. But they are incompatible with the third.

There is yet another sense in which the value pluralism explained above is weak. 'Moral' is here employed in a wide sense in which it encompasses the complete art of the good life, as Mill might have said. It is in fact used in a sense which encompasses all values. The point of keeping the expression 'moral value', rather than talking simply of values, is to avoid two possible misunderstandings. First, 'value' is sometimes used in a relativized sense, to indicate not what is of value but what is held to be so by some person, group, or culture. Secondly, some people hold that some kinds of values, for example aesthetic ones, provide no reasons for action: that they are relevant merely to appreciation. In this paper 'value' is non-relativized and is understood to constitute or imply the existence of reasons for action.

Whatever the truth in any of the strong varieties of moral pluralism, valuing autonomy is compatible with their rejection. It does commit one, however, to weak moral pluralism (and henceforth by 'moral pluralism' I will refer to the weak variety). Autonomy is exercised through choice, and choice requires a variety of options to choose from. To satisfy the conditions of the adequacy of the range of options the options available must differ in respects which may rationally affect choice. If all the choices in a life are like the choice between two identical-looking cherries from a fruit bowl, then that life is not autonomous. Choices are guided by reasons and to present the chooser with an adequate variety there must be a difference between the reasons for the different options.

Furthermore, as was argued above, the options must include a variety of morally acceptable options. So the morally acceptable options must themselves vary in the reasons which speak in favour of each of them.

Plainly the reasons for an option may, but need not, pertain to the object to be realized through its pursuit. They can, for example, pertain to the manner of its pursuit: is it pursued vigorously, carefully, or determinedly; is its object sought through a high risk policy, in a carefully planned way, spontaneously, and so on. There often are reasons to prefer an option because of the manner in which it pursues its object. It seems plausible to assume that autonomy requires a variety in the choices which reflects both kinds of considerations, a variety regarding both what to do and how to do it. Be that as it may, my only assumption is that reliable ability to act for reasons of a particular kind requires a certain disposition. This is true both where the reasons concern the object (for example, generosity) and where they affect the manner of its pursuit (for example, spontaneity). Finally, I am assuming that such dispositions, being dispositions to pursue valuable options, are virtuous, that they constitute so many virtues.

The upshot of the above is that autonomy presupposes a variety of conflicting considerations. It presupposes choices involving trade-offs, requiring relinquishing one good for the sake of another. Since excellence in the pursuit of goods involves possession of the appropriate virtues, the existence of these conflicts speaks of the existence of incompatible virtues, that is of moral pluralism. A person may have an autonomous life without attaining any virtue to any high degree. However, he inhabits a world where the pursuit of many virtues was open to him, but where he would not have been able to achieve them all, at least not to their highest degree. To put it more precisely, if autonomy is an ideal then we are committed to such a view of morality: valuing autonomy leads to the endorsement of moral pluralism.

II PLURALISM AND TOLERATION

It is sometimes supposed that moral pluralism by itself establishes the value of toleration. However, refraining from persecuting or harassing people who possess moral virtues which we lack is not in itself toleration. I do not tolerate people whom I admire and respect because they are generous, kind, or courageous, whereas I am not. Toleration implies the suppression or containment of an inclination or desire to persecute, harass, harm, or react in an unwelcome way to a person. But even this does not yet capture the essence of toleration. I do not tolerate the courageous, the generous, and the kind even if I am inclined to persecute them and restrain myself because I realize that my desires are entirely evil.

Toleration is a distinctive moral virtue only if it curbs desires, inclinations, and convictions which are thought by the tolerant person to be in themselves desirable. Typically a person is tolerant if and only if he suppresses a desire to cause to another a harm or hurt which he thinks the other deserves. The clearest case of toleration, whether justified or not, is where a person restrains his indignation at the sight of injustice or some other moral evil, or rather at the sight of behaviour which he takes to be of this character. Whether a person is tolerant or not depends on his reasons for action. Himmler did not tolerate Hitler when he did not kill him. But an anti-Nazi may have spared his life out of a misconceived sense of duty to let people carry on even when they are in the wrong.

I emphasized the tolerant person's view that in being tolerant he is restraining an inclination which is in itself desirable. The typical cases referred to are cases in which the intolerant inclination is in itself desirable because it is a reaction to wrongful behaviour. Is it then part of our notion of toleration that only the wrongful or bad can be tolerated? Many writers on the subject assume so. But this view is unwarranted. To be sure one cannot tolerate other people because of their virtues. But one can tolerate their limitations. A person can tolerate another's very deliberate manner of speech, or his slow and methodical way of considering every issue, and so on. In all such cases what is tolerated is neither wrong nor necessarily bad. It is the absence of a certain accomplishment. This is not an attempt at hair-splitting. The reason people lack certain virtues or accomplishments may be, and often is, that they possess other and incompatible virtues and accomplishments. When we tolerate the limitations of others we may be aware that these are but the other side of their virtues and personal strengths. This may indeed be the reason why we tolerate them.

Toleration, then, is the curbing of an activity likely to be unwelcome to its recipient or of an inclination so to act which is in itself morally valuable and which is based on a dislike or an antagonism of that person or of a feature of his life, reflecting a judgement that these represent limitations or deficiencies in him, in order to let that person have his way or in order for him to gain or keep some advantage. (As was pointed out to me by P. M. S. Hacker, mercy is sometimes a special case of toleration. One can tolerate out of mercy.)

This characterization of toleration deviates from the view which is most common in writings on political theory in two respects. My explanation relies on four features. First, only behaviour which is either unwelcome to the person towards whom it is addressed or behaviour which is normally seen as unwelcome is intolerant behaviour. Secondly, one is tolerant only if one inclines or is tempted not to be. Thirdly, that inclination is based on dislike or antagonism to the behaviour, character, or some feature of the existence of its object. Finally, the intolerant inclination is in itself worthwhile or desirable.

Political theorists tend to concentrate on one hostile reaction as the only possible manifestation of intolerance: the use of coercion. They are resistant to the thought that an expression of a hostile view, for example, may be intolerant behaviour. Secondly, as was observed above, it is often thought that only if a person judges another or his behaviour to be wrong or evil can he be tolerant of that person or of his behaviour.

I shall say little about the first point. If there is a concept of intolerance according to which only coercive interventions are intolerant then this is not the ordinary notion of intolerance but one developed by political theorists to express a particular point of view. I know of no reason for sharing that point of view. The ideas of toleration and of intolerance identify modes of behaviour by their grounds and object. They do not identify them by the means employed. Saying this is not saying that all the manifestations of intolerance are either equally acceptable or equally unacceptable. It is merely to point out that there are concepts that identify actions by their motives and not by the means those motives lead to.

I have already explained the reasons for rejecting the view that only the bad or the wrong can be tolerated. The fact that intolerance can be directed at people's limitations and that those can be aspects of some other virtues which those people possess acquires special significance for those who believe in moral pluralism. It provides the link between pluralism and toleration.

At the end of this article I shall argue that, within bounds, respect for personal autonomy requires tolerating bad or evil actions. But toleration can also be of the good and valuable when it curbs inclinations which though valuable in themselves are intolerant of other people's morally acceptable tastes and pursuits. While pluralism as such need not give rise to occasions where toleration is called for, some very common kinds of pluralistic moralities do. Let us call them competitive pluralistic moralities (there are competitive moralities which are not pluralistic but they do not concern us).

Competitive pluralism not only admits the validity of distinct and incompatible moral virtues, but also of virtues which tend, given human nature, to encourage intolerance of other virtues. That is, competitive pluralism admits the value of virtues possession of which normally leads to a tendency not to suffer certain limitations in other people which are themselves inevitable if those people possess certain other, equally valid, virtues. The very traits of character which make for excellence in chairing committees and getting things done, when this involves reconciling points of view and overcoming personal differences, those very traits of character also tend to make people intolerant of single-minded dedication to a cause. And there are many other examples, the prevalence of which suggests that most common forms of pluralism are of the competitive kind.

It is possible that all viable forms of pluralism are competitive. Failing that it is likely that the variety of valuable options which is required by the ideal of autonomy can only be satisfied by competitive moral pluralism. This view is plausible given the range of abilities many people have. We assume that moral life will be possible only within human communities, and that means that the range of capacities development of which is to be made possible in order for all members of the community to be autonomous is greater than the range necessary to assure an individual of autonomy. That is a consequence of the fact that both the genetic differences between people and the social needs for variety and for a division of labour lead to a diversity of abilities among people. The moral virtues associated with the diverse forms of life allowed by a morality which enables all normal persons to attain autonomy by moral means are very likely to depend on character traits many of which lead to intolerance of other acceptable forms of life. All those forms of life are not only morally legitimate but also ones which need to be available if all persons are to have autonomy. Therefore respect for autonomy by requiring competitive moral pluralism also establishes the necessity for toleration.

Even if one rejects my supposition that given human nature autonomy can only be realized within a community which endorses a competitive pluralistic morality, even if one thinks that that supposition is based on a misguided view of human nature, that it is perhaps too pessimistic, even if one believes that autonomy and pluralism are possible without conflict, the above conclusion is not undermined. Even on these optimistic assumptions it is still the case that competitive pluralism contributes, where it exists, to the realization of autonomy. Therefore, competitive pluralism provides an argument for a principle of toleration. The only modification is that on the more optimistic assumptions there may be circumstances in which there will be no need to rely on the principle, circumstances in which the conflicts which activate it do not arise. This does not invalidate the principle of toleration. And, of course, in our world it is not merely idly valid; the circumstances for its invocation are very much with us.

III THE SCOPE AND LIMITS OF AUTONOMY-BASED TOLERATION

The previous section argued that competitive moral pluralism of the kind which is required by respect for autonomy generates conflicts between people pursuing valuable but incompatible forms of life. Given the necessity to make those forms of life available in order to secure autonomy there is a need to curb people's actions and their attitudes in those conflicts by principles of toleration. The duty of toleration is an aspect of the duty of respect for autonomy. To judge its scope and its limits we need to look at the extent of our autonomy-based duties generally.

Since autonomy is morally valuable there is reason for everyone to make himself and everyone else autonomous. But it is the special character of autonomy that one cannot make another person autonomous. One can bring the horse to the water but one cannot make him drink. One is autonomous if one determines the course of one's life by oneself. This is not to say that others cannot help, but their help is by and large confined to securing the background conditions which enable a person to be autonomous. This is why moral

165

philosophers who regard morality as essentially other-regarding tend to concentrate on autonomy as a capacity for an autonomous life. Our duties towards our fellows are for the most part to secure for them autonomy in its capacity sense. Where some of these writers are wrong is in overlooking the reason for the value of autonomy as a capacity, which is in the use its possessor can make of it, that is, in the autonomous life it enables him to have.

There is more one can do to help another person have an autonomous life than stand-off and refrain from coercing or manipulating him. There are two other categories of autonomy-based duties towards another person. One is helping in creating the inner capacities required for the conduct of an autonomous life. Some of these concern cognitive capacities, such as the power to absorb, remember and use information, reasoning abilities, and the like. Others concern one's emotional and imaginative make-up. Still others concern health, and physical abilities and skills. Finally, there are character traits essential or helpful for a life of autonomy. They include stability, loyalty, and the ability to form personal attachments and to maintain intimate relationships. The third type of autonomy-based duties towards another concern the creation of an adequate range of options for him to choose from.

As anticipated all these duties, although based on the value of the autonomous life, are aimed at securing autonomy as a capacity. Apart from cultivating a general awareness of the value of autonomy there is little more one can do. It is not surprising, however, that the principle of autonomy, as I shall call the principle requiring people to secure the conditions of autonomy to all people, yields duties which go far beyond the negative duties of non-interference, which are the only ones recognized by some defenders of autonomy. If the duties of non-interference are autonomy-based then the principle of autonomy provides reasons for holding that there are other autonomy-based duties as well. Every reason of autonomy which leads to the duties of non-interference would lead to other duties as well, unless, of course, it is counteracted by conflicting reasons. Such countervailing reasons are likely to be sometimes present, but they are most unlikely to confine the duties of autonomy to non-interference only.

So far I have emphasized the far-reaching political implications of the ideal of autonomy. But autonomy-based principles of toleration have clear limits to which we must turn.

First, while autonomy requires the availability of an adequate range of options it does not require the presence of any particular option among them. A person or a government can take action eventually to eliminate soccer and substitute for it American football, for example. The degree to which one would wish to tolerate such action will be affected by pragmatic considerations which can normally be expected to favour erring on the side of caution where governmental action or action by big organizations is concerned. But it has to be remembered that social, economic, and technological processes are constantly changing the opportunities available in our society. Occupations and careers are being created while others disappear all the time. The acceptable shapes of personal relationships are equally in constant flux, and so is the public culture which colours much of what we can and cannot do. Not everyone would agree that such processes are unobjectionable so long as the government does not take a hand in shaping them. The requirements of autonomy as well as other considerations may well call for governmental intervention in directing or initiating such processes.

It is important in this context to distinguish between the effect of the elimination of an option on those already committed to it, and its effect on others. The longer and the more deeply one is committed to one's projects the less able is one to abandon them (before completion) and pick up some others as substitutes. But even if such a change is possible, denying a person the possibility of carrying on with his projects, commitments, and relationships is preventing him from having the life he chose. A person who may but has not yet chosen the eliminated option is much less seriously affected. Since all he is entitled to is an adequate range of options the eliminated option can, from his point of view, be replaced by another without loss of autonomy. This accounts for the importance of changes being gradual so that they will not affect committed persons.

The second main limitation of autonomy-based toleration has already been mentioned. It does not extend to the morally bad and repugnant. This point raises an issue of great importance to the understanding of the relation between autonomy and other moral values. No one would deny that autonomy should be used for the good. The question is has autonomy any value *qua* autonomy when it is abused? Is the autonomous wrongdoer a morally better person than the non-autonomous wrongdoer? Our intuitions rebel against such a view. It is surely the other way round. The wrongdoing casts a darker shadow on its perpetrator if it is autonomously done by him. A murderer who was led to his deed by the foreseen inner logic of his autonomously chosen career is morally worse than one who murders because he momentarily succumbs to the prospect of an easy gain. Nor are these considerations confined to gross breaches of duties. Demeaning, or narrow-minded, or ungenerous, or insensitive behaviour is worse when autonomously chosen and indulged in.

A second question presents itself now. Could it be that it is valuable to make evil and repugnant options available so that people should freely avoid them? Is the person who rejected a life of mindless idleness, for example, better than one who never had the chance of choosing it? Three reasons are often produced in support of this view. First, people must be tested and prove themselves by choosing good rather than evil. Second, the need to choose refines one's moral judgement and discrimination. Third, the presence of evil provides the occasion for developing certain moral virtues. Whatever sound sense there is in all three considerations derives from the thought that the morally good person not only manages his life morally, but would have done so even if circumstances were less favourable or presented more temptations or pressures for evil.

Opportunities for the immoral and the repugnant cannot be eliminated from our world. It may be possible to develop a new form of tape that will make the copying of music from tape in breach of copyright impossible. One opportunity for immorality, let us assume, would thereby disappear. But the vice that it displayed, the vice of, let us say, dishonest dealing, will still have lots of opportunities to be practised. It may, in principle, be possible to eliminate the opportunities for practising some specialized vices. But then, in a world from which they were well and truly eradicated, the corresponding specialist moral ability, that of being good in avoiding that vice, would not be one the absence of which is a moral weakness or blemish. The morally good, in other words, are those who would have led a moral life even if the circumstances of their life were less favourable, but only in the sense of being able to cope with the temptations and pressures normal in their society.

For the most part the opportunities for dishonesty, indolence, insensitivity to the feelings of others, cruelty, pettiness, and the other vices and moral weaknesses are logically inseparable from the conditions of a human life which can have any moral merit. Given their prevalence one cannot object to the elimination of opportunities for evil on the three grounds cited above. The same kind of considerations show that only very rarely will the non-availability of morally repugnant options reduce a person's choice sufficiently to affect his autonomy. Therefore, the availability of such options is not a requirement of respect for autonomy.

Autonomy is valuable only if exercised in pursuit of the good. The ideal of autonomy requires only the availability of morally acceptable options. This may sound a very rigoristic moral view, which it is not. A moral theory which recognizes the value of autonomy inevitably upholds a pluralistic view. It admits the value of a large number of greatly differing pursuits which individuals are free to choose. But is the principle of autonomy consistent with the legal enforcement of morality? To the examination of this question we must now turn.

IV AUTONOMY AND THE HARM PRINCIPLE

Mill's harm principle states that the only justification for coercively interfering with a person is to prevent him from harming others. My discussion will revolve round the somewhat wider principle which regards the prevention of harm to anyone (himself included) as the only justifiable ground for coercive interference with a person. The harm principle is a principle of toleration. The common way of stating its point is to regard it as excluding consideration of private morality from politics. It restrains both individuals and the state from coercing people to refrain from certain activities or to undertake others on the ground that those activities are morally either repugnant or desirable. My purpose is to compare the scope and justification of the harm principle with those of autonomy-based toleration.

That there may be at least some connection between the autonomy and the harm principles is evident. Respect for the autonomy of others largely consists in securing for them adequate options, that is, opportunities and the ability to use them. Depriving a person of opportunities or of the ability to use them is a way of causing him harm. Both the use-value and the exchange-value of property represent opportunities for their owner. Any harm to a person by denying him the use of the value of his property is a harm to him precisely because it diminishes his opportunities. Similarly injury to the person reduces his ability to act in ways which he may desire. Needless to say, a harm to a person may consist not in depriving him of options but in frustrating his pursuit of the projects and relationships he has set upon.

Between them these cases cover most types of harm. Several

forms of injury are, however, left out. Severe and persistent pain is incapacitating. But not all pain falls into this class and even pain which does incapacitate may be objected to as pain independently of its incapacitating results. The same is true of offence. Serious and persistent offence may well reduce a person's opportunities. It may even affect his ability to use the opportunities he has or frustrate his pursuit of his goals. But many cases of causing offence fall short of this. All offensive behaviour may be reprehensible as offensive, independently of its consequences to the affected person's options or projects. Similar considerations apply to other forms of injury such as hurting people's feelings.

It is of interest to note that pain and offence, hurt and the like are harmful only when they do affect options or projects. For 'harm' in its ordinary use has a forward-looking aspect. To harm a person is to diminish his prospects, to affect his possibilities adversely. It is clear that supporters of the harm principle are also concerned with the prevention of offence and pain. It is not clear whether they extend it to encompass all forms of hurting or adversely affecting people. For clarity's sake we could distinguish between the narrow harm principle which allows coercion only for the prevention of harm in the strict sense of the word and the somewhat open-ended broad harm principle which allows coercion for the prevention of pain, offence, and perhaps some other injuries to a person as well.

I hope that these observations are as uncontroversial as they are intended to be. I have tried to follow the common understanding of harm, but to describe it in terms which bring out the connection between harm and autonomy. They reinterpret the principle from the point of view of a morality which values autonomy. That is, they are not an account of the meaning of 'harm' (only the point about the forward-looking aspect of harm belongs to an account of its meaning). People who deny the moral value of autonomy will not be committed to denying that there are harms, or that harming people is, as such, wrong. But they would have to provide a different understanding of what behaviour harms others. Since 'causing harm' by its very meaning demands that the action is prima facie wrong it is a normative concept acquiring its specific meaning from the moral theory within which it is embedded.

This way of thinking of the harm principle may help resolve our response to two potentially decisive objections to it. First, the principle seems to forbid the redistribution of wealth through taxation, and the provision of public goods out of public funds on a non-voluntary basis, as well as to proscribe such familiar schemes as tax-financed educational and national health systems, or the subsidization of public transport. Secondly, the only reason for coercively interfering with a person in order to prevent harm is that it is wrong to cause such harm. But if coercive interventions are justified on this ground then they are used to enforce morality. If so why stop with the prevention of harm? Why not enforce the rest of morality?

Let us assume that we accept the second objection and maintain that it is the function of governments to promote morality. That means that governments should promote the moral quality of the life of those whose lives and actions they can affect. Does not this concession amount to a rejection of the harm principle? It does, according to the common conception which regards the aim and function of the principle as to curtail the freedom of governments to enforce morality. I wish to propose a different understanding of it, according to which it is a principle about the proper way to enforce morality. In other words I would suggest that the principle is derivable from a morality which assigns high value to individual autonomy and regards the principle of autonomy, which imposes duties on people to secure for all the conditions of autonomy, as one of the most important moral principles.

To derive the harm principle from the principle of autonomy one has to establish that the autonomy-based duties never justify coercion where there was no harm. This brings us immediately to the first objection. Governments are subject to autonomy-based duties to provide the conditions of autonomy to people who lack them. These extend beyond the duty to prevent loss of autonomy. This may seem an endorsement of the first objection to the harm principle. But is it? It is a mistake to think that the harm principle recognizes only the duty of governments to prevent loss of autonomy. Sometimes failing to improve the situation of another is harming him.

One can harm another by denying him what is due to him. That is obscured by the common misconception which confines harming a person to acting in a way which results in that person being worse off after the action than he was before. While such actions do indeed harm, so do acts or omissions the result of which is that a person is worse off after them than he should then be. One harms another by failing in one's duty to him, even though this is a duty to improve his situation and the failure does not leave him worse off than he was before. Consider a disabled person who has a legal right to be employed by any employer to whom he applies and who has fewer than four per cent disabled employees in his work force. If such an employer turns him down he harms him although he does not worsen his situation. If you owe me five pounds you harm me by delaying its repayment by a month.

So if the government has a duty to promote the autonomy of people the harm principle allows it to use coercion both in order to stop people from actions which would diminish people's autonomy and in order to force them to take actions which are required to improve people's options and opportunities. It is true that an action harms a particular person only if it affects him directly and significantly by itself. It does not count as harming him if its undesirable consequences are indirect and depend on the intervention of other actions. I do not, for example, harm Johnson by failing to pay my income tax, nor does the government harm him by failing to impose a tax which it has a moral obligation to impose, even if it can be established that Johnson suffered as a result of such failures. In each case the culprit can claim that the fact that Johnson is the one who suffered was decided not by the guilty action but by other intervening actions (which may not have been guilty at all).

But even though I or the government did not harm Johnson we caused harm. If you like, call it harm to unassignable individuals. The point is that one causes harm if one fails in one's duty to a person or a class of persons and that person or a member of that class suffers as a result. That is so even when one cannot be blamed for harming the person who suffered because the allocation of the loss was determined by other hands. A government which has a moral duty to increase old age pensions harms old age pensioners if it fails to do so, even though it does not harm any particular pensioner.

The upshot of this discussion is that the first objection fails, for the harm principle allows full scope to autonomy-based duties. A person who fails to discharge his autonomy-based obligations towards others is harming them, even if those obligations are designed to promote the others' autonomy rather than to prevent its deterioration. It follows that a government whose responsibility is to promote the autonomy of its citizens is entitled to redistribute resources, to provide public goods and to engage in the provision of other services on a compulsory basis, provided its laws merely reflect and concretize autonomy-based duties of its citizens. Coercion is used to ensure compliance with the law. If the law reflects autonomy-based duties then failure to comply harms others and the harm principle is satisfied.

But the autonomy principle is a perfectionist principle. Autonomous life is valuable only if it is spent in the pursuit of acceptable and valuable projects and relationships. The autonomy principle permits and even requires governments to create morally valuable opportunities, and to eliminate repugnant ones. Does not that show that it is incompatible with the harm principle? The impression of incompatibility is encouraged by the prevalent anti-perfectionist reading of the harm principle. That reading is at odds with the fact that the principle merely restricts the use of coercion. Perfectionist goals need not be pursued by the use of coercion. A government which subsidizes certain activities, rewards their pursuit, and advertises their availability encourages those activities without using coercion.

It is no objection to point out that the funds necessary for all these policies are raised by compulsory taxation. I assume that tax is raised to provide adequate opportunities, and is justified by the principle of autonomy in a way consistent with the harm principle in the way described a couple of paragraphs above. It is in deciding which options to encourage more than others that perfectionist considerations dominate. Here they are limited by the availability of resources mobilised in the above-mentioned way. The harm principle is consistent with many perfectionist policies of the kind required by any moral theory which values autonomy highly. It does, however, exclude the use of coercion to discourage non-harmful opportunities. Can that exclusion be derived from the principle of autonomy?

If the argument of section III is sound, then pursuit of the morally repugnant cannot be defended from coercive interference on the ground that being an autonomous choice endows it with any value. It does not (except in special circumstances where it is therapeutic or educational). And yet the harm principle is defensible in light of the principle of autonomy for one simple reason. The means used, coercive interferences, violate the autonomy of their victim. The coercion of criminal penalties is a global and indiscriminate invasion of autonomy. Imprisoning a person prevents him from almost all autonomous pursuits. Other forms of coercion may be less severe, but they all invade autonomy, and they all, at least in this world, do it in a fairly indiscriminate way. That is, there is no practical way of ensuring that the coercion will restrict the victims' choice of repugnant options but will not interfere with their other choices. A moral theory which values autonomy highly can justify restricting the autonomy of one person for the sake of the

173

greater autonomy of others or even of himself in the future. That is why it can justify coercion to prevent harm, for harm interferes with autonomy. But it will not tolerate coercion for other reasons. The availability of repugnant options, and even their free pursuit by individuals do not detract from their autonomy. Undesirable as those conditions are they may not be curbed by coercion.

V THE HARM PRINCIPLE: WIDE OR NARROW?

Our enquiry is almost complete. We set out to explore the limits of toleration required by a perfectionist political morality, one which not only holds that individuals have moral duties towards others, but that they may use political means in trying to discharge their duties. The required limits of toleration may be wider than this enquiry suggests. There may be other independent arguments for toleration and in some ways the boundaries they dictate may differ from those here indicated. But some alternative arguments are not acceptable if the argument of this paper is sound. Anti-perfectionist arguments are alternatives rather than complementary to ours. The morality whose implications were explored is one which places a very high value on personal autonomy. We saw that such a morality presupposes competitive pluralism. That is, it presupposes that people should have available to them many forms and styles of life incorporating incompatible virtues, which not only cannot be all realized in one life but tend to generate mutual intolerance.

Such an autonomy-valuing pluralistic morality requires a principle of autonomy which will protect people pursuing different styles of life and assure the survival of the options to pursue different forms of life. The principle of autonomy itself generates such a principle of toleration. We explored the limits of the principle which are two. First, it does not protect nor does it require any individual option. It merely requires the availability of an adequate range of options. We saw that this lends the principle a somewhat conservative aspect. No specific new options have a claim to be admitted. The adequacy of the range is all that matters, and any change should be gradual in order to protect 'vested interests'. Secondly, the principle does not protect morally repugnant activities or forms of life. In other respects the principle is a strong one. It requires positively encouraging the flourishing of a plurality of incompatible and competing pursuits, projects and relationships.

It turns out that the boundaries of the autonomy-based toleration are those stated by the harm principle. It allows perfectionist policies so long as they do not require a resort to coercion. Both coercion and manipulation invade autonomy. A morality which values autonomy highly will shun either except where they are required to protect autonomy. The harm principle deserves its place as the liberal principle of toleration not because it is anti-perfectionist, for it is not; but because, as J. S. Mill, its original advocate, and H. L. A. Hart, its leading protagonist in recent times, clearly saw, it sets a limit on the means allowed in pursuit of moral ideals. While such ideals may indeed be pursued by political means, they may not be pursued by the use of coercion (or, as I have mentioned above, manipulation) except in exceptional cases. Those are cases which involve harm and they are exceptional because they typically involve a violation of the autonomy principle. The principle sets a necessary condition only. It does not justify all uses of coercion to prevent harm. But it puts an end to the use of coercion for other purposes.

One last, but crucial ambiguity remains to be resolved. Do these considerations vindicate the wide or the narrow harm principle? The drift of the argument so far shows that if coercion may only be used to protect people's autonomy then the narrow principle is the right one. For 'harm' in the narrow sense is confined to infringement of the conditions of autonomy. But commitment to this conclusion can be justified only if no other moral offence or breach of duty could justify infringement of autonomy. This is tantamount to assigning to autonomy lexical priority in the moral scheme of things. Nothing in this paper justifies this conclusion. Nor has it been the classical liberal position. It has allowed that the prevention of pain may sometimes justify invasion of personal autonomy. If so then the principle to endorse is the wide one.

8

Friendship, truth, and politics: Hannah Arendt and toleration

MARGARET CANOVAN

I

Many of the classic arguments for toleration of intellectual and social diversity share a paradoxical characteristic, which is that when they are stated in their most effective form they edge close to the spirit of orthodoxy. Consider, for example, the relation between truth and the toleration of unorthodox ideas. At first sight it seems clear, as Preston King says, that while intolerance has a natural affinity with faith that we can know the truth, toleration is naturally linked to scepticism.[1] In fact, however (as King goes on to point out), toleration has invariably been defended as a means to the attainment of truth, and the argument is most effective where it is believed that conflict between diverse views will enable truth to emerge as errors are eliminated.[2]

It is not difficult to see why this argument should have been so popular with supporters of toleration ever since Milton, because it neatly pulls the rug from under the supporters of orthodoxy.[3] Since those who wish to enforce uniformity usually justify the repression of dissent by claiming that they already know all the answers, the counter-argument that diversity is the surest road to truth is something of a rhetorical tour de force. Its weakness is that it seems to concede too much to the orthodox desire for consensus, leaving only conditional and temporary reasons for the toleration of diversity. For if it is the case that toleration promotes the discovery of truth, it seems to follow that what we have to look forward to is not an indefinite continuance of diversity, but rather the eventual achievement of a well-founded unanimity. The implication seems to be, that is, that a society in which people's opinions are diverse is

---

[1] Preston King, *Toleration* (London, 1976), 114, 120.
[2] *Ibid.*, 126.   [3] J. Milton, *Areopagitica* (London, 1904), 38, 45.

177

a second best, a temporary means to the unanimity in truth that is ultimately desirable.

Some liberal defenders of diversity have been clearly aware of this implication of their position. For example, Mill admitted that a 'gradual narrowing of the bounds of diversity of opinion' is 'inevitable and indispensable', for 'as mankind improves, the number of doctrines which are no longer disputed or doubted will be constantly on the increase: and the well-being of mankind may almost be measured by the number and gravity of the truths which have reached the point of being uncontested'.[4] Mill was concerned, indeed, about the danger that this progress towards unanimity would turn living truths into dead dogmas, but he did not contest the basic point that the main justification for tolerating diversity of ideas now is to achieve unanimity in the end. He believed that this final solution was a long way off, and deplored Comte's claim that the time for criticism and disagreement was already past, but one is nevertheless left with the impression that what is at issue here is a matter of time-scale rather than anything more fundamental.

Twentieth-century defenders of toleration are much less inclined than their predecessors to capitalise Truth, and much more inclined to lay their stress, as Popper does, on our proneness to error. Even so, it seems difficult for them to avoid the conclusion recently pressed so hard by Habermas, that in so far as communication and the exchange of diverse views is not merely futile, it must point beyond itself to rational agreement on the truth. Even now, it seems, the logic of toleration takes defenders of diversity closer to the spirit of orthodoxy than is entirely comfortable.

A similar paradox can be observed in the relation between toleration of diverse practices and love of humanity. One might expect that tolerance here would be a matter of live and let live, so that intolerance would go with a proselytising zeal to save all mankind, and toleration with an individualistic detachment from one's fellow-men. Compare the dedicated Christian missionaries whose love of humanity wiped out indigenous customs all over the globe with Herzen's ironic comment on the dangers of humanitarianism: 'If only people wanted, instead of saving the world, to save themselves – instead of liberating humanity, to liberate themselves, they would do much for the salvation of the world and the liberation of man.'[5] In practice, however, persuasive arguments for tolerance towards other groups and their alien customs have not relied on

[4] J.S. Mill, *Utilitarianism, Liberty, and Representative Government*, ed. A.D. Lindsay (London, 1910), 103.   [5] In I. Berlin, *Russian Thinkers* (Harmondsworth, 1978), 100.

this cool detachment, but on warmer sentiments of human fraternity, usually culminating in the pious hope that if only people of different groups can be brought into close enough contact to learn from one another, their differences will vanish in universal brotherhood.

Many traditional defences of toleration, that is, betray an unconscious commitment to uniformity which is similar to the outlook of the orthodox save for the important qualification that this uniformity is thought of as something to be achieved gradually and by peaceful means. It is true that voices are occasionally raised within the liberal tradition in defence of sheer diversity for its own sake, but liberals have found it hard to give reasons for this other than aesthetic preference. It is typical that Mill's praise of 'individuality' and 'eccentricity' is never really reconciled with the uniformitarian implications of his notion of progress towards truth, which includes the belief that 'practices' as well as 'wrong opinions' 'gradually yield to fact and argument'.[6] On the whole, the literature gives one the impression that the tolerant and the intolerant disagree about means rather than ends, since the ideal for both is a united mankind living in harmonious brotherhood in accordance with agreed principles.

Historically, these arguments have been effective partly for rhetorical reasons, because they went some way towards reassuring the orthodox. Nevertheless, they retain an unsatisfactory air of somehow missing the point, by failing to articulate why it is that diversity is valuable and ought to be tolerated. Do not most liberal hearts sink at the prospect (however distant) of a united and uniform mankind? But how is it possible to justify this sinking of the heart, if uniformity is what diversity points towards? It is all rather reminiscent of those unsatisfying negative arguments for democracy which depend on showing that none of us is wise enough to rule alone, implying, apparently, that democracy is only a second best that we string along with until the day when a philosopher king arrives. But this parallel suggests that a thinker who has done much in recent times to provide positive arguments for the value of democratic politics – Hannah Arendt – may also be able to shed some light on the dilemmas of toleration. I hope to show that Arendt does indeed have interesting things to say about both of the problem areas we have identified, the relation that is, of diversity to truth and to humanity. On the first of these, whereas most of the great writers of the liberal tradition approached ques-

6 Mill, 82.

179

tions of toleration from a fundamentally intellectual perspective, Arendt looks at similar issues from a specifically *political* point of view, suggesting that the spheres of truth and politics are distinct and in tension. Secondly, in contrast to the ideal of submerging differences in a warm brotherhood of all mankind, Arendt explores notions of public friendship and cool solidarity, again based on a specifically political conception of worldly space between people.

Arendt discussed these issues at many points in her work, but there is one essay in particular concerned explicitly with both: 'On Humanity in Dark Times – Thoughts About Lessing'.[7] In what follows I shall concentrate particularly on this essay, though supplementing the discussion from elsewhere in her writings.

II

When Arendt was invited back to Germany in 1959 to receive the Lessing Prize she was acutely aware of the irony of the occasion. As a Jew she had been forced to flee from her native country in 1933 by a regime that was not prepared to tolerate diversity of any kind, or even, in Arendt's words, 'to share the earth' with people of different blood.[8] Now she found herself summoned by the Free City of Hamburg to receive a prize honouring the memory of that prophet of toleration, Lessing, whom she admired profoundly for his freedom of thought. The address that she delivered on the occasion was an appropriately ironical and allusive piece, in which many themes are interwoven. We shall look in turn at two of them, firstly the relation to truth of the kind of free-thinking Lessing practised, and secondly his understanding of friendship as opposed to fraternity. Let us begin, then, with the issue of free-thought and truth.

One of Lessing's claims to fame is as a controversialist, and he was notorious in his own time for his attacks on orthodox religion. Arendt maintains, however, that his approach to controversy was unusual in that he was not primarily interested in getting at the truth. He was, she says, a polemicist of a peculiarly agile kind, changing his position, sometimes contradicting himself, shifting his ground according to the current state of the controversy. His policy was to attack Christianity when it seemed strong and to defend it when it seemed weak. 'Where everyone else was contending over the "truth" of Christianity, he was chiefly defending its

---

[7] H. Arendt, 'On Humanity in Dark Times: Thoughts about Lessing', in *Men in Dark Times* (London, 1970). [8] H. Arendt, *Eichmann in Jerusalem* (London, 1963), 255.

position in the world, now anxious that it might again enforce its claim to dominance, now fearing that it might vanish utterly.' He was 'taking sides for the world's sake, understanding and judging everything in terms of its position in the world at any given time'. He was less concerned with truth than with freedom – with the 'entirely free thinking' that refuses to be forced to accept a conclusion even by compelling chains of logical argument.[9] Instead, he insisted on thinking for himself – a process, Arendt emphasises, which was not a matter of withdrawing into his own mind, but of moving freely among other thinking men in the public world. The purpose of his arguments was above all to keep this free discussion going:

His thinking was not a search for truth, since every truth that is the result of a thought process necessarily puts an end to the movement of thinking. The *fermenta cognitionis* which Lessing scattered into the world were not intended to communicate conclusions, but to stimulate others to independent thought, and this for no other purpose than to bring about a discourse between thinkers.[10]

In Lessing's play *Nathan the Wise*, the Muslim ruler Saladin challenges the Jew Nathan to declare which of the three religions, Islam, Judaism, and Christianity, is the true one. Nathan replies with the parable of the three rings. Once upon a time a man was given a beautiful ring which had the power to make its wearer pleasing to God and man. At his death, the owner left it to his favourite son, decreeing that he and his descendants should do likewise, and that the wearer of the ring in each generation should be head of the house. Eventually it came to a father who loved his three sons so much that he could not choose between them, but privately promised the ring to each of them in turn. To escape from this embarrassment he engaged a jeweller to make duplicates, so good that he himself could not tell them apart, and gave a ring secretly to each son. When he was dead, each claimed to have the genuine ring, but it was impossible to prove this – just as it is impossible to prove which of the religions handed down by tradition is the true one. The sons appealed to a judge, each swearing that he had his ring direct from his father: but the judge pointed out that since the ring was reputed to make its wearer pleasing to God and man, the true one must have been lost and all three must be imitations. The judge's counsel to the brothers was that each should trust his father,

---

[9] *Men in Dark Times*, 7, 8.   [10] *Ibid.*, 10.

believe his own ring to be the true one, and try to prove this by the manner of his life.

The obvious moral of the parable is that the truth of all the various religions is much too uncertain to justify intolerance. According to Arendt, however, Lessing positively rejoiced in this state of uncertainty. 'He was glad that . . . the genuine ring, if it had ever existed, had been lost; he was glad for the sake of the infinite number of opinions that arise when men discuss the affairs of the world. If the genuine ring did exist, that would mean an end to discourse and thus to friendship and thus to humanness.'[11]

Arendt considered that Lessing's suspicion of single, compelling truth and his concern to promote discourse amongst men indicated his profoundly *political* approach to the world. Instead of approaching issues from the philosopher's point of view and looking for a truth that would transcend opinion, he rejoiced in the 'unending discourse among men' that constitutes political life, and it was precisely this joy in the free movement of discourse that constituted his tolerance.[12] She agrees that his fight against the exclusive claims of religious orthodoxy may seem dated and irrelevant, but suggests that we transpose the issues to the sphere of science. It is generally held that the pursuit of scientific truth is an obligation that overrides the claims of freedom and humanity: but suppose, for example, that scientific evidence were to show decisively that one racial group were inferior to another in some highly valued respect. Lessing's views, says Arendt, would still be that relationships between free men are more important than truth, and that no scientific doctrine, however convincingly proved, could be worth the sacrifice of even a single friendship between two men.

Arendt ends the essay with the claim that Lessing's greatness and his specifically political perspective lie precisely in this 'astonishing lack of "objectivity" ' which enabled him to set discourse and friendship amongst men above truth. The notion of exclusive truth, she concludes, is inhuman – not, as one might at first sight suppose, because it tends to create hostility and to separate people, but, on the contrary, because it brings them too close together: 'because it might have the result that all men would suddenly unite in a single opinion, so that out of many opinions one would emerge, as though not men in their infinite plurality but man in the singular, one species and its exemplars, were to inhabit the earth'.[13]

[11] *Ibid.*, 26. [12] *Ibid.*, 27. [13] *Ibid.*, 31.

III

We shall need to return later to the Lessing essay to explore the other connected theme, friendship, but let us first attempt to clarify what Arendt is getting at in attributing to Lessing this puzzling opposition between truth and politics. One of the main concerns of her political writings was an attempt to defend an authentic understanding of politics against the misleading preoccupations imported by philosophers who were more interested in thought than in action, and she had two reasons for claiming that the traditional ideal of truth threatened authentic politics: truth implies unanimity rather than plurality; furthermore, in the place of freedom it puts coercion, or constraint to accept what has been demonstrated to be true. Now, plurality and freedom are according to Arendt the very basis of the political condition. Human beings are in the first place essentially plural, that is different from one another as well as akin. Arendt often expressed this point by saying that, 'Men, not Man, live on the earth and inhabit the world.'[14] We are plural in the sense that each of us is a person in his or her own right, possessing his or her own viewpoint on the common world that we share. Secondly, we are not only plural but free. That is to say, we are capable of *acting* among our fellows, of taking initiatives, interposing new moves, turning the events that happen amongst us in new and unpredictable directions.

If a political structure is to do justice to these human qualities, it must enable persons to live together without crushing their plurality and freedom. This clearly rules out despotism by one over the rest: less obviously but more significantly, it also rules out Rousseauian (or Habermasian) notions of establishing a General Will to which all unanimously consent, after which they can in effect act as one person.[15] If they are to realise their plurality and freedom, people need to be held together not by a common outlook inside all their minds, but by a common world of institutions that lies outside and between them. Where they are gathered around a public political arena, their common affairs can appear in it and be seen by each person from a different perspective; the citizens can move about amongst one another, talking about public affairs, forming and propounding their opinions in the light of the perspectives of

---

[14] H. Arendt, *The Human Condition* (Garden City, 1959), 9.
[15] See M. Canovan, 'Arendt, Rousseau, and Human Plurality in Politics', *The Journal of Politics*, 45 (1983), 297.

others. In other words, *space* between people is a requirement of satisfactory politics.

According to Arendt, the traditional ideal of truth is unpolitical and anti-political precisely because it threatens this space of free movement. In the place of a constantly changing plurality of perspectives it sets unanimous recognition of the right answer, while in the place of freely chosen opinions it sets arguments which demand assent as the reward of logical proof. It replaces the endless talk of politics with the single voice of all rational men.

It must be admitted, I think, that there is a certain ambiguity in Arendt's position here. Although she continually refers to the 'coercion' inherent in logical reasoning, it often seems that the dangers she has in mind belong not so much to genuine truth as to blinkered deductions from false premises. She often speaks, for example, of the ideological reasoning characteristic of totalitarian movements which imprisons the mind within an arbitrary system, shutting out any sensitivity to the viewpoints of others and the common sense that flows from that sensitivity. Fanatical Nazis and Stalinists seemed to her to be people who had accepted certain premisses – like the Nazi premiss that Jews are inherently inferior to Aryans – and then prided themselves on behaving as much like computers as possible, remorselessly following the implications of these premisses to their ultimate conclusions, no matter how preposterous and inhuman these might be. She suggested in *The Origins of Totalitarianism* that this kind of crazy logic is characteristic of a mass society in which individuals are isolated from one another, so that they cannot move amongst their fellows in a common political world and check their own judgements against the perspectives of others. As Martin Luther had said, 'A lonely man . . . always deduces one thing from the other and thinks everything to the worst.'[16]

She later attributed much the same unthinking, machine-like mental processes to the American military strategists who controlled the war in Vietnam. These also, she claimed, prided themselves on their 'rationality', but succeeded only in following logical trains of thought unchecked by reality and common sense:

One sometimes has the impression that a computer, rather than 'decision-makers', had been let loose in South-east Asia. The problem solvers did

[16] H. Arendt, *The Origins of Totalitarianism* (London, 1967), 458, 469–77. H. Arendt, 'Understanding and Politics', *Partisan Review*, 20 (1953), 287.

not *judge*; they calculated. Their self-confidence . . . relied on the evidence of mathematical, purely rational truth. Except, of course, that this 'truth' was entirely irrelevant to the 'problem' at hand.[17]

These examples suggest that what Arendt is opposing as a danger to free politics and human plurality is often not truth itself (in so far as this is attainable) but rather an *ideal* of truth and certainty that continually tends to distort human affairs. Mesmerised by the notion of absolute truth, people cling to the areas where certainty seems to be attainable (notably logic and mathematics) and ignore or despise the modes of thinking that are actually appropriate to the political capacities of human beings. For politics is a matter of plural opinions rather than a single truth, common sense rather than certainty, persuasion rather than proof, and judgement rather than calculation. If we look a little more closely at what Arendt has to say about political opinion and judgement we shall be in a better position to understand her opposition between truth and politics and her contribution to the defence of toleration.

The picture Arendt paints of the political aspect of the human condition is one of plural persons ('Men' rather than 'Man') moving about amongst one another in a common world which they see from different angles. It is natural for them therefore to form different opinions about their common affairs. These opinions are not simply dictated by interest or ideology, neither are they given and unalterable except where the individuals concerned are isolated from one another. On the contrary, Arendt stresses that opinions are characteristically formed *between* people, in the course of discussion. This plurality of opinions offers the necessary basis for the exercise of political judgement, which is never capable of proof, but is far from being arbitrary or subjective.

Arendt's starting-point in talking about political judgement was Kant's *Critique of Judgement*. This may seem a surprising choice, but Arendt maintained that this book actually contained Kant's real contribution to political philosophy, even though she admitted that Kant himself 'did not recognise the political and moral implications' of his own ideas.[18] Kant was concerned there with aesthetic judgements that are not merely subjective but do not consist in the

[17] H. Arendt, *Crises of the Republic* (New York, 1972), 37.
[18] H. Arendt, 'Truth and Politics', in *Philosophy, Politics and Society*, 3rd Series, ed. P. Laslett and W.G. Runciman (Oxford, 1967), 115; 'The Crisis in Culture: Its Social and Political Significance', in *Between Past and Future* (London, 1961), 219; *Lectures on Kant's Political Philosophy*, ed. R. Beiner (Chicago, 1982), 31.

application of a universal rule, and he suggested that such judgements are made possible by an 'enlarged mentality' which enables one to 'think in the place of everyone else'. To judge properly, one must liberate oneself from a narrowly subjective point of view and take account of the opinions of others.

Precisely the same considerations seemed to Arendt to apply to political judgement. As she put it in an essay entitled 'Truth and Politics',

Political thinking is representative. I form an opinion by considering a given issue from different viewpoints, by making present to my mind the standpoints of those who are absent. . . The more people's standpoints I have present in my mind while pondering a given issue and the better I can imagine how I would feel and think if I were in their place, the stronger will be my capacity for representative thinking and the more valid my final conclusions.

During this process 'our thinking is truly discursive, running, as it were, from place to place, from one part of the world to the other through all kinds of conflicting views, until it finally ascends from all these particularities to some impartial generality'.[19]

The test of political thinking is not 'truth' but 'common sense' – by which Arendt does not mean folksy intuition or populistic consensus, but the firm hold on the many-sidedness of reality that comes from sharing a world with others. It is the direct opposite of the insane logic of a paranoiac who 'lives in a world of his own'. Since judgements of this kind cannot be proved, they can never compel assent. Instead, they are persuasive; as Kant says, they 'woo the consent of everyone else',[20] and there is no question of their ever replacing the diversity of opinions with unanimity. They are themselves, indeed, the fruit of that diversity, of the existence of a plurality of perspectives on the common world. Their lack of compelling proof should not, therefore, be regarded as a reproach against them. Arendt claims, indeed, that statements that *can* be proved 'possess a peculiar opaqueness' compared with this discursive process of political thinking 'in which a particular issue is forced into the open that it may show itself from all sides, in every possible perspective, until it is flooded and made transparent by the full light of human comprehension'.[21]

The things Arendt has to say about political judgement remain highly suggestive remarks rather than amounting to a fully worked

---

[19] 'Truth and Politics', 115.
[20] 'The Crisis in Culture', 222.   [21] 'Truth and Politics', 116.

out theory. Her last book, the tripartite *Life of the Mind*, was to have culminated in a volume entitled *Judging*, but she died just as she was about to start writing it. In any case, as Ronald Beiner points out, her interests had by that time shifted away from concern with the forward-looking prudential judgements involved in action to the retrospective judgements passed by an impartial spectator upon events.[22] Her earlier discussions nevertheless make clear her view that the ideal of absolute, rational truth which has been so influential in Western traditions is thoroughly misleading for politics in that it threatens the space of plurality and freedom within which authentically political thinking takes place. (She maintained elsewhere that this ideal of truth is also misleading for philosophy, since genuinely philosophical thinking produces no results – but that is another story.)

Although Arendt's position is intuitively persuasive, it appears to be open to attack on the grounds that her opposition between the realms of opinion and truth is incoherent. Once one accepts that judgements are corrigible, then one is surely reintroducing the notion of truth into the realm of opinion and judgement, though it is a conception of truth reached by means of discourse rather than via single-track reasoning. Habermas in particular, while acknowledging a profound debt to Arendt, claimed that she did not fully appreciate the implications of her own conception of discourse amongst plural individuals, and that 'an antiquated concept of theoretical knowledge that is based on ultimate insights and certainties keeps Arendt from comprehending the process of reaching agreement about practical questions as rational discourse'.[23] According to Habermas, of course, 'all speech . . . is orientated towards the idea of truth', that is towards 'a consensus achieved in unrestrained and universal discourse'[24] – a position which takes us right back to the point with which I began this chapter, since Habermas's theory is a particularly clear example of the paradox whereby free exchange of opinions is defended on the grounds that it will eventually abolish itself in rational unanimity.

To pursue this issue adequately would be to embark upon alarmingly deep philosophical waters, but there are two points in Arendt's defence which I would like to make briefly here. The first

[22] R. Beiner, 'Interpretive Essay', in *Lectures on Kant's Political Philosophy*, 91.
[23] J. Habermas, 'Hannah Arendt's Communications Concept of Power', *Social Research*, 44 (1977), 22.
[24] J. Habermas, 'Towards a Theory of Communicative Competence', *Inquiry*, 13 (1970), 372.

is a debating point addressed to Habermas's insinuation that Arendt was being merely old-fashioned, since recent developments suggest that her approach may actually be the more up-to-date of the two. She herself made little attempt to defend her paradoxical views on opinion and truth against philosophical objections, but rather similar views have recently been comprehensively defended by Richard Rorty[25] while according to Richard Bernstein it is possible to discern a convergent movement in contemporary philosophy (to which Arendt has contributed) 'beyond objectivism and relativism' to 'the central themes of dialogue, conversation, undistorted communication, communal judgement, and the type of rational wooing that can take place when individuals confront each other as equals and participants'. Bernstein agrees with Habermas that Arendt exaggerated the opposition between truth and opinion, partly because she did not appreciate the degree to which judgement has a place even in supposedly 'objective' fields like natural science. However, he also regards Arendt as a useful corrective to Habermas, in that she is more sensitive to the 'nonreducible plurality of opinions that is characteristic of politics and action'.[26]

Strictly speaking, however, whether or not Arendt's views are coming into fashion in philosophical circles is beside the point. Arendt's strongest defence against Habermas's style of criticism, as I have argued elsewhere, is that his approach is excessively intellectualist, and shares the defects of an entire tradition that has insisted on thinking about politics in terms of philosophical truth.[27] Habermas claims that the possibility of rational agreement between the participants is inherent in communication, and that this possibility can be realised through 'discourse' in which the participants set aside considerations of immediate practical relevance, and prepare to question everything in the search for truth. Clearly, this leisurely search for ultimate principles has very little to do with the problems of forming sound judgements of particular situations in the constantly changing world of politics, for even if such ultimate principles were to be attained, their application in practice would still be a matter of judgement. There is therefore little connection, and no logical implication, between the possibility Arendt points to – that there may be common-sense agreement that a particular political

---

[25] R. Rorty, *Philosophy and the Mirror of Nature* (Princeton, 1980).

[26] R. Bernstein, *Beyond Objectivism and Relativism: Science, Hermeneutics and Praxis* (Oxford, 1983), 221–3.

[27] M. Canovan, 'A Case of Distorted Communication: A Note on Habermas and Arendt', *Political Theory*, 11 (1983).

decision was prudent or imprudent – and Habermas's ideal of establishing general principles that all rational men must accept.[28]

To return from this digression, then, although one may feel that Arendt's terminology of 'truth' versus 'opinion' is in some ways rather misleading, her central point – that the ideal of absolute truth threatens the political space between citizens – is clear enough. There is another area of possible conflict between truth and politics, however, in which (moving, like Lessing, from one side to the other to redress the balance) she felt that it was truth that needed to be defended. The issue here was the vulnerability of accurate information about facts and events, given the far-reaching possibilities of political distortion in the modern world. Dr Goebbels's lying propaganda, Stalin's rewriting of history, the deceptions practised by the U.S. government over the Vietnam war, all brought home this point, which she examined particularly in an essay entitled 'Truth and Politics'.

For the purposes of that discussion she made use of the traditional distinction between rational and factual truth, and where rational truth was concerned she reiterated the point we have already explored, namely that an absolutist ideal of truth is at odds with the diverse opinions that constitute the realm of political discourse. Her main concern in the essay, however, was with facts – true information about what Hitler or Trotsky or Nixon actually did – and with the ways in which they conflict with the demands of politics.

Fundamentally, she says, what sets truth and politics at odds is that truth of any kind is coercive. It is *given*: it makes no concession to conflicting opinions: 'seen from the viewpoint of politics, truth has a despotic character'.[29] She suggested, by contrast, that lying has a strong affinity with the capacity for free action that makes politics possible, because both depend on the ability to imagine that things could be otherwise.[30] Factual truth is under threat not only in totalitarian states but even in free countries, where unwelcome facts are often neutralised not by suppressing them, but by treating them as if they were only opinions which one is free to ignore if one so chooses.[31]

What makes factual information so particularly vulnerable is its contingency. There is nothing self-evident about facts, and what really happened is sometimes much less plausible than what one

---

[28] Arendt's intimations on the subject of judgement have been taken up and carried further by R. Beiner in *Political Judgement* (London, 1983).
[29] 'Truth and Politics', 114.   [30] *Ibid.*, 122.   [31] *Ibid.*, 111.

could make up. (As Jeffrey Archer recently remarked when discussing the implicit rules of writing good political novels, the writer must avoid obviously implausible incidents, such as the entry of an intruder into the Queen's bedroom.) Nevertheless, the factual information that is at the mercy of political pressures is also essential to politics. Realistic, informed political judgement is impossible without it, as even totalitarian rulers tend to discover.

In speaking of the 'non-political and potentially even anti-political nature of truth', therefore, Arendt was certainly not endorsing lying for political ends. What she *was* concerned to do was to defend the space between people within which free politics can be carried on against the vision of unanimity based on undeniable reasoning that is the ideal of so much Western political thinking, including arguments for toleration. But this aspiration to universal truth did not seem to her the only well-meant ideal that threatens free politics. She felt obliged also to defend the space between people against an even more insidious danger: the ideal of fraternity. To see what she had to say about this, let us return to her essay on Lessing.

IV

Arendt's Lessing essay was entitled 'On Humanity in Dark Times': times, as she said, in which the public realm is obscured; in which people do not have the sense of sharing a common world and being able to look at its affairs in the light of a public arena; in which free action and free discussion are impossible. Those who live in such dark times, she says, often come to feel that the world of public affairs and public appearances does not really matter, and, as she puts it, they 'reach behind' the world into a special kind of humanity, a set of close human relationships based on compassion and expressed in fraternity.[32] This warm brotherhood is particularly likely to appear among deprived and persecuted groups who have been forcibly excluded from the world of politics and culture, and Arendt (who was drawing on her own experience among Jewish victims of Nazism) described it in ambivalent terms, as a form of human closeness that produces great warmth but excludes light.

It is as if under the pressure of persecution the persecuted have moved so closely together that the interspace which we have called world . . . has simply disappeared. This produces a warmth of human relationships

[32] 'On Humanity in Dark Times', 11.

190

which may strike those who have had some experience with such groups as an almost physical phenomenon.[33]

Such human warmth, she agrees, is in many ways a marvellous thing, breeding kindness, goodness, and vitality, and by its charm attracting people outside the ranks of the oppressed who seek to share in it through 'that enthusiastic excess in which individuals feel ties of brotherhood to all men'.[34] Fraternity of this sort, however, is irrelevant and misleading in politics. For one thing, it is produced by conditions of persecution and does not outlast them: 'the humanity of the insulted and injured has never yet survived the hour of liberation by so much as a minute'.[35] More seriously, it is bought at the price of 'worldlessness' – lack of participation in a common public realm – and it involves the loss of those capacities that can develop only where plural men can move about freely in a common world and see it from different perspectives: capacities such as common sense, realism, impartiality, and political judge-ment (all of which had been disastrously lacking among the Jews as a result of their history).[36]

In opposition to the seductive vision of fraternity with all its warmth and closeness, Arendt sets a much cooler and more distant relationship which she calls 'friendship' and finds celebrated in Lessing's writings. *Nathan the Wise* is, she says, 'the classical drama of friendship'. This 'friendship' (to which Nathan and Lessing are ready to sacrifice religious truth) should not be understood in terms of the post-Rousseauian ideal of intimates opening their hearts to one another, but as a relationship mediated by talk and argument about public affairs, a sense better understood by the Greeks. Aristotle, for instance, saw 'friendship' among citizens as one of the fundamental bases of the *polis*, and Arendt takes this to mean con-stant talk between citizens about the common political world lying between them, a discourse which itself humanises this common world. The Romans expanded this friendship into *humanitas* when they found that 'in Rome people of widely different ethnic origins and descent could acquire Roman citizenship and thus enter into the discourse among cultivated Romans'.[37]

'Humanity' in this sense is exemplified not in an emotional identification with others but in a 'sober and cool' friendship which allows and requires space between people. It therefore allows room

---

[33] *Ibid.*, 13. [34] *Ibid.*, 16. [35] *Ibid.*, 16.
[36] See Arendt's *The Jew as Pariah: Jewish Identity and Politics in the Modern Age*, ed. R. Feldman (New York, 1978). [37] 'On Humanity in Dark Times', 24–5.

for disagreement and dispute about the affairs of the common world, and does not regard impartial judgement as disloyalty. Arendt remarked that Lessing had found it hard in the dark times in which he lived to find people prepared to be friends with him on these terms: 'where people moved together in order to warm one another, they moved away from him'.[38] She herself continually felt and struggled against 'the excessive closeness of brotherliness' within her own Jewish community, which meant, for example, that her attempt to look coolly and impartially at the trial of Eichmann was very widely regarded as a betrayal of communal loyalty.

The difference between her position and that of most of her fellow-Jews emerged very clearly in an exchange of letters on the subject of *Eichmann in Jerusalem* between her and Gershom Scholem. Scholem accused her of being deficient in '*Ahabath Israel*: "Love of the Jewish people" ', and in *Herzenstakt*. Arendt replied by denying the appropriateness of either in politics: love, she said, makes sense only between individual persons, and not when directed towards collectives such as peoples, while as for *Herzenstakt*, 'the role of the "heart" in politics seems to me altogether questionable'. [39] She added that she had described elsewhere the disastrous political results of displaying private emotions in public, and it will help us to understand her conception of 'friendship' if we explore this aspect of her thought a little further.

As Ronald Beiner has convincingly argued, Arendt's is a politics of 'mediation' rather than 'immediacy' (in striking contrast to Rousseau's, for instance), and the medium which links people together while holding them at arm's length is above all discursive talk.[40] The powerful emotions that unite individuals in private life, such as love and compassion, are out of place in politics because they abolish 'the distance, the worldly space between men where political matters, the whole realm of human affairs, are located'. Such emotions are inarticulate: they do not lend themselves to 'argumentative speech, in which someone talks *to* somebody *about* something that is of interest to both'.[41] Attempts to act on the basis of compassion in politics merely distort the genuine, inarticulate emotion of sympathy with the sufferer into a sentiment of pity. Pity is certainly talkative, but it is dangerously false: it directs itself towards generalised groups rather than real individuals, it comes to be enjoyed for its own sake and therefore exploits its objects, and it

---

[38] *Ibid.*, 30.   [39] *Eichmann in Jerusalem*, 51–4.
[40] R. Beiner, 'Political Judgement', unpublished Oxford D. Phil thesis, 1980.
[41] H. Arendt, *On Revolution* (London, 1963), 81.

provides excuses for all kinds of cruelties. Arendt claimed in *On Revolution* that the French Revolution and its successors had degenerated into tyranny partly because the revolutionaries had been misled by compassion, which turned into a sentimental and shallow pity when they brought it into politics. She quotes a petition addressed to the National Convention: 'Par pitié, par amour pour l'humanité, soyez inhumains.'[42]

In place of this misguided attempt to conduct public affairs on the basis of emotions that can be genuine only in private, she suggested that the proper public equivalent of compassion is 'solidarity'. This is not an emotion, like compassion, or a sentiment, like pity, but a *principle* which establishes 'deliberately and, as it were, dispassionately a community of interest with the oppressed and exploited'.[43] Solidarity is not a matter of immediate identification with a particular sufferer, or of revelling in sentimental pity for the unfortunate, but is a cool, reflective, impartial concern for 'the dignity of man'. Taking its place in the worldly space between people, it allows for discursive talk and can inspire judicious political action.

Like her reflections on opinion and judgement, Arendt's thoughts on compassion, pity, and solidarity are meditations rather than a theory. In *On Revolution* they are developed mainly by means of interpretations of two literary masterpieces, Dostoevsky's story 'The Grand Inquisitor' and Melville's *Billy Budd*, both of which Arendt treats as allegories of the French Revolution. Her analyses are complex and allusive, but the relevant points for our present purposes are clear, and reinforce her views on truth and politics. Where both truth and humanity were concerned, she wanted to defend the political space between people: a space in which there is room to consider different perspectives and reach sound political judgements, and room to stand back from one's immediate feelings and loyalties and strive for impartiality.

V

Let us now try to draw the threads of this discussion together and consider more directly what we can learn from Arendt that will help us in thinking about toleration. As I suggested at the beginning of this chapter, Arendt's approach is unusual. Unlike so many of the saints of liberalism, she does not believe that toleration of diversity

---

[42] *Ibid.*, 85.   [43] *Ibid.*, 84.

will eventually lead to truth and harmony. She had no more in common, however, with that sceptical version of liberalism according to which views and practices are not amenable to debate, and relations between them are a pragmatic matter of power-struggles and economic trade-offs. The distinctive features of her vision of politics are first her conception of 'public space', which holds plural individuals together at the same time as separating them, and secondly her claim that the debate within this public forum is to be seen as something worth engaging in and preserving for its own sake.

What, then, are the implications of this position for questions of toleration? Some of them are obvious enough. Where intellectual freedom and the toleration of intellectual diversity are concerned, for instance, she echoes Lessing in insisting on the intrinsic value of public debate. Her position has equally obvious implications for the toleration of political differences. As we have seen, her claim is that the very nature of politics and the condition of man as a political animal demand diversity. This is not an evil to be endured because the alternatives are worse, but a positive good, constitutive of authentic politics. Toleration of political diversity cannot of course be unbounded, but its limits can themselves be deduced from the nature of politics. For instance, formation of realistic opinions and judgements about public affairs requires access to the facts, and while this is an argument that must be chiefly directed against governments and in favour of freedom of information, it is also an argument for not tolerating blatant distortions of the facts where these can be established. Furthermore, the political condition of plurality and freedom depends upon a commitment by all those concerned to maintain the common political world that guarantees rights as citizens to all of them. Where groups endeavour to destroy that common political world, or refuse to allow certain others to share it, their right to toleration must be forfeit. Arendt concluded her study of the trial of Eichmann with a judgement on him framed in these terms:

just as you supported and carried out a policy of not wanting to share the earth with the Jewish people and the people of a number of other nations . . . no one, that is, no member of the human race, can be expected to want to share the earth with you. This is the reason, and the only reason, you must hang.[44]

[44] *Eichmann in Jerusalem*, 255.

194

The basic principles limiting political toleration are not difficult to elicit, though each particular case must be a matter of judgement, open to discussion and dispute.

Arendt's concepts of plurality and public space do, I think, help us to understand more clearly why it is that the intellectual and political freedom we tend to take for granted are valuable, and why it is worth tolerating unpalatable opinions and attitudes for their sake. As I have stressed, however, her approach is essentially a political one, whereas most of the issues of toleration that we are likely to be concerned about at present are social issues with moral overtones. Arendt did not directly discuss such issues as abortion and vivisection, but her position does have certain implications for contemporary debates.

In order to see what these are, it is important to realise that Arendt's conception of politics as free action and debate within a public space was accompanied by a sharp distinction between politics and society. Both, according to her account, are modes of public existence, in contrast to private life, but whereas in politics citizens are united by the affairs of the public world that lies between them, in society what holds them together is the interdependence of their private wants: their material needs and their life-styles. Society seemed to her inherently conformist and stifling, and one of her most persistent aims was to defend the free space of politics against social pressures.

This distinction between politics and society provides grounds for a wide toleration of social as well as political pluralism. As we have seen, Arendt claims that where a political structure is true to the human condition of plurality and freedom, what holds it together is not that its members resemble one another but that they are gathered around a common public arena. Political unity is therefore compatible with a high degree of social diversity.

When Arendt arrived in America as a refugee, one of the first things that struck her was the immense diversity of social and ethnic groups coexisting within the framework of a single republic. This was in sharp contrast not only to Nazism, which made common blood a condition of citizenship, but to a European political tradition which the Nazis had caricatured and pushed to extremes – the notion that a state needs to be built upon a homogeneity of people, culture and way of life, and is threatened by social or ethnic diversity. The U.S.A. was a visible demonstration that as long as all the various groups shared a commitment to a common political arena, they could be quite different from one another outside that arena, in their social life. Arendt tried to apply this lesson when the Israeli state was founded after the Second World War, arguing that it should not be patterned on the nation states from which the Jews had been driven. What she recommended was a federal structure accommodating both Jews and Arabs and placing the state above ethnicity and religion. Needless to say, her arguments went unheeded.

Arendt's conception of politics as an autonomous sphere therefore allows for a good deal of mutual distancing between politics on the one hand and social arrangements on the other, thereby providing an argument for the public toleration of practices by one group that are offensive to others. One controversial implication of this principle is that some cases of *intolerance* between social groups do not count as political matters either, and are none of the state's business unless they either deprive individuals of their rights as citizens or threaten the continuance of the public arena itself.

In a notorious article published in 1959, 'Reflections on Little Rock', Arendt applied this principle to the black struggle to integrate American schools, then in its early stages.[45] It caused a storm in the American liberal community because Arendt opposed forced integration, thereby apparently siding with Southern racists against all right-thinking people.

Arendt surely took up this position, as she took up many other controversial positions, partly for Lessing's reason – in order to re-dress the balance in a one-sided argument. Her position was quite coherent, however. Distinguishing between politics and society, she set out to look at the issue from a political point of view, focusing upon the principles and interests of the American Republic. It was, she said, quite clearly the duty of the Federal authorities to ensure that all citizens, including blacks, were allowed to exercise their constitutional rights, and therefore the authorities should override Southern rules preventing blacks marrying whites or voting in elections. Having overridden unconstitutional laws, however, and guaranteed the blacks equal citizen rights, the political authorities should, Arendt maintained, keep out of questions of social discrimination, and not risk the stability of the Republic in futile efforts to iron out the differences between social groups. While it is the state's duty to guarantee the citizen a right to marry as

---

[45] H. Arendt, 'Reflections on Little Rock', *Dissent*, 6 (1959).

he pleases, it is none of the state's business to *make* blacks marry whites in the interests of integration: and, similarly, it is not the state's business to make them mix socially, for instance in schools. Social mixing always does involve conformism inside particular groups and discrimination against those outside, and so long as the equal rights of citizens in politics are safeguarded, these social differences are irrelevant.

Arendt's position therefore seems to provide a defence not only of social pluralism, but also of social discrimination by intolerant groups. Unpalatable as her views on this issue may seem, however, it is important to realise that the dilemma involved here is a real and intractable one. Tolerance of social diversity, for instance in the education system, inevitably does to some extent mean tolerance of discrimination, while effective efforts to get rid of that would involve the wholesale intolerance involved in imposing social uniformity. Since toleration means, by definition, not repressing ideas or practices of which one disapproves, it must inevitably have costs, and the implication of Arendt's approach is that when we are deciding in any particular case whether the price is worth paying, there are political as well as moral considerations to be taken into account, for we must consider whether toleration or suppression favours the interests of the free political realm itself.

There is an interesting passage in another essay, 'Civil Disobedience', in which Arendt contrasts the moral individual whose only concern is to live at peace with his conscience with the citizen whose concern is the welfare of the public realm. She quotes Abraham Lincoln, who said that he went to war not to abolish slavery (for all his abhorrence of it) but to save the Union.[46] While her claim that conscience is 'self-interested' may seen unnecessarily provocative,[47] the implication for the present discussion is that there is another context besides moral approval and disapproval within which specific issues of toleration need to be considered, namely our obligation as citizens to safeguard the vitally important realm of free debate and action. This principle is relevant not only to disputes about the toleration of extremist political movements but also to many other cases. Consider, for example, a case where a democratic state is deeply divided over the issue of abortion. A citizen convinced that abortion is wrong might nevertheless oppose legislation by the Moral Majority on the grounds that such

---

[46] *Crises of the Republic*, 61.
[47] G. Kateb, *Hannah Arendt: Politics, Conscience, Evil* (Oxford, 1984).

intolerance threatens the common commitment to the public realm which makes free politics possible. Similarly, an animal rights campaigner outraged at the toleration of cruelty to animals in scientific laboratories, and tempted to take direct action, needs to consider the implications of such law-breaking for the maintenance of the public sphere of free action and discussion.

Clearly, decisions in such cases are matters for political judgement in the light of public debate. This is linked to a final implication of Arendt's approach – an implication unwelcome to philosophers but nevertheless persuasive – which is that where political dilemmas such as the limits of toleration are concerned, we cannot expect to find an agreed philosophical principle that will settle our problems for us. This is not to fall into scepticism and to suppose that there is no point in going on discussing such issues, or to claim with cynical 'realism' that they are always resolved by power struggles between factions. It is to recognise that political debate is neither futile *nor* conclusive: that it issues in political decisions which are ad hoc, contingent and always liable to be challenged: but nevertheless that the process of public debate – for example over where the limits of toleration should be drawn – is something valuable in itself.

Faced with the search for a philosophical answer to our dilemmas, Arendt could perhaps echo Lessing's admission that, given the choice, he would choose the search for truth in preference to the possession of Truth itself. Since constant readjustment of the limits of the tolerable is itself one of the major components of that public debate between plural persons that constitutes politics, the problem of endlessly redefining those limits is perhaps preferable to the discovery of some ultimate principle that would silence the debate for ever, and reduce plurality to uniformity.

9

Dissent, toleration, and civil rights in communism

G. W. SMITH

I

I take it that the typical liberal view of dissent is roughly that the individual citizen has a right to oppose the laws or policies of his state, and that he has a right to express his opposition by attempting to persuade others to share his views, but that he has no right to disobey any constitutionally valid law to which he might happen to object. Nor has he any right to disobey such laws, even if he doesn't happen to object to them, as a way of making a public point or protest against some other aspect of the law or of governmental policy. The position is even more restrictive in that the right to dissent is strictly derivative in the sense that it exists only as embodied in a number of crucial individual or civil rights— freedom of speech, of assembly, of association, and the right to the suffrage. Indeed, the right to vote represents the most vital avenue through which opinion may be translated into actual legal or political reform. Taken together, then, this constellation of rights secures to the individual the right to engage in effective dissent, but no further right to disobedience.[1]

Even so, the liberal more often than not tends to look upon acts of civil disobedience in a markedly lenient manner, in particular by insisting upon distinguishing them from criminal acts and by mitigating the usual sanctions applied to law-breakers. Why? Well, one reason is surely that civil disobedience is, in an important sense, merely an extension of the practice of dissent and is, for the liberal,

I should like to thank both participants in the Morrell Conference on Toleration held in the Department of Politics and Institute for Research in the Social Sciences at the University of York (1985), and staff and students in the Research Seminar in the Department of Political Science, University of Nebraska, Lincoln (1986) for their helpful comments.
[1] The fact that the civilly disobedient are required voluntarily to accept punishment for their actions suggests that they cannot be said to have a *right* to disobey.

grounded in basically the same ethical rationale. For, at least ideally, the agent who takes his civic duties seriously exercises valued powers of individual autonomy in making up his own mind on issues and in employing (and thereby developing) his powers of independent reason and judgement. And as there can be no guarantee that persons exercising these valued powers must always arrive at positions in conformity with whatever happens to be the moral or political orthodoxy of the time, a commitment to the value of dissent implies at least a predisposition in favour of tolerating disobedience (particularly, of course, if it takes a conventionally non-violent 'civil' form). Even so there exists a manifest tension here, between on the one hand considerations of political stability, which preclude any actual right to conscientious disobedience to law, and on the other a form of activity which exemplifies precisely the human capacities and powers which, in the liberal view, ground the value he accords to individual rights.

The usual liberal view of civil disobedience, then, is that it is not something in which the individual has a right to engage, but rather something which deserves fairly positive toleration. Hence, toleration of serious dissent, dissent likely to develop into outright disobedience, flourishes in the penumbra of established rights to freedom of speech, assembly, the suffrage, and so on. That is to say, it is the kind of activity which extends to the limit those values secured by the effective exercise of these individual rights. We might say that toleration of civil disobedience and respect for political dissent flourish best when the moral reasons for recognising individual rights (especially the value of individual autonomy) are clearly understood and more or less widely accepted. This might go some way to explaining why the fate of the dissentient is often so uncertain: it depends at least to some degree on the underlying ethos of the society in which he lives as much as on his formal rights themselves.

If this is correct and the scope of legitimate dissent and of tolerable disobedience is fundamentally determined by a conception of what is involved in respect for the autonomous personality, then the liberal's response to the marxian vision of communism must be significantly affected by the manner in which this value is handled, especially by Marx himself. In particular, we may ask whether the marxian notion of autonomy differs from the liberal ideal, and if so, in what respects. Are the conditions for the development and exercise of autonomy altered in the epochal transformation from capitalism to communism, and if so, how? Does the marxian conception of autonomy imply or presuppose the existence and recognition, in a communist society, of the civil rights the liberal associates with dissent? And, if it does, does it carry the implications for the acceptance of individual dissent and the slightly begrudging toleration of disobedience which are amongst the deepest values of liberalism?

II

Marx never explicitly addresses himself to the question of individual dissent in a well-established communist society – whether it ought to be tolerated, and if so, what its proper limits might be, or through what kinds of practices it might legitimately be expressed. Although it is pretty clear what he thinks should be done with counter-revolutionary dissidents during the post-revolutionary period of the dictatorship of the proletariat, he says nothing about how members of a solidly established communist society should respond to any of their number conscientiously refusing to conform to important norms of communist social practices. His silence can be explained in a number of ways: in part by his pragmatic rejection of the so-called 'utopian' practice of writing blue-prints for future societies; in part by his polemical interest in attacking what he regarded as the politically tendentious concern of liberals for the individual at the expense of the majority. But the reason perhaps most commonly invoked is connected with his views about material abundance in communism and the absence therein of class conflict. The line here is that by abolishing private property in capital and by rationalising production material scarcity will be eliminated and with it the root cause of social conflict – the clash of opposing economic interests. Moreover, in the course of this social transformation, the circumstances which give rise in liberal societies to the problem of individual dissent and raise the question of the limits of toleration will also be removed. For, whereas in class-divided capitalism individual autonomy and social solidarity are necessarily irreconcilable, in communism the social circumstances will be such that, in the exercise of individual autonomy of judgement and choice, agents will face no fundamental obstacles to the achievement of unanimity. Marx is himself perhaps never quite as explicit as this, though some of his followers undoubtedly are.[2]

The element of realism here undoubtedly lies in the view (by no means original with Marx) that important moral and political disputes may often be illuminated by connecting them with the class positions and interests of their proponents. Even so, it is one thing to admit that this may be useful as a guide to understanding disputes in a class society, but manifestly quite another to maintain that it has any relevance to a classless one. For, what reason is there for thinking that differences of this kind can arise only from differences of economic interest? And even if they did, what reason is there for believing that people sharing the same values because they share the same economic position would necessarily order their values in the same schedule of priority? Perhaps it might be replied that such questions cannot arise in a situation of material superabundance, where all needs may be satisfied. But, apart from the fact that this involves invoking one highly utopian belief in support of another, at the very least in any society time will always remain scarce in that opportunity costs have to be borne in any decision.

The intuitive attractiveness of what we might call the 'Coincidence of Interests thesis' lies in the fact that it involves no compromise with, or qualification of, a straightforwardly liberal conception of individual autonomy. The idea is that in communism people will develop and exercise precisely the same capacities and powers of judgement and choice that are held supremely valuable in a liberal society, the only difference being that once the conditions dividing their interests have been eliminated and the veil of false-consciousness and ideology torn aside, they will all spontaneously cleave to the same 'human' values, any differences between them that remain being strictly instrumental and in principle resolvable by non-political, technical, means. It is understandable why, in these circumstances, problems of private conscience and toleration might be thought simply not to arise. The difficulty with the Coincidence thesis lies, however, in its manifest incredibility.

[2] Thus Agnes Heller: in communism 'every individual strives for the same thing . . . and the manner in which decision-making is carried out is of no importance whatever. Whether the decisions are made by means of referendum or through rotating representatives, every individual expresses the needs of all other individuals and it cannot be otherwise. In "socialized" man, the human species and the individual represent a unity. Every individual represents the species and the species is represented in every individual' (*The Theory of Need in Marx* (London, 1974), 124–5).

III

It might well be argued, in defence of Marx, that this reading is simplistic in that it ignores the extent of the *conceptual* transformation which Marx believes will occur in the passage from capitalism to communism. After all, political dissent and civil disobedience are practices which carry with them extensive presuppositions and cannot even be thought without invoking such notions as the state, authority, obligation, and law. But Marx's position is surely that these apparently basic categories, far from being transcendental preconditions of social experience as such, are merely transient features of class societies, destined to disappear with the advent of communism. From this perspective the marxian line is not so much that the problem of toleration is solved by way of the simple, and highly implausible, idea that individual autonomy and social solidarity may be effortlessly integrated as an aspect of the purely economic revolution, but rather that the entire liberal problematic is dissolved by way of a radical reconceptualisation of the whole basis of the relation between the individual and society.

In broad terms the marxian strategy is fairly clear and goes something as follows. Capitalist systems are rent by an irreconcilable division between civil society, the sphere of economic egoism and competition, and the state, the sphere of apparent political altruism and illusory community. Hence the individual cannot but be pulled in contrary directions – towards the assertion of individual independence on the one hand, but also in the direction of political conformity on the other. Hence the unavoidable tension between the conflicting imperatives of individual judgement and public compliance which expresses itself in the typical liberal preoccupation with dissent and disobedience. However, in the transition from capitalism to communism the dichotomy of economics versus politics is dissolved and the entire character of social cooperation between persons redefined by the creation of a completely novel set of social practices. And it isn't simply that individuals will come to live an entirely different form of life in which the tensions marking capitalism have been removed by a merely social transformation. Marx's treatment of religion is perhaps the best clue to follow here. Just as the theologian agonises fruitlessly over the relation of the individual soul to God, so the liberal philosopher strives to define the proper relation between the individual and the state. But in an unalienated, humanly emancipated, society it is not only God and the state which are revealed as

203

projections of ideology and false consciousness; the notion of the individual conscience goes the same way as the idea of the individual soul. For in both cases what is essentially at issue is a fundamental misconception concerning what the 'person' really is. For, in reality, he is neither soul nor conscience, but basically a social individual who finds his being in and through his relations with others. Properly understood, then, the nature of the relation of the individual to his community is such that the problem of individual dissent cannot even be conceived.

In broad terms, then, the alternative to the Coincidence thesis takes the form of the claim that to raise the question of toleration in communist societies is to commit a fundamental category mistake. The difficulty is in making the claim more specific. After all, if Marx learned any lesson from Hegel it was of the futility of attempting to anticipate in thought the development of an entirely novel form of social life – hence his conviction that the outcome of a social transformation on the scale of that between capitalism and communism must be lived through before it can be adequately theorised. Yet by the nature of his radical political commitments Marx cannot acquiesce in the Hegelian corollary, namely that those who make history cannot understand it. His ambition to unify theory and practice results in his thought being caught in a basic tension between his insistence on the novelty of the social arrangements of communism (and hence of the nature of personality therein) in contrast with anything with which we might be familiar and his need to furnish at least some kind of picture of the society towards which the proletariat is to strive. Indeed, to raise the question of the fate in communism of the liberal practices of civil dissent and toleration perhaps serves to highlight this tension as clearly as anything can.

IV

What I want to do now is to approach this issue by considering two attempts to articulate the transformation of the liberal notion of the individual as an autonomous bearer of rights into the idea of a social individual. The first is that offered by Evgeny Pashukanis in his book (first published in 1929 and reissued in English in 1978) *Law and Marxism.*[3] The second is an account developed from Gerry Cohen's interpretation of the Marxian 'dialectic of labour'.[4]

---

[3] Ed. C. Arthur (London, 1978).

[4] G. A. Cohen, 'Marx's Dialectic of Labour', *Philosophy and Public Affairs*, 3 (1974), 235–61. (A similar argument can be found in his *Karl Marx's Theory of History: A Defence* (Oxford, 1978), ch. 1.)

The nub of Pashukanis' position is that the individual, understood in the way the liberal conceives of him – as an autonomous bearer of individual rights – is nothing more than a historically temporary phenomenon, a function of capitalism. Consequently, when capitalism is finally abolished, the liberal conception of the individual will necessarily evaporate along with it and will be replaced by a categorically different conception of man. The 'Evaporation thesis', as we may call it, pivots upon an analogy between the abstract commodity form which productive values take in capitalism and the abstract form of the legal individual. According to Marx, goods produced for exchange must all be capable of falling under a common measure in terms of which they can be seen to exchange equal value for equal value. But between all the variety of specific things actually produced for exchange there can be found only very general or abstract similarities. Hence the fact that things are produced for exchange means that they can be identified as commodities only in the most abstract way. Marx of course maintains that commodities have their values measured in terms of the amount of socially necessary labour required to produce them, i.e. in terms of the amount of average labour-time embodied in their production. Commodities are thus essentially abstract values, detached from the specific circumstances of their production and from the concrete circumstances of their consumption.

And so, argues Pashukanis, with the bourgeois individual. As exchange requires abstraction in relation to things exchanged, so likewise it requires abstraction in respect of the agents who do the exchanging. A system of commodity exchange necessarily rests upon the practice of contractual agreement between agents who must be characterised in similarly abstract terms precisely because the operations of the market demand a set of conditions which enable reciprocal agreements to be made which are generally enforceable by authority. Hence the inevitability within the market system of the abstract individual – the bearer of individual rights (especially, of course, of the right to own property) – assumed to be self-interested, free to engage with anyone on the basis of reciprocity, and presumed to be capable of legal responsibility for his acts and omissions. In other words, the autonomous bearer of rights, the liberal paradigm of the 'person', is, according to Pashukanis, by no means a natural phenomenon; neither are his credentials grounded in any objective moral imperative. On the contrary, his identity is merely the result of a set of social stipulations embedded in practices required for the functioning of a system of abstract market

205

exchanges. A system which has as its main rationale, of course, the exploitation of labour.

According to the doctrines of marxism, exploitation can be abolished only by the elimination of the system of commodity exchange – both the elimination of the market in products and labour-power and of the social identity of the agents who traffic in them. Hence, Pashukanis insists, the necessary extinction of the abstract individual, the bearer of individual rights. Who takes his place? Well, just as production in socialism is detached from the demands of the market and devoted to the satisfaction of particular needs, so the individual is extricated from the system of exchange relationships, in which he appears simply as an abstract legal personality, and is recognised in all his concrete specificity and uniqueness. What Pashukanis has in mind here is perhaps best brought out in his treatment of criminality.[5] The liberal attitude to punishment, he argues, reflects the presuppositions of the exchange economy. In a bourgeois system of justice the judicial aim is to find the precise abstract equivalent to be extracted from the offender as reciprocal payment for the wrong done – so many years for this offence, so many for that. Though an offender might be found non-responsible for his act, and this will affect the penalty, the general presumption in bourgeois civil law – that the individual is responsible for his actions – is carried through into the criminal jurisdiction. In socialism, however, though individuals may act in such a way as to pose a 'social danger', they will be dealt with as a managerial rather than as a legal problem. What does this mean? It means basically that the aim will not be to find some general rule of criminal responsibility under which the offender can be punished; instead he will be treated as a concrete individual whose social deviancy arises from a specific constellation of social circumstances, and who is therefore in need of individually tailored reform or re-education. The deviant in communism is a whole person who must be treated 'scientifically' in relation to the totality of the specific social and psychological causes of his deviancy – i.e., to use Pashukanis' phrase, in 'Medical-ethical' terms. 'Due process of law', as the liberal understands it, is a right only of abstract and alienated individuals – the activities of the lawyer and the judge give way to the ministrations of the psychiatrist and sociologist.

All this must, of course, strike the liberal as being pretty sinister, particularly in the light of the uses to which criminal psychiatry has

---

[5] *Law and Marxism*, ch. 7.

in fact been put in the U.S.S.R.[6] But Pashukanis' proposals are perhaps equally remarkable for their pathos. The discussion of the abstract individual of liberalism, when taken together with Marx's views concerning the revolution in social relations (and hence in the nature of personal identity) involved in the transition from capitalism to communism, promises an entirely novel conception of individuality. But the outcome is disappointing. For what we are in fact offered is a familiar rehash of basically eighteenth-century Enlightenment materialism, according to which men are 'creatures of circumstance', incapable of autonomy and therefore not responsible for their actions. Hence the 'managerial' approach to the social deviant – he must be retrained or reconditioned, either medically or educationally, into new patterns of socially orthodox behaviour. It is difficult to avoid the impression that Pashukanis' 'new man' of communism isn't more of a man because he is treated concretely and in the round rather than abstractly; on the contrary, he is treated on the basis of a set of categories which imply that he is in reality less like a man and more like an animal.

V

The reader of *Law and Marxism* may well feel that we are faced with a stark choice: either liberal individualism, with its notion of the abstract bearer of rights and its commitment to a narrowly juridical treatment of persons, or socialist collectivism, with its view of the concrete individual, enmeshed in a net of social circumstances and subject to the attentions of scientific experts in deviancy. It may be argued, however, that Pashukanis displays a peculiarly one-dimensional view of capitalism and its effects; a view, moreover, by no means obviously Marx's own.

There is perhaps a tendency to come away from Marx with the conviction that he is prepared to reject capitalism root and branch as the worst possible form of social system short of actual slavery, as an absolute and unmitigated decline even from feudal circumstances of labour, a condition unrelieved by any redeeming features at all, except possibly by the fact that it is the necessary precursor and cause of a proletarian revolution, and therefore of a society entirely purged of all signs of its predecessors. But it is no longer plausible to say that Marx regarded capitalism in a totally negative way, even in respect of its constitutive values. A number of recent commen-

---

[6] See e.g. S. Bloch and P. Reddaway, *Russia's Political Hospitals* (London, 1977).

tators on Marx, amongst whom G. A. Cohen is perhaps the most influential, have argued that Marx did not regard the labour of the Victorian factory as an unqualified decline from the circumstances of feudal and craft labour, nor did he think that capitalism was merely a slate fit only to be wiped clean. In a brilliant essay Cohen argues that it is fruitful to see Marx's three great social epochs, feudalism, capitalism, and communism, as forming a dialectical triad. According to Cohen's interpretation 'a subject undergoes a dialectical process if it passes from a stage where it is undivided from some object, through a stage where it divides itself from it in a manner which creates disunity, to a stage where distinction persists but unity is restored'.[7] These three stages he terms 'undifferentiated unity – differentiated disunity – differentiated unity'. And the three categories, when applied to social forms, produce three types or stages of social relationships, stages characterised by 'engulfment', 'separation', and 'community'. The three stages are instantiated in the three epochs – feudalism, capitalism, and communism.

Cohen applies his schema to Marx's theory of labour. On its positive side, the alienation of labour in capitalism represents the extrication of the individual from the engulfing tradition and custom of feudal craft labour, releasing the worker from the ties of narrow economic relationships. On its negative side, however, it also alienates him from all social responsibilities and results in a social condition of disunion and detachment. Communist conditions of labour, on the other hand, recapture the essentially social nature of feudal production, but in circumstances which incorporate the universality and autonomy gained through the capitalist productive experience, and hence achieve a form of social production which unites a sense of individual autonomy with a sense of the essentially social nature of productive individuality. Cohen confines himself to Marx's theory of labour, but it is by no means impossible to extend the approach to Marx's critique of political liberalism and individual rights, especially as we find it developed in the 1843 work *On the Jewish Question*.[8] For, in this piece, Marx makes two sets of very interesting contrasts, between feudal and bourgeois political institutions on the one hand, and between the rights of man and the rights of the citizen on the other. Though (perhaps for the methodological reasons alluded to earlier) Marx

---

[7] 'Marx's Dialectic of Labour', 237.
[8] In *The Writings of the Young Marx on Philosophy and Society*, ed. L. D. Easton and K. Guddat (New York, 1967), 216–48; and see R. Keat, 'Individualism and Community', in J. Mepham and D. H. Ruben (eds.), *Issues in Marxist Philosophy*, 4 (Brighton, 1981).

never elaborated his position, the perspective on individual rights sketched here suggests that there might be room for individual dissent even in the materially and conceptually revolutionised conditions of an established communist system.

The first contrast goes briefly as follows. In feudalism, the relation between the individual and the state is 'immediate' or 'direct' in the sense that political and legal rights and liberties are attached directly to economic function and social status. Each trade, craft, occupation, or social rank is accorded a distinct and corresponding political identity: an arrangement exemplified in the feudal 'estates', where various socio-economic groups 'represent' their particular interests to the prince. But though political alienation is absent in feudalism, the effect of the immediate link between the individual and the state is merely to confirm the former in the narrowness and particularism of his economic function or social status. In being associated directly with the state through the avenue of socio-economic rights, the individual is, to use Cohen's terms, 'engulfed' by its particularism. That is to say, the self-identity of the feudal individual is primarily that of the occupier of a socio-economic role, and not that of an individual citizen of a universal state. Marx doesn't specify a feudal conception of liberty as such but it presumably may be said to be a matter of possessing status privileges – the rights of the guildsman, the cleric, the landowner, and so forth.

However, just as the onset of capitalism dissolves the engulfment of the individual in rural or craft labour, liberating him from the mental and moral stagnation of tradition and precedent, so the advent of liberalism corrodes the related feudal political forms. The alienation of wage labour is accompanied by alienation in political life.[9] In one respect this is undesirable: the economic and political alienation expressed in the associated political and legal institutions and practices of the bourgeois state imply frustration and conflict for the individual. But each has a positive side too. Just as feudal craft labour had to be destroyed for the labourer to develop his universal productive powers, so liberal political forms guarantee the individual a universality unknown to feudal man. For the developed liberal state ensures to all its citizens without distinction

---

[9] Thus 'The political revolution . . . *abolished* the *political character* of *civil society*. It shattered civil society into its constituent elements – on the one hand *individuals* and on the other the *material and spiritual elements* constituting the vital content and civil situation of these individuals . . . A *particular* activity and situation in life sank into a merely individual significance, no longer forming the general relation of the individual to the state as a whole.' *Ibid.*, 235. Italics in the original.

identical civil rights and liberties, irrespective of their differing economic or social positions. Political and legal rights thus cease to be attached to economic function or social status, which are relegated henceforth to the private sphere of civil society. Hence Marx recognises what many marxists, including Pashukanis, apparently ignore, namely that political liberalism represents a real advance in self-consciousness over feudalism. For, through the possession of these individual rights, the citizen is able to extract himself from the web of feudal social relations and from the feudal political state of mind. He can come to see himself and others in the political sphere as *individuals* – independent, self-directed, all equally bearers of rights. Not the particular rights of the cleric, or of the guildsman, but the universal rights of *man*.

But though Marx clearly presents this as a vital historical advance in human self-consciousness, it none the less in his view remains defective, in two main respects. Firstly, the sense of autonomy and individuality is achieved only at a cost, namely by abstracting political and legal freedom from the concrete circumstances of civil society, where inequality and particularism remain. Indeed, the effects of these circumstances are exacerbated because they are now untrammelled by any restraints of custom or political duty. Secondly, the rights thereby formally guaranteed by the state are in fact rights which are incompatible with genuine social unity. Admittedly, individuals in capitalism enjoy the universal rights of man rather than the particularistic rights of the landowner or the charter-holder, and this affords scope for the exercise of individual autonomy otherwise denied to them. But a common enjoyment of formally universal rights cannot ensure social unity, for the rights of man sustain and protect institutions and practices within civil society which are, to Marx's mind, manifestly anti-social. Marx's opinion of the typical liberal rights to private property, to privacy, to religious conscience and so on is that 'none of the so-called rights of man goes beyond the egotistical man, withdrawn into himself, his private interest and private choice and separated from the community as a member of civil society'.[10] To use Cohen's terminology once more: feudal political engulfment only gives way to liberal detachment (political alienation) and not to genuine community. For, though liberal rights undoubtedly represent an advance over feudal privileges – they are after all rights accorded to

---

[10] *Ibid.*, 236–7. And 'liberty as a right of man is not based on the association of man with man but rather on the separation of man from man. It is the right of this separation, the right of the *limited* individual limited to himself.' *Ibid.*, 235. Italics in the original.

all men equally, thus enabling them to develop and sustain a sense of their universality – they do so only abstractly, in the sense that they remain divorced from the concrete realities of actual economic life in capitalism. They are, in addition, anti-social and hostile to community in that they merely reflect the contradictions of a competitive economic system.[11]

Is there any place, then, in Marx's conceptual universe for a set of individual rights which are both universal and concrete – rights which could be presented as the dialectical reconciliation of individuality and community? There are two obvious difficulties facing any such programme. The first is Marx's rejection elsewhere in his writings of juridical and political practices as forms historically restricted to class societies and hence necessarily absent in communism. How, we may ask, are individual rights possible if rights *tout court* are impossible? In this regard it is perhaps worth distinguishing what Marx says about distributive rights (rights of justice) and civil rights. In his most outright rejection of rights in the 'Gotha Programme' Marx in fact confines himself to attacking the former, objecting to them on the grounds that, in a society where scarcity and selfishness have been transcended, rules of justice, that is to say rules for distributing goods between competing claimants, are simply redundant. Leaving aside the tenability or otherwise of his position, this clearly need not apply to individual civil rights, which are not distributive.[12] The second difficulty arises from Marx's rejection of the whole dimension of the 'political', even in *On the Jewish Question*, where he is quite explicit – 'Only when he has recognised his own powers as *social* powers, so that social force is no longer separated from him as *political* power, only then is human emancipation complete.'[13] If the political realm disappears with the advent of communism how can there be any prospect of, so to speak, 'distilling' the rights characteristic of feudalism and capitalism into an entirely novel form combining universality and concreteness?

In respect of this difficulty it is perhaps worth remembering that in the 1840s Marx was by no means alone in advocating the abolition of politics. The French Positivists and Proudhon envisaged a similar prospect. They equate politics with government and government with the coercion and exploitation of the governed,

---

[11] For an illuminating discussion of this aspect of Marx's position see also R. Keat's 'Liberal Rights and Socialism', in K. Graham (ed.), *Contemporary Political Philosophy: Radical Studies* (Cambridge, 1982).   [12] See e.g. A. Buchanan, *Marx and Justice* (London, 1982), ch. 5.
[13] *On the Jewish Question*, 241. Italics in the original.

and they foresee the abolition of politics through the establishment of a society characterised by voluntary cooperation and social harmony. But, for them, this by no means implies a society bereft of rules or laws; only one without laws enforced in the interests of one class against others by state power. Now, both feudalism and liberalism are, in Marx's view in *On the Jewish Question,* 'political' in this fairly specific sense. Each frustrates the human 'species capacity' for uncoerced social cooperation, with the result that social unity is either rendered impossible (as in the feudal state, which remains a mere aggregation of particular interests without ever attaining universal sovereignty) or spurious (as in the abstractly universal political state of liberalism). Whereas feudal rights are commendably concrete, in that they give direct expression to the actual economic circumstances of those who hold them, they do so in a particularistic manner, a manner which precludes any achievement of social unity – for in relation to others the feudal individual remains privileged, rather than a person united with others in the common enjoyment of the same rights. Liberal rights, on the other hand, are commendably universal, but this is achieved only by abstracting the individual from his concrete and divisive economic circumstances, and hence they can do no more than offer an illusion of social unity. According to this reading, then, the nub of Marx's claim about the achievement of 'social' powers in communism involves the key idea that the concreteness characteristic of feudal rights will be combined with the universality of liberal rights to produce a social framework within which individuality will be able to flourish without need for the coercion required to protect earlier forms of rights which, in the one way or the other, deny man's human essence.[14]

This, in broad terms, is the programme implied by what we might call the 'Distillation of Rights' thesis, undoubtedly a much more humane position than that represented by Pashukanis'

---

[14] Thus schematically:

Undifferentiated Unity (feudalism)
Status rights: concrete particularity: political engulfment
Differentiated Disunity (liberalism)
Rights of Man: abstract universality: political separation
Differentiated Unity (communism)
Rights of social man: concrete universality: social unity
(Any attempt to impute such a line to Marx without a great deal more argument would be rash. It is offered here merely as a way of sympathetically illuminating what must surely be seen as one of Marx's main theoretical ambitions – namely to characterise a society which can accommodate *both* individuality *and* social unity.)

'Evaporation of Rights' thesis and philosophically less naive than the 'Coincidence of Interests' theory. But is it tenable? Firstly we may ask precisely what kinds of individual rights would notionally be encompassed by this argument. Clearly, the egotistical and divisive 'rights of man' are excluded. But, as was mentioned earlier, Marx distinguishes two species of rights: the rights of man and 'citizen rights'. In Marx's view the former may be reduced to one basic one – the right to private property, an exclusive and unsocial right expressive of alienation. However, he also says that liberal constitutions provide for '*political* rights that can be exercised only in community with others. *Participation* in the community constitutes their substance.' [15] Although he is extremely cryptic about what these are it seems fairly clear that Marx is thinking mainly of the democratic aspects of liberalism, especially the universal right to vote – a right enshrined in all developed liberal constitutions, but none the less one consistent with (indeed necessary for) the achievement of genuine social unity. In this regard it is worth noting that the right to the suffrage has a number of significant features: (1) As it is a right which can be consistently ascribed universally to all individuals irrespective of their particular economic functions, it can (unlike the rights of man) survive the abolition of economic inequality. (2) The elimination of such inequality is indeed necessary, for then the vote can be used effectively rather than (as in capitalism) as a fairly meaningless ritual by the great majority of the poor. (3) The right can be exercised universally, i.e. one person's exercising his right to vote in no way impedes the exercise of the same right by others. (4) Its exercise is thus at least formally consistent with the maintenance of social harmony. (5) Hence it seems fairly plausible to say that the suffrage, exercised under the material conditions of genuine economic equality, may be seen as representing a dialectical achievement, the reconciliation of individual

---

[15] *On the Jewish Question*, 233. Italics in the original. *cf* Ruth Anna Putnam's claim at the one extreme with Alasdair MacIntyre's at the other. Putnam: 'Perhaps this [i.e. the 'fact' that the socialist's basic theory of persons and of society is incompatible with the theory which underlies the liberal tradition] is seen most clearly when one considers the theory of alienation found in the writings of the young Marx. One could add to the traditional list of rights . . . the right not to be alienated? The suggestion is absurd. Rights are the prized possessions of alienated persons.' 'Rights of Persons and the Liberal Tradition', in T. Honderich (ed.), *Social Ends and Political Means* (London, 1976), 102. MacIntyre: 'Marx was throughout his career a radical democrat, who believed that all that was wrong with the liberties of bourgeois parliamentary regimes was that their enjoyment was effectively restricted to a minority and who wished all to enjoy the liberties of that minority', *Marcuse* (London, 1970), 59.

autonomy (displayed in and through the exercise of individual rights) and social unity.

But it may be thought that even assuming that the right to vote can be interpreted in this way, this cannot itself satisfy the liberal concern about the prospects for political dissent in a communist society. For crucial here, as we have seen, are the allied rights to freedom of speech, to civic association and political assembly and so on, which reflect the value typically placed by liberals upon the opportunity for the individual to develop and display his autonomy of judgement and choice, and which constitute the conceptual framework within which the liberal view of toleration makes sense. Of course, Marx might reasonably be thought to expect that communism, being an economically and socially far more homogeneous society than capitalism, will not experience the kinds of exhibitions of individual disobedience which often occur in liberal systems. In considering just how far to carry their dissent, disaffected members of a communist society (if such there be) might well be thought to be inhibited by a strong sentiment of loyalty to the democratic practices of their system. Moreover, and more significantly, the communist's conception of the nature of his own autonomy might well be very different from that of the liberal dissentient. He may well feel himself to be an intrinsic part of his society in a kind of intimate way that the liberal may well find difficult to understand. Indeed, the very boundaries of the self may be conceived in a much wider and more social manner: communist man might not even identify himself as an 'individual', at least as we now understand the term. It is not at all easy to be specific about the change in self-consciousness involved here, precisely because we are probing an entirely novel form of life.[16] But even so, it can scarcely be argued seriously that individuality (whatever form it takes) could be preserved in a system which, whilst recognising the formal right to the suffrage for all, denied the rights of free speech, association, and assembly.[17] The essential question, then, is not whether these associated rights are implied by 'community', understood as the dialectical transcendence of feudal engulfment and bourgeois alienation, but whether the existence of these rights in communism

[16] For an attempt to elucidate the idea of personality in communism see my 'Marxian Metaphysics and Individual Freedom', in Marx and Marxisms, ed. H. Parkinson (Cambridge, 1982), 229–42.

[17] Thus Lord Acton expresses the basic liberal conviction when he identifies recognition of the right of free speech as the essence of the democratic credo. See 'The History of Freedom in Antiquity', in The History of Freedom and Other Essays (London, Macmillan, 1907), 1–29.

carries the same implications for the *recognition of dissent* and for the *toleration of disobedience* as it does in liberalism.

VI

It is often said that there are two main ways in which social cohesion may be maintained. One, the liberal way, is to focus loyalty upon the institutions and practices which are designed to moderate and conciliate, without eliminating, differences of interest or disputes over ethical, religious, or political principles. This is the approach of political pluralism. Central here are the procedures of the law and of the courts. Procedural fairness and justice are the main values around which a liberal society coheres. The other model of social cohesion is to seek consensus, not in a common commitment to procedures, but by way of allegiance to some substantive goal or value. Whereas in a liberal society individual dissent is accepted as a natural or inevitable incident in political life, in an end-directed or 'enterprise' society dissent from its constitutive values is often regarded as representing an attack on the society itself. Typically, communism is, of course, seen as a system in which the procedures of law are discounted in favour of social organisation for the realisation of a common end – the achievement of the values implied in Marx's picture of man as a 'species-being'. From this point of view the idea that a communist society could accommodate the rights implied in the 'Distillation of Rights' thesis, and hence afford a sphere of toleration of dissent, may well seem unlikely. On the other hand, in the light of the foregoing argument, it might be thought that this is misleading. Could there not be a third form of society, one which would reconcile the recognition of individual rights and individual autonomy with the idea of a common commitment to a substantive principle of social living?

The attractions, and the dangers, of this possibility are perhaps best exemplified in Hegel's political philosophy. For Hegel clearly aims at a society which is designed to reconcile individual rights with the achievement of a particular substantive vision of the good life for man. The tensions involved in this project reveal themselves particularly clearly, however, in his treatment of individual conscience.[18] On the one hand, he insists that the rational state must recognise the right of conscience in the name of freedom and autonomy. However, conscience comes for Hegel in two very

[18] *The Philosophy of Right* (Oxford, 1967), 91–2.

different varieties: 'formal' and 'true'. Formal conscience amounts to nothing more than the expression of a purely 'subjective' and capricious will; whereas true conscience is equated with the 'ethical disposition' and with subscription to the substantive principles embodied in the state. In effect Hegel manipulates his definitions in such a way that the rights of conscience can never be exercised in such a way as to bring the individual into serious collision with the 'rational' state.[19] For genuine independence of judgement, that is to say judgement which could put the individual at odds with the state, is necessarily devalued as 'subjective' and defective from the higher point of view of dialectical rationality. The effect is to invest individuals, not with rights but rather with pseudo-rights. For rights which evaporate at precisely the point at which they are needed to guarantee the individual agent freedom against the state are clearly not really rights at all. Indeed, the only place where Hegel is willing to permit the genuinely free exercise of individual judgement and choice as the liberal understands it is in the inferior sphere of civil society– where it takes the politically innocuous form of freedom of contract and the career open to talents.

There is, of course, nothing about the liberal view of individual rights that requires that right-bearers must always, or even usually, be claiming, defending or enforcing them. A morally solidaristic community, in which individuals rarely stand on their rights because they don't need or don't want to do so, is logically an entirely intelligible liberal idea. But, at the very minimum, the liberal will insist that before someone can properly be described as a bearer or possessor of rights, he must be *capable* of claiming or exercising them on the appropriate occasions. Like Hegel, the liberal thus links the capacity for autonomy with the capacity for rights. A crucial difference arises, however, over the question of the *identification* of the capacity for rational autonomy. To put it baldly, whereas Hegel identifies the capacity for rationality with subscription to specific substantive principles of 'ethical life', the liberal characterises the autonomous agent in terms of formal criteria consistent with the possibility of autonomous dissent. Typically, the liberal strategy has been to circumvent controversy over definitions by simply stipulating some conventional index of rationality, for example in respect of the right to the vote (which gains the

---

[19] 'When I will what is rational, then I am acting not as a particular individual but in accordance with the concepts of ethics in general ... in doing a perverse action, it is my singularity that I bring onto the centre of the stage. The rational is the high road where everyone travels, where no one is conspicuous.' *Ibid.*, 230.

individual a place in the forum with the right to have his voice heard), the absence of 'dependent' or 'servile' status, a property qualification, eligibility for military service, or latterly simply legal majority. Within the ranks of citizens formally so defined the liberal approach is simply strongly to presume the existence in individuals of a capacity for rational autonomy and to permit the presumption to be defeated only by a short list of conditions, for instance insanity. In particular, precisely because he believes that there is no one form of life which can be rationally demonstrated to be superior to all others, and hence necessarily the preference of all rationally competent agents, he will refuse to include in his list of defeating conditions reference to specific substantive ethical or political values.[20]

Should we regard Marx's 'citizen's rights' as being logically more akin to Hegel's pseudo-rights of conscience or to the liberal's conception of individual rights? On the basis of the dialectic of rights intimated in *On the Jewish Question* we must assume that Marx's position is that a full right-bearer must be an autonomous agent capable of rational judgement and choice, and hence the crucial question concerns not whether Marx is prepared to countenance the idea of a right of conscientious dissent but rather the criteria for identification of rational autonomy. Although Marx is almost entirely silent on the question of the status of agency in communism, it is possible to attempt some tentative comment on this question by way of a modest extrapolation from his view of the nature of autonomy in class society and of the effects of ideology upon the capacity of rational judgement.

The first point to note is that Marx's conception of rational autonomy is but one element within an internally complex conception of freedom. Persons who are free from alienation and exploitation are free in three distinct but related senses. They are (1) free from the frustrations characteristic of capitalist production, (2) free to choose what kind of life to live, and (3) free to live the 'truly human' life of communism. In effect, Marx runs three analytically distinct notions of freedom in troika, so to speak: 'psychological freedom' – freedom to do what one wants; 'social freedom' – freedom to choose between socially available options; and 'ideal freedom' – the attainment of human self-realisation. Now it is true that, even in his maturity, Marx believed that the immiserating con-

---

[20] The contrast is elegantly articulated by R. Dworkin in his 'Liberalism' in S. Hampshire (ed.), *Public and Private Morality* (Cambridge, 1978).

ditions of capitalist production would compel the working class to develop its powers so that it would eventually put itself in a position to reject capitalism and opt for socialism, and that when given the opportunity it would actually choose the latter. However, he was also of course much alive to the circumstances in capitalism which might limit the horizon of perceived possibilities for the proletariat, and which might corrupt its values. For the tendency of bourgeois ideology is always to engender compliance in the working class. Hence, for succeeding marxists if not for Marx himself, the theory of ideology has furnished a ready source of explanations for the lack of proletarian militancy and communist consciousness.

Given the three-fold nature of freedom, we can see Marx as implicitly extending the range of influences which can undermine an agent's autonomy of choice (i.e. (2)) from the basic liberal set of outright censorship, indoctrination, and propaganda, to include more indirect and insidious factors such as ideologically constricted ideas about what is possible or practicable in the way of social change, culturally specific conceptions of human nature, its powers and needs, and the general effect of social atmosphere and ethos upon the subject's self-image and upon his understanding of the range of desirable and realisable alternatives to the bourgeois status quo.[21] In effect, then, the assumption that individuals choose autonomously becomes defeasible by reference to an entirely new dimension of conditions, defined largely of course in terms of Marx's conception of 'normal' human nature and 'normal' social circumstances.

Clearly, the longer the list of disabling conditions on autonomy, the less tenable the original presumption in its favour. In particular, given the assumption that human beings have certain distinctive and characteristic needs and purposes which can be fully satisfied only in communist society, there must exist a fairly strong and persistent theoretical pressure to explain apparently willing compliance with capitalism by workers by appeal to the effects of 'unnatural' social influences upon their capacities of judgement and choice. In one respect this may simply give rise to what might be considered to be a perfectly proper attempt to seek otherwise elusive causes of false consciousness by taking the theory as a guide for empirical investigation. But if the grip of the theory prevails it may simply be used to license the imputation of such influences in the absence of empirical backing. If this occurs autonomy ceases to

---

[21] See S. I. Benn and W. L. Weinstein, 'Being Free to Act, and Being a Free Man', *Mind*, LXXX (1971), 194–211.

be a matter of the ability to choose between alternatives (i.e. (2)) and becomes identified with one particular preference or option – namely that specified as rationally desirable in the theory of human nature underlying the 'ideal' element in the portmanteau notion of freedom (i.e. (3)).

The pressure on marxists to take this line when faced with the problem of proletarian passivism may be resistible (though elsewhere I have argued that other factors, internal to marxian theory, must push clear-minded and consistent marxists in this direction).[22] Clearly, however, it must be resisted if anything like a liberal conception of autonomy is to be preserved even in a modified form in marxian theory and the notion of the individual as a bearer of effective rights is in any way to be carried over into the socio-political practices of communism. The danger here, however, is clearly that the strategy developed to handle the uncharacteristic behaviour of unmilitant proletarians in class society may be transferred to explain, or explain away, the equally uncharacteristic behaviour of dissenting and militant individuals in an established communist society. True, the social conditions which create false consciousness can no longer, *ex hypothesi*, apply. There can be no social explanation of irrationality in communism, but in so far as autonomy continues to be identified in terms of an agent's subscription to substantive social values and ends (those of man as a 'species-being'), Marx's categories will ensure that the orthodox construe the dissentient's condition in terms of individual irrationality – rather than as representing a clash of basic values to be resolved through the liberal practices of political compromise and toleration. In effect the outcome is much the same as that found in both Hegel and Pashukanis – the dissident is ipso facto defined out of the 'rational community'. It surely cannot be denied that communists equipped with the theoretical insights of marxism will certainly be predisposed to construe dissent in this manner; and given that dissent, if it occurs, cannot be accommodated in the way the liberal responds to it, but must nevertheless be handled if the coherence of society is to be preserved, then what else may we expect but that intolerance will emerge, notwithstanding the rhetoric of 'individual rights' which might, *à la* Hegel, surround it?

---

[22] 'Must Radicals be Marxists?', *British Journal of Political Science*, XI (1981), 405–25.

VII

In sum, then, I have suggested that the liberal ideal of freedom involves the recognition of certain crucial individual rights, and implies both a respect for individual dissent through the exercise of these rights and positive toleration of disobedience arising from the value typically placed upon the development and exercise of powers of individual autonomy presupposed by the ascription of the rights in question. I have asked whether marxian social theory can accommodate a similar view of individual liberty. Three positions on personal autonomy and rights in communism were then considered. The 'Coincidence of Interests' thesis, according to which autonomy will always as a matter of contingent fact eventuate in common agreement and the absence of individual dissent, was rejected as incredible. The more sophisticated 'Evaporation of Rights' thesis of Pashukanis, which argues that individual autonomy is a transient phenomenon, a corollary of the abstract commodity form, and destined to disappear in socialism, was also found to be inadequate on the grounds that, as well as manifestly implying a dehumanising attitude to 'deviancy', it involves an overly narrow interpretation of Marx's view of the value of the kind of individual autonomy achieved in capitalism. Hence the 'Distillation of Rights' thesis, which represents an attempt to articulate what Marx apparently sees as the positive features of liberalism, and hence the claim that the 'citizen's rights' specified *On the Jewish Question* – precisely those typically associated with dissent by liberals – might imply the kind of dialectical transcendence of the egoistic 'rights of man' that Marx's historical method suggests we should seek in communism. Finally, I raised the question whether the formal recognition of these rights – the right to vote, to freedom of expression and association – could be said to be grounded in the kinds of considerations which the liberal typically invokes, especially their function as being instrumental to the development and exercise of the valued personality capacities of autonomy of choice and judgement. A distinction was made between rights and pseudo-rights, the latter being such as are only apparently based on genuinely liberal values – giving the appearance that autonomy is regarded as legitimate, but in effect always defined as being exercised in conditions of political or social conformity and never as an instrument of independent dissent. And it was concluded that though our evidence is necessarily scanty (given Marx's self-denying ordinance about what can be said about communism), the fact that the coherence of a communist society must rest largely upon the existence of a moral consensus as to its substantive values, a central one of which is a theory of human nature which implies a restrictive conception of what can count as the rational ends of human beings, strongly suggests that the prospect for citizen's rights operating as effective defences of individual dissent in a recognisably liberal manner is, to say the least, slight. Indeed, it is surely difficult to avoid the most sinister conclusion from all this, namely that the adoption of the 'psychiatric attitude' towards troublesome political dissent is more an implication of than an aberration from marxian social principles.[23]

It may be objected, of course, that the argument rests upon exiguous textual evidence and involves heavy interpretation of some of the vaguest of Marx's ideas – personality, freedom, the principles of communist social organisation etc.; and that, consequently, it implies very little, if anything, about the logic of toleration in communism. To the charge of addressing an issue to which Marx's own writings only permit an essentially debatable response the answer must be that it is not simply a theoretical question, but an increasingly pressing practical one, especially for liberals contemplating the dire civil rights records of *soi-disant* socialist countries, or wondering what to make of the current flurry about *glasnost*. Moreover, in the absence of an alternative account of the connection between these crucial marxian ideas and the ideal of toleration (and short of most implausibly imputing to the inhabitants of a well-established communist society an unthinkingly tenacious piety towards the liberal practices of their historical forerunners), what grounds do we have for drawing a less dismal conclusion?

[23] The strategy here – to identify the irrational *agent* in terms of the irrationality of his *desires* – comes in a variety of guises not restricted to marxism. Thus in Freudian psycho-therapy the patient's rejection of the therapist's interpretation of his unconscious motives may be construed as a further 'symptom' of his heteronomy – the Freudian view of the 'good life for man' being thus imposed in the form of criteria for identifying rational autonomy. In marxism it manifests itself in its most blatant form of course in the practices of the Soviet penal psychiatry clinics, where political dissent is taken as sufficient to diagnose schizophrenia or paranoia and to license a stripping of civil rights – see Bloch and Reddaway, *passim*.

10

Liberalism, marxism, and tolerance

GRAEME DUNCAN AND JOHN STREET

A Soviet broadcaster once explained the official policy on the content of radio programmes:

Absolute freedom is an invention of lovers of bombastic phraseology. Freedom of individuality is only permissible within a definite framework, not detrimental of society . . . That's why in providing broad vistas for the flight of creative fantasy we do not permit propaganda of violence, we ban pornography, we do not approve of works that contradict moral principles and negate values common to humanity.[1]

It is an argument which typically finds no favour with liberals, not least because the official policy seems to express intolerance for any view which does not accord with those laid down by the state. Soviet claims upon the word 'toleration' are seen, by the liberal, as a cynical exercise in redefinition: the Soviet state tolerates only that which it approves. But is the gap between the two views as wide as it sometimes seems? This is the question to which this chapter is directed.

Tolerance is most commonly referred to as a liberal value. It is held to epitomise the liberal's concern for freedom of speech and action, for free choice and intellectual scepticism. Marxism seems almost to confirm this link between liberalism and tolerance by the disdain it expresses for the institutions and assumptions which enshrine liberal values. As Merleau-Ponty once wrote: 'To tell the truth and to act out of conscience are nothing but alibis of a false morality; true morality is not concerned with what we think or what we want.'[2] In so far as marxists discuss tolerance, their task often

---

[1] Quoted in J. Sapiets, 'Extolling the Party', *Index on Censorship*, vol. 11, no. 5 (October 1982), 14.
[2] From 'Humanism and Terrorism', quoted in S. Lukes, *Marxism and Morality* (Oxford, 1985), 134.

appears only to be to dismiss liberal versions of it, to label it as 'repressive tolerance', and to develop their own account of a real tolerance.

On the basis of such assumptions about the distinctions between marxism and liberalism, it might be presumed that marxism and liberalism hold to radically different conceptions of the value and content of tolerance. Where liberals would seem to value tolerance as an end in itself, marxists are more inclined to treat it instrumentally, as a means to some pre-established end. Where liberals appear to view tolerance as a necessary corollary of intellectual scepticism and moral uncertainty, marxists are more inclined to regard tolerance as a tactically useful method of realising a particular truth. Such distinctions are here baldly over-stated, but the impression remains that marxism and liberalism regard tolerance quite differently. This chapter is an attempt to suggest that the difference between the two conceptions of tolerance is not as great as has been supposed, and that each tradition shares much in common theoretically and that they are being pushed closer to each other by political reality.

LIBERALISM AND TOLERANCE

If 'liberalism' is just short-hand for the freedom of individuals to choose their own values, beliefs, and life-styles, then it is clear that tolerance is a central liberal tenet. Entailed in this version of liberalism is the claim that no one value, belief, or life-style can be said to be superior to another. This means not only that government, if it is to act on liberal principles, must not bestow advantages on any particular choice, but also that there is no absolute truth or set of moral standards which can arbitrate between competing choices. In pursuit of this kind of liberalism, tolerance is fundamental simply because there is no justification for intolerance. There must be a plurality of choices from which individuals can select, and any attempt to limit the range will constitute a breach of liberal principles. Intolerance is just such an attempt. Tolerance involves allowing all possibilities. From within this vision of liberalism, an intolerant society is authoritarian; it engages in suppression, censorship, witch-hunts, and the like. In contrast, a tolerant society is open; it is a place in which ideas compete, but in which there are no outright winners. Underlying this liberalism and its view of tolerance is a sceptical approach to truth which recalls Popper's view of the scientific method. We know when we are wrong; we can never be sure that we are right.

Of course, this version of liberalism does not come without qualifications and modifications. Liberal tolerance has to face the constraints of practical reality. This intrudes in one obvious guise: some freely made choices are incompatible. This problem may be resolved within the theory in one of two possible ways. It depends on where the problem is located: in the incompatibility or in the choices. The elimination of incompatibility is achieved by arguing that the source of conflict is not the choices themselves but the context in which they are made. For example, disputes over the distribution of resources in a society are treated as problems of scarcity, rather than incompatibility. The answer is to improve economic growth.[3] Resolving the conflict in this way ceases to make it an issue for tolerance. Smokers and non-smokers can live together if they are given a sufficiently large, air-conditioned room. Where incompatibility cannot be explained away or redefined, the second strategy is called into play. Here rights are allocated, or rules made, to resolve the conflict. Racism tends to be treated in this way. The rights of blacks are protected against the claims of those who would favour discrimination. It is worth noting here that while the practice of racism is restricted, racist ideas are tolerated. This suggests a further point about the characteristics of this version of liberal tolerance.

Toleration is concerned with speech and thought. The assumptions underlying this are, first, that ideas do not automatically inform action; secondly, that in the free exchange of ideas the good survive the bad; and thirdly, that the suppression of ideas does more damage than the ideas themselves. The idea of free choice remains the foundation of tolerance, and the burden of the argument falls to those who wish to restrict ideas and actions. The defence of pluralism, and the epistemological scepticism of this approach to liberalism and tolerance, should not, however, be confused with moral scepticism or indifference. As Dworkin points out, while this version of liberalism holds to the view that governments should make 'political decisions . . . independent of any particular conception of the good life, or of what gives value to life', this is not an excuse for moral scepticism. Liberalism's 'constitutive morality provides that human beings must be treated as equal by their government, not because there is no right and wrong in political morality, but because that is what is right'.[4] In this account of

---

[3] See, for example, W. Beckerman, *In Defence of Economic Growth* (London, 1974); and the counter-argument in F. Hirsch, *Social Limits to Growth* (London, 1977).

[4] R. Dworkin, 'Liberalism', in S. Hampshire (ed.), *Public and Private Morality* (Cambridge, 1978), 127 and 142.

liberalism, tolerance is built upon the ethical and epistemological assumptions which underpin the value placed on pluralism. Tolerance is an end in itself, the principal embodiment of pluralism.

This version of liberalism, with its particular emphasis on toleration, is not, however, the only version. The 'pluralist' account can be compared with an alternative liberalism which might be labelled 'monist'. In this version tolerance is not an end in itself, but a means to an end. J. S. Mill is the most obvious representative of this view.

In many respects, Mill shares the features of pluralist liberalism, as in this familiar passage from *On Liberty*:

If all mankind minus one were of one opinion, and only one person were of the contrary opinion, mankind would be no more justified in silencing that one person, than he, if he had the power, would be justified in silencing mankind . . . We can never be sure that the opinion we are endeavouring to stifle is a false opinion; and if we were sure, stifling it would be evil still.[5]

However, what distinguishes Mill's liberalism from the conventions of pluralist liberalism is its willingness to recognise that not all choices are of equal weight, that they can be compared and judged, and that a good society is one which favours the 'better' choices. Conflicts cannot, or need not, be resolved by resort to the technical or legal solutions offered by pluralist liberalism. The value of liberalism becomes not so much its ability to provide a setting for the individual pursuit of individual truths, but rather its ability to create the conditions for individuals to realise a single truth. This truth is reached through the intellectual activity of free, equal, and rational people. Instead of a plurality of ideas coexisting, they are in permanent conflict, competing for attention and confirmation. This is the way the truth is attained. The value of truth is such that all ideas must be considered. A single dissenter is valued as much as a crowded consensus because of what he or she may represent for the discovery of truth.

The use of tolerance as an instrument for revealing the truth needs to be distinguished from a more cynical use of intolerance: as an instrument for maintaining social order. Such an idea seems to lie behind the argument of one of liberal tolerance's sternest critics, Herbert Marcuse: tolerance is 'first and foremost for the sake of

---

[5] J.S. Mill, *On Liberty*, in Everyman edition of *Utilitarianism*, etc. (London, 1972), 79.

heretics'.[6] And it fits with seventeenth-century uses of the idea, when, as Richard Tuck illustrates, toleration was applied pragmatically to defuse fanatical commitment to certain political beliefs.[7] Scepticism was used to subvert threats to the dominant orthodoxy. Mill's liberalism, though vulnerable to a cynical reading, is expressed in quite different terms. For him, tolerance is linked to truth rather than to social order, even if that truth might sustain a particular social order.

This can be illustrated by Mill's emphasis on the need for tolerance in matters of both opinion and scientific truth. Different opinions must be tolerated since they admit of no final resolution – there is no answer; while scientific theories are to be questioned precisely in order to establish the answer they provide.[8] Tolerance, in both cases, is not so much valued in its own right, but rather because it furnishes the conditions appropriate to the material being handled. More precisely, the value and use of toleration are determined by the epistemological status of the discourse. But whether dealing with fact or opinion, toleration is important for the way it allows facts to be established or opinions to flourish. In 'monist liberalism', the value of tolerance is determined by the context in which it operates.

From these brief summaries, we can see that just as there are different accounts of liberalism, so there are different versions of tolerance within liberal theory. The liberal theories share a common ground. They place considerable emphasis on the value of 'tolerance', and they both see it as essential to the successful realisation of a liberal society. They also agree that the point of tolerance lives in the way it allows ideas and activity to inhabit the public realm. But there is also considerable disagreement over the value and meaning of tolerance. According to which theory we take, tolerance is either an end in itself or a means to an end.

Having sketched the rough outlines of two different accounts of liberal tolerance, we can now turn our attention to marxism and marxist views of 'tolerance'.

MARXISM AND TOLERANCE

While it may be true that liberalism cannot be described as a single coherent set of ideas, the different strands of liberalism remain

---

[6] H. Marcuse, 'Repressive Tolerance', in P. Connerton (ed.), *Critical Sociology* (Harmondsworth, 1976), 307.
[7] See Chapter 1 in this volume.   [8] J.S. Mill, *On Liberty*, ch. 2.

united by common themes which distinguish these different liberalisms from marxism. Indeed, the very idea of tolerance seems to serve as an illustration of this point. Many marxists express disdain for the particular features of 'bourgeois morality', or in some cases of morality in all its forms.[9] In its most extreme form, this analysis informed the crude cynicism of terrorist groups like the Baader-Meinhof group, who used acts of terror to induce acts of repression from the state, and thereby to expose the 'true' character of the liberal state and its much vaunted tolerance. Without drawing the same practical conclusions, Althusser's treatment of ideology suggests a similar argument about the status of tolerance.[10] Tolerance serves a functional role in the operation of the state and society; it has no value in itself. This is true both for capitalism and communism: in the former, tolerance simply oils the wheels of repression; in the latter, formal moral codes become redundant in a society where rationality dictates the social order. But to see all marxists like this, or to see the distinction between marxism and liberalism as being fixed in this way, is to miss too much.

However obvious the difference between marxist and liberal views of tolerance appears to be, we need to look beyond this apparently fundamental divergence to enquire whether the lack of a common front is inevitable, is a feature of particular marxists, or is a result of particular marxist concerns. To answer these questions, we have chosen to concentrate on one aspect of tolerance: its practical application; on two marxists who have written on this: Leon Trotsky and Herbert Marcuse; and on three different contexts for the application of tolerance: capitalism, revolution, and communism. Our exposition is organised around the last three.

Tolerance under capitalism

Marcuse, both in 'Repressive Tolerance' and in *One-Dimensional Man*, makes much of the idea that the apparent tolerance of capitalist society is no more than a sham. His portrait of modern capitalism is of a society which, through its abundant material wealth, systematically incorporates all potentially subversive forces. In the name of diversity, capitalism creates uniformity. In the name of democracy, it creates tyranny. In the name of tolerance, it practises oppression. Capitalism's insidious achievement has been to

---

[9] For a discussion of this see Lukes, *Marxism and Morality*.
[10] L. Althusser, *For Marx* (London, 1969).

allow a form of tolerance, recognisable as the 'pluralist liberal' view, in which the choices are much more apparent than real. The available alternatives are ones which can have no significant effect upon the dominant – capitalist – structure of society.

Capitalism, in the guise of technological rationality, has penetrated the 'inner space' of the mind. This process has effectively destroyed people's capacity for critical reasoning, which was based on the ability to conceive of a better world than they already inhabited. Instead, the dominant view is that there is only one world and only one way of organising it; and that the only choices and possibilities are those that already exist within it. By securing itself in this safest of ways, capitalism can easily afford to be tolerant: to allow, even encourage, people to read Marx. For Marcuse, there is a yet more frightening side to this kind of tolerance. It is a tolerance which treats all ideas equally. Fascism and democracy are treated as equivalents, as are racism and egalitarianism, militarism and pacifism. Tolerance in the service of such equality becomes, according to Marcuse, the 'instrument of servitude' and an enemy of progress.[11]

Marcuse's critique of tolerance within liberal capitalism denies any substantial moral content to the idea as it is practised, but Marcuse is not dismissive of the value itself. His essay on repressive tolerance is also a defence of partisan tolerance, under which intolerance is extended to those policies and opinions which are outlawed and suppressed.[12] Universal tolerance is 'possible only when no real or alleged enemy requires in the national interest the education and training of people in military violence and destruction'.[13] Underlying this argument, and implicit in the idea of universal tolerance, is an account of tolerance which would be recognisable to the monist liberal. Truth sets the standards and the limits of tolerance: 'There is a sense in which truth is the end of liberty, and liberty must be defined and confined by truth.'[14] Unlike the pluralist, Marcuse argues for tolerance on the grounds that it enables truth (which is 'the end of liberty') to be ascertained. Free speech is necessary '*not* because there is no objective truth . . . but because there *is* an objective truth which can be discovered'. 'The telos of tolerance is truth.'[15] Truth is not discovered by the impartial balancing of two sides but by the rationality exposed by disinterested enquiry. Thus Marcuse's criticism of tolerance within

---

[11] Marcuse, 'Repressive Tolerance', 317–22. [12] *Ibid.*, 301. [13] *Ibid.*, 303.
[14] *Ibid.*, 304. [15] *Ibid.*, 307.

capitalism can be seen as a critique of 'pluralist liberalism'. It is much less an attack on the tolerance of 'monist liberalism'. This is an issue to which we shall return when considering tolerance within communism. But first we need to consider marxist views of tolerance in the transition to communism.

Tolerance in the revolution

The Bolsheviks' criticisms of 'bourgeois' democracy are similar to those of Marcuse. What differentiates the Bolsheviks is the particular perspective from which they view their target. Not only did they see liberal democracy as being fraudulent in its promise of social change, but they also saw its political freedoms as damaging to the revolution. Though the Bolsheviks were aware of the need for mass support, they were worried that paying heed to every dissenting voice or alternative plan could distract them from their revolutionary course.[16] Trotsky explains the harsh logic of Bolshevism. A revolution requires the use of unsocialist practices to achieve socialism. (In the familiar aphorism, just as you cannot make an omelette without breaking eggs, so you cannot make a revolution without breaking heads.) In propounding such an argument, Trotsky set himself apart from the arguments of marxists like Rosa Luxemburg who saw political freedoms as essential to the success of the revolution.

Trotsky argued that Bolsheviks could not tolerate those who raised doubts about the efficacy of violence and terrorism: 'The man who repudiates terrorism in principle – i.e. repudiates measures of suppression and intimidation towards determined and armed counter-revolution, must reject all idea of the political supremacy of the working class and its revolutionary dictatorship. The man who repudiates dictatorship of the proletariat repudiates the socialist revolution, and digs the grave of Socialism.'[17] For Trotsky, the revolutionary path is clearly defined, the value of communism widely accepted. This certainty allows him to label those who dissent as either wrong or as enemies. The military comparison is obvious. Making a revolution is no different from waging a war. And just as armies cannot be organised along liberal democratic lines (without defeating the purpose of military organisation), so the revolutionary party can be run only on

[16] See M. Brinton, *The Bolsheviks and Workers' Control, 1917–1921* (Toronto 1972).
[17] L. Trotsky, *Terrorism and Communism* (Michigan, 1961), 23.

military lines. Tolerance is ruled out by the explicit comparison with military practice.

Intolerance is defended, therefore, in terms of the tactical need for effective coordination. But this pragmatic justification is grounded in the higher claim that the revolution is 'right' or 'correct'. Bolshevik intolerance is justified by reference to the 'higher' democracy it creates by denying a 'lower' form. Instead of 'statically reflecting' an existing majority, Trotsky argued that the Bolsheviks were 'dynamically creating' a new majority.[18]

Trotsky's argument was cast in terms of means and ends. Papers had to be closed down in order 'to throttle the class lie of the bourgeoisie and to achieve the class truth of the proletariat'.[19] Like Marcuse, Trotsky saw tolerance as being intimately linked to the truth as represented by the ideal of communism and the cause of the working class. Intolerance was justified by reference to its necessity in achieving the goals of the revolution. For Trotsky, tolerance is justified – or denied – according to the end it achieves. Under capitalism, tolerance is seen by both Trotsky and Marcuse as a device for propping up a corrupt order. The end determines the means. The same link is drawn in turn by Trotsky in justifying intolerance in pursuit of the revolution. This parallels Engels's familiar views in 'On Authority'. There he argues that expert knowledge (which is 'correct') entitles the holders of it to wield power without recourse to democratic processes.[20]

What is significant about Trotsky's view of tolerance is that its worth is determined by its role in the attainment of the specified ends. It exists to be used or ignored according to the circumstances. Although Trotsky and Marcuse conceive truth differently, its status in their theories necessitates tolerance to be moulded by it. In this sense, while they remain distanced from the arguments of pluralist liberalism, they share some of the features of monist liberalism. The structure of their arguments are similar, even if their conclusions, and the implications for political action, are different.

The element of common ground can be further explored in the context of the post-revolutionary world. Do liberals and marxists find themselves united in the value they place on tolerance when marxists describe their ideal society?

[18] *Ibid.*, 45.   [19] *Ibid.*, 180.
[20] F. Engels, 'On Authority', in K. Marx and F. Engels, *Selected Works*, 1 (London, 1958).

231

Tolerance within communism

Trotsky's views on the place of tolerance within communism follow from his arguments about the conditions necessary for a successful revolution. The difference between the two is marked by a shift of emphasis. Where intolerance within the revolutionary struggle rests on the analogy between revolutionary and military conduct, intolerance under communism is determined by the higher form of democracy represented by the new social order. Of course, the argument is not phrased in quite these terms. Trotsky's case does not accept that 'tolerance' is an ideal or value to be treasured. Thus, the idea that he condones 'intolerance' is a matter of little importance. There is no value in a practice – toleration – which simply allows experts in 'spiritual slavery' to keep popular consciousness in a conservative state, while the 'safety-valves' and 'lightning-conductors' of a tolerant society accommodate dissatisfaction.[21] Tolerance is the ideal only of dominant, anti-communist forces and hypocritical Quakers. By both dissociating himself from the value of tolerance and by arguing for the higher value represented by communism, Trotsky appears to dispense with all arguments about, or claims for, tolerance. The term seems to have no meaning, except in the mouths of others. And what these others would describe as tolerance, Trotsky would see as necessary for some preconceived purpose. The principles of democratic centralism serve to capture the limits of tolerance within Trotsky's communism. Dissent and discussion precede a decision; they do not follow it.

Marcuse's view of tolerance within communism echoes Trotsky's. But though they reach similar conclusions, they come by slightly different routes. Marcuse's dismissal of capitalist tolerance as 'repressive' is premised on the idea that there is an alternative, higher form of tolerance. He calls this 'pure tolerance', and he traces it from the ideas of J. S. Mill. 'Pure tolerance' is employed in the pursuit of truth; and where 'repressive tolerance' is conservative, 'pure tolerance' is progressive.[22] And it is the latter that is to be practised in the transition to, and realisation of, an emancipated society. Marcuse argues for the application of 'discriminating tolerance'. By this he means that ideas and values should be encouraged in so far as they lead to a true understanding of society and a proper respect for persons; ideas and values which have the

[21] Trotsky, *Terrorism and Communism*, 78.
[22] Marcuse, 'Repressive Tolerance', 319–21.

opposite effect should be condemned. In this respect, tolerance for Marcuse has a status and function very similar to those it has for Trotsky. It is a device for achieving a preordained goal. They differ only in the duty they feel to justify themselves against the claims of those who advocate tolerance. Where Trotsky argues in the face of an immediate practical need, Marcuse addresses a less precise but more pervasive social value. Where Trotsky's enemy are the Mensheviks and other 'reactionary' forces, Marcuse's antagonist is liberalism.

But while Marcuse attacks contemporary liberalism and is dismissive of current notions of tolerance, and while in this sense his ideas are akin to Trotsky's, it is clear that the ideas of liberty and toleration exercise a far greater hold over Marcuse than they do over Trotsky. Marcuse, unlike Trotsky, is concerned to establish his vision of communism as a proper and fit descendant of liberalism. 'Pure tolerance' sets the standard for that society. It ceases to be a device, and becomes a practice in its own right. His vision of society, pictured in his *Essay on Liberation*, is of individuals giving expression to their true feelings, unconstrained by the social, institutional, or psychological ties with which technological rationality had bound them. It is a vision that owes much to the politics of the late sixties and to the apparent boundlessness of America's resources. What it presumes is the compatibility of and the ability to fulfil the manifold aspirations released in the newly emancipated society. But what is interesting for us is that, were it possible to realise Marcuse's world, there would be no call for tolerance ('pure' or otherwise). Tolerance entails allowing a person to do something which, in some way, adversely affects you. In Marcuse's vision, no such activities are countenanced. Society is the happy result of individual free expression. Like some pluralist liberals, Marcuse eradicates the issue of tolerance by supposing the compatibility of all choices.

It is easy to be dismissive of Marcuse's utopian vision, but its treatment of tolerance must necessarily characterise all liberationist theories. The 'truth', which allows for the exposure of the hypocrisy and corruption of existing, unliberated society, presumes the possibility of a consistent and uncorrupt alternative society. It also provides a means of legitimating intolerance. It establishes some claim about what it is right for people to know or want. The decisive character of this knowledge eliminates the need for toleration, other than as an indulgence or as part of a patterned education.

LIBERALISM, MARXISM, AND TOLERANCE

In the sense that tolerance is concerned with the practice of allowing for competing or alternative views and activities, its form and character seem to ally easily with liberalism. Both the political principles and the intellectual assumptions of liberalism provide an obvious home for tolerance. But as we showed earlier, we have to be wary of assuming any simple link between tolerance and liberalism. First, liberalism itself has no neatly defined boundaries; and secondly, the role and definition of tolerance varies with the different readings of liberalism. On the other hand, it appears that marxism does not place any great store by tolerance. Under capitalism, it disguises oppression; in times of revolution, it is inefficacious; within communism, it is unnecessary. In the face of liberalism's indecisiveness and marxism's indifference, tolerance may fall to liberalism by default, and give credence to the criticism commonly made by liberals of the U.S.S.R. (in Tom Stoppard's words: 'what they call their liberty/is just the freedom to agree/that one and one is sometimes three' (*Every Good Boy Deserves Favour*)). To allow this, however, is to overlook the problems tolerance poses for both ideological positions.

Recalling the distinction between pluralist and monist liberalism, we can see that marxist views of tolerance have something in common with each. The goal-directed character of monist liberalism has a similar theoretical form to marxist arguments. They differ only in the goal anticipated and in the claims used to put this goal above all others. In contrast, the emphasis on individual choice and self-interest in pluralist liberalism is paralleled by Marcuse's vision of a liberated society. In both, self-directed activity is the ideal. Marxism's similarity with liberalism in these respects is reflected in its treatment of tolerance. Both monist liberalism and marxism treat tolerance instrumentally; both pluralist liberalism and marxism regard tolerance as having limited relevance in ideal conditions.

However, these similarities might be said to rest on the weakest points of each theoretical position. The chance of spontaneous, compatible claims emerging from individual actions seems, at best, unlikely; and in a world in which the limits to growth are social as well as physical, the chance becomes zero.[23] Thus, both marxism and liberalism have to generate valid principles and legitimate political structures by which to identify and resolve rival claims.

[23] L. Thurow, *The Zero-Sum Society* (Harmondsworth, 1981); see also Hirsch, *Social Limits to Growth*.

Tolerance cannot be avoided, it must be actively practised. This then leads to the other common problem: establishing which ideas and activities are to be preferred, which to be condemned, and which to be tolerated. To be able to do this, liberalism has to generate a moral foundation which, according to MacIntyre, it lacks;[24] and marxism is forced to re-examine both its 'scientific' character and its vision of communism.

Within contemporary marxism, these theoretical enquiries are paralleled by practical political changes. There is, for example, the growing disenchantment of marxists with the treatment of minorities and dissidents within 'actually existing socialist states'. There is also the growing pressure on marxist parties to adapt to the demands and concerns of feminists, ecologists, and others.[25] In so far as these changes argue for diversity, and a move away from a theory of social change based solely on class, toleration would seem to become an integral part of marxist political practice. The 'rainbow coalition' envisaged by the new marxists presumes an ethic of cooperation and compromise.[26] It is not just a matter of qualifying Trotsky's ruthless instrumentalism, Marcuse's helpless fatalism, or their expectant utopianism. At the level of marxist theory, it requires an introduction of political eclecticism and intellectual scepticism. Marxism is then left with the task of establishing the form and character of tolerance itself. Toleration can neither be ignored nor derided.

If tolerance is to have any substance within this revised marxism, then marxists will have to engage in the arguments which have typically been the preserve of liberals. Tolerance will have to be taken seriously, and not dismissed as a superficial good or a cynical device. It means acknowledging a place for a tolerance in which the tolerated have a real choice, and in which the tolerator makes a real sacrifice. Tolerance cannot simply involve a willingness to hear what others say; it requires a preparedness to listen and to act. It cannot be a tactic used in the pursuit of the 'higher' goals of communism, because those goals have themselves to be subject to debate and disagreement. Tolerance must be respected in its own right. The problem becomes that of identifying the limits to

[24] A. MacIntyre, *After Virtue* (London, 1981).
[25] See, for example, J. Cocks, 'Hegel's Logic, Marx's Science, Rationalism's Perils', *Political Studies*, XXXI, 4 (1983), 584–603; R. Bahro, *The Alternative in Eastern Europe* (London, 1978); and M. Barratt, *Women's Oppression Today* (London, 1980); L. R. Bahro, *Socialism and Survival* (London, 1982).
[26] The most obvious expression of this trend can be found in the pages of *Marxism Today*, and particularly in the writings of Stuart Hall.

tolerance. The rights to dissent will be in conflict with other rights. That these will be differently ascribed by liberals and marxists does not change the fact of their common difficulty: the claims of tolerance run counter to the claim that there is a moral code by which to judge competing demands. The right of the feminist to be heard and heeded over, say, pornography, has to be judged against the right of the racist to be heard and heeded over, say, repatriation. The ability to separate these two examples depends on a certainty which the idea of tolerance seems to deny. Yet if marxism is to avoid charges of determinism or utopianism, it has to allow for the scepticism and doubt which tolerance enshrines. And if liberal tolerance is going to involve more than benign indifference, then it has to allow for the ideas of 'correctness' which marxism is under pressure to reject.

11

Socialism and toleration

DAVID MILLER

Let me begin with a traveller's tale, set in the mid 1980s, that may serve to introduce our problem. A visitor from the West to, let us say, Moscow will observe a number of unfamiliar features in his new surroundings. He will notice, for example, the absence of *The Times* – unless he happens to be on the streets in the early hours of the morning, during that brief interlude between one van delivering the papers and another collecting them for transmission to the government department that has purchased all the copies. This he will probably have anticipated. He may, however, be a little more struck by the lack of cultural variety in his surroundings. There are no ostentatious youth subcultures; no quarters of the city where ethnic shops and restaurants flourish; no streets where gay pride is on show, or bookshops barred to men. Religious practices have not entirely disappeared, but church and synagogue are very largely the preserve of the elderly and there are no orange-robed monks parading in the streets. In short, the impression received is of a society where not only opinion but also culture is pressed as far as possible into a single mould that bears the label 'socialism'.

Back home again, and opening *The Times* over breakfast, our traveller is quite likely to be confronted by a large advertisement from the G. L. C., fighting for its survival, and the standard-bearer of what is currently referred to as 'municipal socialism'. The ad may perhaps be the one that lists 167 organisations whose survival (it is claimed) has been ensured by cash handouts from the Council. Looking down the list he finds the Black Londoners Action Group, the Lesbian Feminist Writers Conference, the Union of Turkish Workers, the London Gay Teenage Group, the Chilean Cultural Committee, the Conference of Ethnic Minority Senior Citizens – to say nothing of the Welsh Harp Society and many other such organisations.

This is a puzzling contrast. In the East, socialists discourage minority cultures, either suppressing them forcibly or exerting pressure of a more discreet kind (in the job market, for instance) to dissuade potential adherents. In the West, socialists encourage a hundred flowers to bloom – with cash subsidies. Now there are two simple-minded responses to this paradox that I want to reject. One maintains that what our traveller has experienced is nothing more than the contrast between socialists in and out of (effective) power. Socialists sign up racial, sexual, religious, and other minorities in the service of the revolution; once the great event has occurred, they reveal their true colours and stamp down hard on their erstwhile allies. That is the first response. The second, diametrically opposed, maintains that cultural oppression in the East has nothing to do with socialism as such. It is an excrescence resulting from the economic backwardness of the socialist states, from the despotic political tradition of Russia, or from some other such factor. Authentic socialism, it is implied, is really a superior version of liberalism. Despite liberal claims that cultural diversity flourishes best under liberal institutions, it is in fact only with a socialist transformation that hitherto repressed minority cultures will enjoy equal status with the dominant culture. Socialism will deliver what liberalism only promises.

In my view this second response is no more adequate than the first. It fails to ask how a shift from liberal to socialist principles changes the manner in which the issue of toleration is addressed. I shall argue that socialism carries with it practical commitments that limit the scope of toleration – as indeed does liberalism, though this will not be my concern here. In order to mark out these limits, we need to sketch in the essential elements of a socialist position, highlighting those features that are critical from the point of view of toleration.[1] But we must begin with some memoranda concerning the idea of toleration itself.

First, although the issue of toleration first arose in relation to

This paper was prepared for the Morrell Conference on Toleration, University of York, 24–6 September 1985. I should like to thank the participants in the Conference for their helpful comments, and also audiences at the Universities of Essex and Melbourne, where the paper was later read. Bob Goodin and Bhikhu Parekh generously sent me written comments.

[1] Socialism appears in many guises, and there is no space here to provide a full justification for the version that I favour. I am currently working on a book which I hope will go some way towards meeting this deficiency. In the present chapter I simply take certain premises for granted (for example that socialists are commited to the distribution of at least some benefits on the basis of need) and explore their implications for the idea of toleration.

matters of belief, especially religious belief, it clearly extends to many other aspects of human life – including, for instance, personal dress and appearance, social practices of various kinds, forms of art, and so on. In all these areas, toleration means permitting activities to flourish that diverge from those that the tolerator himself regards as correct or valuable. Second, although the simplest way to be intolerant is to suppress the disapproved-of activities by force – that is either through direct physical force, or through the force of law – toleration as an ideal appears also to exclude other ways of discouraging deviant behaviour; for instance withholding benefits or services from those who engage in certain practices in cases where there is no internal connection between the practice itself and the benefit or service that is refused (an obvious case would be the exclusion of Catholics from public office in England prior to 1829). Third, to extend this line of thought still further, the values that underlie toleration appear to point beyond toleration itself towards the idea of a society that is equally hospitable to all the beliefs and activities that its members espouse, at least in so far as these beliefs and activities do not impinge adversely on the lives of other members; in other words to an image of society as a neutral arena in which the success or failure of different forms of life depends only on factors internal to those forms of life, with social institutions themselves not being biased in favour of any practices in particular. Although a view of this kind does admittedly go beyond mere toleration, if we base our commitment to toleration on, for instance, the idea of respect for persons, this seems to require arranging our institutions so that, as far as possible, they do not discriminate between the plans of life that people have chosen – since discrimination would imply that the favoured plans of life and/or their adherents were seen as more worthy of regard than the disfavoured.[2]

Whether in the end such an extended ideal of toleration is viable is an issue that requires careful discussion. I draw attention to these matters here because, in approaching the question of socialism and toleration, it seems preferable to begin with as broad an understanding of toleration as possible. Socialists, after all, often point out that to treat issues of freedom and tolerance in relation only to legal permissions and prohibitions is to ignore all those other factors – economic factors especially – that promote or dis-

---

[2] For an example of this position, see A. Weale, 'Toleration, Individual Differences and Respect for Persons', in J. Horton and S. Mendus (eds.), *Aspects of Toleration* (London, 1985).

courage particular practices and forms of thought.[3] A tolerant society must do more than provide the legal freedom to engage in unconventional activities. That point having been made, let me now turn to those components of the socialist idea that appear to pose problems for toleration.

The key component, for present purposes, is the socialist ambition to create a society embodying a strong sense of common citizenship. Each member of this society should ideally see himself as bound to the other members in such a way that he feels himself responsible for their welfare. In addition, his identity is at least partially constituted by his social membership; in answer to the question 'Who are you?', he says, among other things, 'I belong to . . .'. His society does not appear to him merely as an arena in which he pursues his own personal projects; rather, how well his life goes depends in part on how well his society as a whole fares. His fate is bound up with the fate of his fellows, and he is willing to act – in politics especially – for the common good.

This idea is sometimes expressed by saying that socialism must be communitarian. Provided 'community' is used to refer to the idea of common citizenship sketched in the last paragraph, the formulation is unobjectionable and may conveniently identify the gulf that separates a socialist from a liberal outlook. But the communitarian label is also misleading, in at least three ways. First, it may suggest that the socialist's aim is to create a monolithic form of community, an all-inclusive, organic society whose internal relations are all of the same kind.[4] While there is certainly a tradition of socialism (perhaps more accurately, of communism) which is simple-mindedly communitarian in this sense, there is no good reason for socialists to align themselves with it. On the contrary, a socialist society ought to be institutionally plural, containing a number of separate spheres with different organising principles; in particular there should be a large area of what might be called 'civil society' in which market relationships and private associations are the dominant elements.[5] Second, although citizenship is a form of community in so far as it embodies a shared sense of identity and mutual concern between citizens, it is clearly very different in

[3] See Chapter 10 in this volume.
[4] As Plant emphasises, with particular reference to the German tradition, 'the idea of community involved some notion of the whole man, in which men were to be met by other men in the totality of their social roles and not in a fragmented or segmented way'. R. Plant, *Community and Ideology* (London, 1974), 16.
[5] I provide a partial defence of this view in 'Marx, Communism and Markets', *Political Theory* (forthcoming).

character from more traditional, *Gemeinschaftlich* forms of community; in particular, it is not dependent on physical location, on kinship, or on direct personal relationships between members.[6] Citizenship depends on a shared understanding of what it means to be a member of this particular society, an understanding which is developed consciously through debate and discussion, particularly political debate; in this respect it contrasts with unreflective forms of community based, so to speak, on natural facts. Third, the socialist idea of citizenship is egalitarian, in the sense that each citizen acknowledges an equal obligation to contribute to the welfare of the remainder; and each has an equal right to participate in the deliberations through which the general shape of his society is continually reviewed. Here again, there is a clear contrast with older ideas of community, which often incorporated hierarchical authority relations, with the controlling upper rank taking a paternal interest in the welfare of their dependants.

Why should socialists be committed to this idea of citizenship? There is a direct reason of a somewhat abstract kind, and also an indirect reason that is more mundane. The direct reason is that citizenship, if successfully established and practised, reconciles people to their social environment to the fullest extent that a modern society allows. They are no longer faced with an external world that lies beyond their control and whose processes appear to them to be meaningless. Implied in this is a view of human personality that receives its strongest formulation in Marx's theory of alienation. The full-blown marxist view seems to me to be indefensible.[7] The idea that we might identify completely with our social environment overlooks the fact that that environment is unavoidably made up of other persons whose purposes are not necessarily in tune with ours; and that in large areas of social life we experience outcomes that are the unintended results of the joint activities of many other people. But even if the idea in its strongest form must be discarded, a weaker version still resonates through the socialist tradition. It may be possible to see the social world as subject to human control in its overall pattern, even though unplanned and spontaneous in its details. Translating this into practice implies political control of the economy and other institutions that shape social life. But political control alone, in the absence of citizenship, does not resolve the problem of alienation. An order imposed by a political body

---

[6] The best-known elucidation of the idea of community in this traditional sense is F. Tönnies, *Gemeinschaft und Gesellschaft*, translated as *Community and Association* (London, 1955).   [7] See 'Marx, Communism and Markets'.

remains external unless the subject concerned can identify with it. Nor is democratic machinery sufficient by itself to overcome this problem. A policy that is adopted by majority decision may appear to those who dissent from it as nothing more than an alien imposition. A genuine solution demands that each person identify with the body making the decision in such a way that, while dissenting from particular outcomes, he still regards the resulting order as one that he has helped to create. This is admittedly a difficult cheque to cash, and, as readers of Berlin and Talmon will readily appreciate, the idea expressed here may be developed in sinister directions.[8] But the idea itself is not completely baseless. If we identify with collective bodies – groups, institutions, and so forth – we may come to feel involved in their decisions and to feel, in some cases, ashamed of them, even when we disagree with what has been decided. The socialist wants to amplify and extend this experience. Moreover, it is important that identification should occur at the level at which most major decisions affecting the shape of society are made – meaning, in practice, at the level of the nation state. Thus small-scale forms of community, although valuable for other reasons, are not sufficient for this purpose. To solve (or at least mitigate) the problem of alienation, the socialist will look for communal identification at the national level.

The indirect reason for seeking to establish citizenship has to do with the distribution of welfare. It is a commonplace that socialists are committed more or less strongly to the principle of distribution according to need. Some portion of social resources is to be allocated on this basis. Now at first sight it may seem that all that is necessary to achieve this goal is to set up a welfare bureaucracy with the appropriate policy directives. But in fact such a proposal would be quite inadequate unless it were backed up by a popular consensus about the distributive principle in question. For, to begin with, we may take it that socialists will want the welfare system to be democratically supported and not merely the work of a high-minded elite. More subtly, the relationship between those who are at any moment the recipients of welfare and those who contribute, directly or indirectly, to its provision will alter according to the generally prevailing ideology of welfare. Socialists would like to see recipients viewing their claims as matters of justice rather than as benevolence or charity. This requires that the prevailing view among both recipients and donors should be that distribution

---

[8] See I. Berlin, 'Two Concepts of Liberty', in his *Four Essays on Liberty* (Oxford, 1969); J. L. Talmon, *The Origins of Totalitarian Democracy* (London, 1952).

according to need is a requirement of social justice. Now although almost everyone would acknowledge a general humanitarian obligation to aid people in life-and-death situations, the much stronger idea of distribution according to need – where 'need' is stretched beyond biological survival to include items that are necessary only from the point of view of a socially defined manner of life – is rooted in a social context. All the evidence suggests that people give greater weight to this notion to the extent that they see themselves as bound to the beneficiaries of the principle by common ties. The more communal the relationship, the more need displaces merit (in particular) as a criterion of justice.[9] Thus the kind of underpinning for a welfare state that socialists will look for can only be provided through a widespread sense of common membership throughout the society in question.

It is once again worth stressing that this common identity must exist at national level. Small-scale or local communities may of course practise distribution according to need internally, and there is ample historical evidence of this occurring.[10] But there is no reason to believe that separate distributions at this level will add up to a just distribution overall, when one takes into account local and regional variations in productive wealth, in population profile, and so forth. Only a national distributive mechanism can guarantee fairness; and this requires ideological support at the same level.

Given that, for these two reasons, socialists are committed to the idea of common citizenship, what does this imply for their attitude to toleration? As indicated earlier, it is important to see the problem of toleration as extending beyond the narrow question of freedom of speech and its limits. Far more important, for the socialist, is the issue of how to respond to cultural diversity. By cultural diversity I mean the coexistence within a society of distinct patterns of belief and behaviour such that normally a person is a participant only in one subculture. These subcultures are sustained by social pressures of various kinds; people may be born into them or decide to become participants at some later point, but once inside it becomes costly to move out, in the sense that one will be

---

[9] There is, for example, evidence from empirical social psychology that people give less weight to merit and more weight to equality in distribution when they believe that they will be interacting with their partners over a period of time (the experiments were not set up in such a way as to allow differences in need to affect the outcome). See E. C. Shapiro, 'Effect of Expectations of Future Interaction on Reward Allocation in Dyads: Equity or Equality', *Journal of Personality and Social Psychology*, XXXI (1975), 873–80; M. J. Lerner, 'The Justice Motive: "Equity" and "Parity" among Children', *Journal of Personality and Social Psychology*, XXIX (1974), 539–50.   [10] See M. Walzer, *Spheres of Justice* (Oxford, 1983), ch. 3.

regarded as a traitor or a lost sheep by those remaining inside whose comradeship one values (I don't mean that the costs are always deliberately imposed). Now, why should cultural diversity pose any problem for the socialist view? In the light of what has already been said, the answer is easily anticipated. Subcultures threaten to undermine the overarching sense of identity that socialism requires. They are liable to do so in two ways: they give participants a narrower focus of loyalty that may pre-empt commitment to the wider community; and by way of reaction people outside a particular subculture may find it difficult to identify with those who are seen as in some way separated off.

These claims are made by way of hypothesis at the moment, and I shall return to the arguments for and against them later. Let me now put some flesh on these rather abstract bones by considering the example of ethnicity, which I think poses the most acute problems for socialism. Ethnicity involves two elements. First, a belief in common descent, leading to a historically given identity. Second, possession of a common culture, involving belief and behaviour that sets the ethnic group off from the larger society to which it belongs. Precisely how this cultural separation is manifested will vary a great deal from case to case. In some cases the key element will be language (French and English communities in Canada), and in some cases religion (Hindus, Muslims, and Sikhs in India); in some cases the weight will largely be carried by descent plus social rituals (Jews and Italians in America). Race may become an element, but it is important not to confuse race with ethnicity as such. Ethnicity requires belief, whereas a person of any race may in theory assimilate to a culture dominated by people of another race. In practice there may be difficulties posed by *other people's* beliefs. A black Englishman, for example, who wants to see himself simply as English may be hindered by others, black and white, who identify him as a West Indian. Even here, however, it is clear that in the last resort no one can have an ethnic identity foisted on him against his will.

As far as I can see there is nothing in the idea of ethnicity as such that a socialist should find objectionable. Historically many socialists (like many liberals) have been inclined to see ethnic identities as involving a sort of false consciousness, to be dissolved away painlessly with the coming of a Rational Society. But socialism is not harmed by abandoning this profoundly mistaken belief. Socialists can afford to be agnostic as to whether it is intrinsically better to have a culturally homogeneous society or a society with a rich ethnic patterning, just as they can afford to be agnostic over many questions of private taste and belief. It is not ethnicity *as such* that should concern them.[11] What they *should* be concerned about are the possible political effects of ethnic divisions.

There are two, partially separable, sources of difficulty. One is the relation between ethnic identity and communal identity *qua* member of the wider society. There is no reason, of course, why narrower loyalties should not serve to strengthen wider ones, as commonly happens in the case of local and national attachments. Burke made this point:

We begin our public affections in our families. No cold relation is a zealous citizen. We pass on to our neighbourhoods, and our habitual provincial connexions . . . so many little images of the great country in which the heart found something which it could fill. The love to the whole is not extinguished by this subordinate partiality. Perhaps it is a sort of elemental training to those higher and more large regards, by which alone men come to be affected, as with their own concern, in the prosperity of a kingdom.[12]

But here it is important that the small should be made in the image of the great. With ethnic identities this may not always be the case. The clearest example is where the ethnic identity contains within it a loyalty to some other community in another place. Familiar examples here would be Jews in the Diaspora and Israel, the Asian communities in Britain and parts of the Indian subcontinent, and more generally people who, say as a result of the redrawing of national boundaries in war, find themselves on the wrong side of a border. But the problem goes somewhat further than this. Communal identity is not merely an abstract notion; it needs to be embodied in particular symbols, practices, and beliefs. Where one ethnic group is dominant, it is almost certain that the form in which communal identity is expressed will embody elements of the majority culture. Where the dominant group is Christian, for example, Christian rituals will be used to mark important national occasions (for instance remembrance of war victims). To the extent that maintaining ethnic identity requires rejecting such cultural practices, members of minority groups will be alienated from the

[11] They may of course be concerned about particular ethnic practices, such as the subordination of women in traditional Muslim families, that appear to be incompatible with the general principles underlying socialism.
[12] E. Burke, *Reflections on the Revolution in France* (London, 1967), 193.

rituals, and will find it correspondingly harder to identify strongly with the wider community.

I do not want to make more of these points than they deserve. It is clearly possible to feel strong loyalties to more than one place, and it is a matter of common observation that many Jewish people (for example) are strongly committed both to Israel and to the country they inhabit. Equally it may be possible to forge a national identity that draws rather little on the beliefs and practices of any one ethnic group in particular; the obvious instance here would be the U.S., where national loyalties are patently strong, but where the focus of loyalty appears to be fairly abstract: the Constitution and the 'American way', which involves opportunities for individuals to strive for success. It would therefore be wrong to regard the identity problem as completely insoluble; but equally wrong to suppose that there is no problem in the first place.

The second difficulty posed by ethnicity is one of distributional conflict. On the assumption (which socialists must make) that the state will be a major distributor of resources, whether in the form of direct employment, or capital investment, or of welfare benefits such as subsidised housing, ethnic divisions are likely to lead to political competition to enhance the share of resources flowing to each group. Two main outcomes are on the cards, depending on whether or not a single ethnic group can establish a dominant position. If it can, a likely outcome is exploitation of the minority community or communities by the dominant community, a case classically illustrated by Northern Ireland in the period before direct rule was imposed; the power of the state is used to direct a disproportionate share of resources to members of the majority group. If no single group is dominant, the response may well be a general agreement, born of mistrust, to starve the state proper of resources, and instead to organise distribution on a community basis, either through local government or through voluntary organisations within each ethnic group. In this way each group retains control of the resources that broadly speaking it raises itself – a solution that, as I have already pointed out, does nothing to correct underlying imbalances in the living standards of the various communities. This is often advanced as at least a partial explanation of the low level of welfare expenditure on the part of the federal government in the U.S.[13]

[13] For a good presentation of this argument, see G.M. Klass, 'Explaining America and the Welfare State. An Alternative Theory', *British Journal of Political Science*, 15 (1985), 427–50.

Besides these two unattractive possibilities, there is a third, namely consociational democracy (a model developed by the Dutch political scientist Arend Lijphart to explain the relative stability of democratic regimes in socially divided European nations, especially Austria, Belgium, the Netherlands, and Switzerland).[14] The essence of the consociational model is collaboration between political elites representing the various communities to ensure that each has its vital interests safeguarded when government policy is made. It may also involve some devolution of decision-making to political bodies in which one or other community is dominant – for instance a form of federalism. In this way, it appears, distributional conflict can be handled in such a way that each community gets its fair share of resources, with the state still playing a large role in resource allocation. The magnitude of welfare state expenditure in Holland and Belgium could be cited as a supporting example.

For a socialist, this third alternative is clearly preferable to either majority rule by the dominant community or contraction of the distributive role of central government. The cost, however, is rule by elites. The consociational solution depends on bargaining between a small number of decision-makers, each holding an informal power of veto in case a decision appears to him to damage seriously the interests of the group he represents. Bargaining of this sort is necessarily confined to relatively small numbers. The consociational model conflicts with the ideal I have been sketching of a society in which each person plays an active role in deciding its future shape. Thus for socialists it can only be seen as a second-best solution, a realistic way of coping with cleavages that forestall the emergence of a more participatory form of democracy.

If we want both to have democracy of a more radical kind *and* envisage a fairly extensive redistributive role for the state, it is essential that people should participate politically, not as advocates for this or that sectional group, but as citizens whose main concerns are fairness between different sections of the community and the pursuit of common ends. This is not to say that everyone has to agree at the outset on a common set of principles; on the contrary, the aim of political debate is to reach a rough consensus, starting from a great variety of opinions as to what ought to be done. The point is that the content of the debate has to be a dialogue in which each

---

[14] A. Lijphart, *Democracy in Plural Societies* (New Haven and London, 1977). For a critical appraisal, see B. Barry, 'Political Accommodation and Consociational Democracy', *British Journal of Political Science*, 5 (1975), 477–505.

tries to persuade his fellows that the reasons for his views are good ones, not a process of bargaining in which each tries to attract support for the interests he represents by offering reciprocal support for the sectional interests of others. Now, clearly dialogue and bargaining are ideal types, and we should expect actual political systems to blend elements of both; it is equally clear, however, that the composition of the blend varies a good deal in practice, and there is nothing absurd in trying to promote the dialogue ideal as far as possible.

This brings us directly back to the question of identity. For the dialogue ideal to have a chance of success, participants must share a common identity as citizens that is stronger than their separate identities as members of ethnic or other sectional groups. Thus we now have a second argument to set alongside the first. The first argument, to recall, was that ethnic divisions may directly undermine the overall sense of common membership that socialists value; the second is that they may foster a factionalised form of politics which, at best, amounts to horse-trading between the various groups. The solution to both problems must lie in creating and maintaining an over-arching identity which is more salient for all communities than their separate ethnic identities. But this immediately raises a further problem, addressed in the remainder of this chapter, namely whether this requires any limits to the toleration that can be extended to subcultures and their expression.

There are two areas in which socialists ought to value toleration as strongly as liberals. One is freedom of speech, in particular freedom to express dissenting political opinions. The dialogic conception of politics that I have just outlined assumes that each person can participate in political debate on an equal footing, and with an equally authentic voice. Plainly any bar on the expression of political views would offend against that assumption and discriminate against those whose opinions were suppressed.[15] The second is what one might call the realm of private culture; how a person chooses to dress, what life-style he adopts, what sexual relationships he engages in, what religious beliefs he holds, and so forth. The reason here is simply that socialism holds no brief in this area; it recognises (or ought to recognise) the value of the private realm, but it has nothing directly to say about its substantive con-

---

[15] I omit any discussion of the special case of views whose expression threatens to subvert the conditions for future dialogue. This is the familiar problem of whether toleration should be extended to the intolerant; my sense is that the socialist will address it in much the same terms as the liberal.

tent. This point is sometimes expressed by saying that socialism contains no conception of the good life. Such a formulation is potentially misleading, because as I have been at pains to stress, socialism does have a clear view about the importance of citizenship to human fulfilment; but it is agnostic about specific modes of life within that setting.

There is, however, an important qualification to be entered. Socialists may be agnostic about the content of the private realm itself, but they are clearly interested in the impact that private culture has on the public realm. Now, participants in particular sub-cultures may well make demands on the state for support in one form or another – for legislation that makes it easier to engage in certain practices, or for financial assistance for modes of life (such as living on remote islands) that would otherwise be very costly to engage in. It is tempting to try to keep this particular genie very tightly stoppered up, to say that the proper distributive policy should be to give each person the same basic set of resources, and leave it to him to decide what style of life to follow. But this response cannot really be sustained. For one thing it may not be possible to define a set of resources that are equally basic for all modes of life in a culturally plural society – witness the criticisms attracted by Rawls's attempt to couch the problem of distributive justice in terms of a set of 'primary goods' that are supposed to be equally essential for each person's 'plan of life'. For another, certain modes of life may require special resources, not because they are in any way luxurious but simply for technical reasons, as in the case of the remote islanders. It must therefore be open to anyone to make out a case for support in the political arena, a case that will ideally be judged according (a) to the depth of commitment to the mode of life that its adherents evince, and (b) to the reasonableness of the form of support requested. But this in turn implies that people may have to act politically as spokesmen for a particular form of private life, raising once again the spectre of a factionalised form of politics in which people participate not as citizens but as group representatives.

This places the socialist in a quandary: he recognises (a) that it may well be desirable for many forms of private culture to flourish; (b) that fairness may require differential support for these sub-cultures; and (c) that nevertheless politics should not take the form of bargaining between competing interests. To escape from it he needs to rely on a sense of common citizenship that transcends cultural differences. But such an understanding will not simply appear spontaneously; it needs to be fostered through appropriate background institutions. Here at least the socialist has an advantage over the liberal. For whereas liberals tend to regard cultural identities as given, or at least created externally to the political system, socialists have usually possessed a stronger sense of the malleability of such identities, that is the extent to which they can be created or modified consciously. The practical question is: which institutions are likely to be crucial in fostering the sense of citizenship?

First, the institutions of politics themselves: the way in which political activity is organised will influence the way in which participants regard their roles. Consider as an example the party system. It is hard to conceive of political debate and decision-making in a large society without people who share broadly speaking the same set of beliefs forming organisations to promote them. Socialists should have no quarrel with parties that approximate to Burke's classical definition: 'a body of men united for promoting by their joint endeavours the national interest, upon some particular principle in which they are all agreed'.[16] Such parties, to underline the point, are held together by principles, and their aim is to promote the public interest as it appears to them in the light of these principles. Very different considerations apply where parties become no more than umbrella organisations for advancing a range of sectional interests, or worse still for advancing one particular sectional interest. In this case the party, instead of serving as a bridge between personal beliefs and public principles, will tend to strengthen sectional identities at the expense of shared ones. Suppose that someone belongs to a Muslim minority in a predominantly Christian society. If a party is formed that aims explicitly to promote the interests of Muslims, which he joins, he will find his political experience shaped by that purpose. He will interpret his political role as one of advancing a minority interest; he will not be encouraged to see himself as a citizen who has to make principled decisions on a wide range of issues facing his society as a whole.

Socialists should be concerned about such possibilities. They ought to be completely tolerant and even-handed in their dealings with parties of principle, but they should be prepared to design a constitution that discourages sectional parties. It would probably be unwise to attempt to ban such parties outright, for two reasons. First, it is difficult to legislate for such prohibitions in a way that

---

[16] E. Burke, cited in F. O'Gorman, *Edmund Burke* (London, 1973), 31.

does not exclude legitimate forms of association. Second, sectional identities may already have become so strong that what we have is really two separate nationalities living side by side, in which case the final best outcome is likely to be the secession of one community. Here a sectional party will be the natural expression of the national aspirations of the secessionist community. Discouragement without banning might take the form (for example) of requiring parties to fight seats in a certain number of geographical areas before any candidates could be elected or of refusing public funding to parties that could not show that they were genuinely national parties.

Such policies are not inherently desirable, but they may sometimes be necessary if the sense of citizenship that socialists depend upon is to be sustained. I am attempting here to sketch in possible limits to toleration from a socialist perspective, and so I am considering the worst case. Let me now turn to a second institutional locus that is likely to be important for citizenship, the education system. In particular, I want to ask how far socialists should go in embracing 'multi-cultural education', as it is often now called, given a society that is already culturally pluralistic.[17] Multi-cultural education may be interpreted in different ways. It may imply that children from all backgrounds should be introduced to the various cultures, systems of religious belief, and so forth that are found in their society, with the aim of increasing mutual understanding and thereby tolerance. This seems a rather desirable goal, and may indeed indirectly help to foster a greater sense of unity between cultural groups. On the other hand multi-cultural education may be taken to mean that the offspring of each culture should be instructed in that culture alone. Again that might seem unobjectionable or even desirable if it referred only to matters that were essentially private – for instance social mores or religious practices. It will be difficult, however, to keep these private questions separate from the broader issue of the group's relation to the wider society. How in particular will political education be handled? Will politics be looked at from the point of view of the cultural group, or will it be treated quite separately, from the standpoint of common citizenship? If the latter, how will the two visions of the child's place in the world – as Muslim, let us say, and as British – be harmonised?

It is interesting to see how this issue is skirted round in the recent

[17] The case for multi-cultural education is usefully presented in B. Parekh, 'The Concept of Multi-Cultural Education', in S. Modgil and G. Verma (eds.), *Multi-Cultural Education: The Interminable Debate* (London, 1986).

Swann Report on the education of children from ethnic minority groups. Swann, it should be said at once, endorses the first of the two views of multi-cultural education sketched above.

In our view an education which seeks only to emphasize and enhance the ethnic group identity of a child, at the expense of developing both a national identity and indeed an international, global perspective, cannot be regarded as in any sense multicultural . . . We would instead wish to see schools encouraging the cultural *development* of all their pupils, both in terms of helping them to gain confidence in their own cultural identities while learning to respect the identities of other groups as equally valid in their own right.[18]

The question of political education is then raised, particularly in relation to the perceived alienation of young members of ethnic minorities from the political system. The problem is seen, however, as one of increasing their instrumental effectiveness as participants.

the political education offered to ethnic minority youngsters can play a major role in countering their sense of alienation, by informing them about the institutions and procedures available within the political framework for making their opinions known, and opening their minds to the possibility that existing practices may, and sometimes should, be altered or replaced. Effective political education can also provide ethnic minority youngsters with the skills necessary to participate in political activities, thus helping to channel their energies into positive rather than negative forms of expression.[19]

This is an impeccably liberal view. The state is a piece of machinery for producing policies favourable to this or that constituency, and here is a group who lack the information and skills to extract a fair deal from it; clearly we must set about providing them. There is nothing wrong with this as far as it goes, but it makes no attempt to get to grips with the idea of citizenship and the beliefs that support it. Citizenship is not just a matter of knowing how to be effective politically, but of identity and commitment. In order to see his fate as bound up with the fate of the rest of his people, a citizen must have some understanding of the collectivity to which loyalty is owed, which will normally include some understanding of its history. Citizen identity cannot be divorced entirely from cultural identity, as I argued earlier. Thus whereas political education in the Swann view can be regarded as an extra element added on to a cultural education which tries to be neutral as between all cultures

---

[18] *Education for All: The Report of the Committee of Inquiry into the Education of Children from Ethnic Minority Groups*, Cmnd. 9453 (London, 1985), 322–3.   [19] *Education for All*, 339.

that happen to exist in a society, political education in this larger sense must try to shape cultural identities in the direction of common citizenship. It must try to present an interpretation of, let us say, Indian culture in Britain that makes it possible for members of the Indian community to feel at home in, and loyal to, the British state. In so far as there are elements in Indian culture that are at odds with such a reconciliation, the interpretation must be selective or, if you like, biased.

In case this should sound a conservative view, it may be worth reiterating the point that the sense of common identity which socialists wish to foster is not simply an historically given identity. Although historical continuity is normally to be welcomed rather than despised, since shared memories are a powerful force working for social unity, citizens will continually reshape their collective identity through democratic debate. The past is to be appropriated consciously rather than taken on board unconsciously. As new minority cultures appear, they may be expected to contribute to this reshaping. Thus the relationship between cultural identity and national identity is not to be regarded as fixed; nor, therefore, should the content of political education.

Education does, in any case, pose in an acute form the issue of wider and narrower senses of toleration raised at the beginning of this chapter. In a narrow sense, educational toleration might simply mean that no pupil who held dissenting opinions was prevented from airing them in class; in a somewhat broader sense, that pupils were encouraged to respond critically to the views expressed in text-books or by the teacher, rather than learning them by rote. But it might well be observed here that the content of what is taught, in contentious subjects such as politics and history, is still going to have a large impact on pupils' beliefs and attitudes. Is it then possible to practise toleration in the widest sense in which it comes to mean neutrality between the various points of view on offer – in this case between different interpretations of the historical and political context in which the pupil finds himself?

Advocates of multi-cultural education seem to envisage a form of comparative study in which the history, culture, and politics of one's own society are treated alongside those of many others, particularly of others with contrasting traditions.[20] The pupil is invited to identify with each in turn and to examine the remainder critically from that perspective. But it is very doubtful whether such

---

[20] See Parekh, 'The Concept of Multi-Cultural Education'.

proposals could be successfully implemented or, if they were, whether the outcome would be a desirable one. For the relationship between the (future) citizen and the history and so on of his own country is not merely academic: an understanding of that history and so on tells him (in part) who he is and how it is appropriate for him to behave. Were he really to achieve the detached perspective favoured by the multi-culturalist, he would ipso facto be alienated from the public culture of his own society – a free-floating, deracinated individual. This itself would be a politically charged outcome, albeit an improbable one.

The upshot is that in the case of educational subjects which have practical implications, such as politics and history, toleration in the strong sense in which it aspires to neutrality is impossible. The pupil may be taught to admire or despise the public culture and practices of his society, but he must be taught something (as indicated above, there is still room for toleration in the narrow sense: he may be given the opportunity to question what he is taught). This poses no problem for the socialist, of course, who in any case favours a form of political education geared to common citizenship. The argument is directed rather against liberal aspirations to neutralist toleration, which appear very often to underlie proposals for multi-cultural education.

To return finally to our bewildered traveller, and the alternatives he faces: there are no good grounds for socialists to follow the Eastern road, namely deliberate suppression of minority cultures within the boundaries of the state. Socialism, I have claimed, embodies no full-blown conception of the good life which might justify the imposition of one particular culture on all citizens. On the other hand, the view that socialist society should be no more than an arena in which many disparate forms of life coexist is seriously flawed. It overlooks all the difficulties involved in creating and maintaining the kind of common identity that socialist principles require. This problem sets the parameters for the socialist view of toleration: there is no case for suppressing minority views and cultures, but at the same time the institutions of a socialist society should aim to foster a sense of common citizenship which may in practice require some discrimination between cultures. This conclusion also carries implications for the socialist movement. Although it may seem politically expedient to try to build a so-called 'rainbow coalition' through a policy platform that appeals to the special interests of many diverse groups, it is far from clear that a politics of this sort could provide the underpinning for a socialist state. Citizenship is not something that can be built in a day.

Index

255